About Island Press

Island Press, a nonprofit organization, publishes, markets, and distributes the most advanced thinking on the conservation of our natural resources—books about soil, land, water, forests, wildlife, and hazardous and toxic wastes. These books are practical tools used by public officials, business and industry leaders, natural resource managers, and concerned citizens working to solve both local and global resource problems.

Founded in 1978, Island Press reorganized in 1984 to meet the increasing demand for substantive books on all resource-related issues. Island Press publishes and distributes under its own imprint and offers these services to other nonprofit organizations.

Support for Island Press is provided by the Geraldine R. Dodge Foundation, The Energy Foundation, The Charles Engelhard Foundation, The Ford Foundation, Glen Eagles Foundation, The George Gund Foundation, William and Flora Hewlett Foundation, The John D. and Catherine T. MacArthur Foundation, The Andrew W. Mellon Foundation, The Joyce Mertz-Gilmore Foundation, The New-Land Foundation, The J. N. Pew, Jr. Charitable Trust, Alida Rockefeller, The Rockefeller Brothers Fund, The Rockefeller Foundation, The Tides Foundation, and individual donors.

THE *NEW* COMPLETE GUIDE TO ENVIRONMENTAL CAREERS

THE *NEW* COMPLETE GUIDE TO ENVIRONMENTAL CAREERS

The Environmental Careers Organization

John R. Cook, Jr.
President

Kevin Doyle
Project Director

Bill Sharp
Principal Author, Second Edition

ISLAND PRESS
Washington, D.C. □ *Covelo, California*

© 1993 The Environmental Careers Organization

Library of Congress Cataloging-in-Publication Data

The new complete guide to environmental careers / the Environmental Careers
  Organization ; John R. Cook, Jr., president, Kevin Doyle, project director, Bill Sharp,
  principal author.
      p.   cm.
    Includes index.
    ISBN 1-55963-178-3 (paper).—1-55963-179-1 (cloth)
    1. Environmental sciences—Vocational guidance.   I. Cook, John, Jr.   II. Doyle,
  Kevin.   III. Sharp, Bill, 1952–   .   IV. Environmental Careers Organization.
  GE60.C66   1993
363.7'0023'73—dc20   92-34855
                                                                              CIP

Printed on recycled, acid-free paper

Manufactured in the United States of America

10 9 8 7 6 5 4 3 2 1

Contents

WITHDRAWN

NOV - 1997

Preface

Congratulations! By picking up this book you have shown interest in the most dynamic and diverse profession of the 1990s. Concern about the environment and a desire to make a difference are at an all-time high. Americans are grappling with the dilemmas of how to manage our incomparable land, water, and wildlife resources, how to provide for increased demands for outdoor recreation, and how to balance growth with the preservation of open space. Cleanup of our polluted air and water still eludes the nation. We remain in the middle of a crisis in hazardous and solid waste management and are painfully aware of the many toxins in our environment.

A large part of our success in addressing these issues will depend on the intelligence and creativity of environmental professionals. Given the work to be done, there is something for everyone, whether one's interests lie in developing new pollution control technologies, studying the habitats of endangered wildlife, teaching ecology to schoolchildren, or pursuing one of the hundreds of other opportunities.

When the first edition of this book was released in November 1989, comprehensive information on environmental careers was difficult to find. There was not one popular book for the environmental job seeker. The response to the first edition of *The Complete Guide to Environmental Careers* has been extremely gratifying. It has been used by career advisors at high schools, community colleges, universities, and training centers throughout the country. We regularly hear from students, job seekers, professionals, and others who have used the book to define their careers and find satisfying environmental jobs.

ix

Today, environmental careers are big news. Books, magazine articles, conferences, career fairs, newsletters, job listings, and word of mouth are spreading the word and attracting talented people to the field. The secret is out.

This new edition of *The Complete Guide to Environmental Careers* retains the basic structure and much of the text from the original book. There are chapters presenting detailed information about the major environmental career opportunities of the 1990s—in such areas as planning, education and communication, environmental protection, and natural resource management. In addition, the book gives you a broad overview of the environmental professions, career search strategies, and information about education, volunteering, and internships.

The chapters on specific career areas are structured to give you easy access to the information you need. Each chapter contains the following sections:

- *At a Glance.* A quick snapshot of employment in the field.
- *What Is . . . ?* A definition of the career area.
- *History and Background.* Includes key laws creating jobs.
- *Issues and Trends.* The main concerns facing the profession.
- *Career Opportunities.* Types of work available in government, business, and nonprofit organizations.
- *Salary.* Current earnings at the entry level and beyond.
- *Getting Started.* Educational needs and other advice.
- *Resources.* Organizations to contact for more information.

What set the first edition of *The Complete Guide to Environmental Careers* apart from other career guides, however, was its focus on *people* through Profiles and Case Studies that show current environmental professionals in action. This second edition has a completely new set of 11 case studies and 34 profiles to bring the diversity of environmental work to life.

The Complete Guide to Environmental Careers has grown naturally out of the work of the Environmental Careers Organization. Established in 1972, ECO is a national nonprofit organization and a respected leader in the development of new environmental professionals. Over the past two decades, the Environmental Careers Organization (formerly the CEIP Fund) has launched the careers of more than 5,000 college students, recent graduates, and others by providing paid, short-term environmental jobs with hundreds of agencies, corporations, consulting firms, and nonprofit organizations. Many of the people profiled and interviewed for the book were participants in ECO programs. More information about the organization is given in the section that follows.

The advice of hundreds of environmental professionals from every conceivable discipline went into this book. If one central theme emerged, however, it is this: The only limitations to your success in an environmental career are the scope of your vision and the level of your persistence. Everyone can make a difference. Welcome aboard, and good luck!

ABOUT THE ENVIRONMENTAL CAREERS ORGANIZATION

The mission of the Environmental Careers Organization is to "protect the environment through the promotion of careers, the development of professionals, and the inspiration of individual action." To achieve that goal, ECO operates four interrelated programs through its regional offices in the Pacific Northwest (Seattle), California (San Francisco), the Northeast (Boston), Florida (Tampa), and the Great Lakes (Cleveland). The four ECO programs are:

Environmental Placement Services (EPS) helps environmental employers get important projects done and at the same time provides crucial on-the-job experience to college students, recent graduates, and entry-level job seekers. Every year, more than three hundred environmental scientists, engineers, planners, communicators, managers, technicians, and generalists are placed in paid, short-term "associate" positions of 3 to 18 months' duration with federal, state, and local agencies, major corporations, consulting firms, and nonprofit groups. Associates' salaries range from $300 to $700 per week or more.

After their projects are completed, ECO associates return to college to finish undergraduate or graduate degrees, take permanent positions with the organizations that sponsored their jobs, or use the experience they gained as associates to land positions elsewhere. Nearly all of the thousands of ECO associates of the past two decades are still working in the environmental field.

What do ECO associates do? They work in hazardous waste management, land and water conservation, parks and outdoor recreation, planning, air and water quality management, education, and all of the other fields detailed in this book. Later, they often sponsor associates of their own, helping to support the next generation of environmental workers.

Environmental Career Services (ECS) provides advice and information to job seekers, teachers, career advisors, working professionals, and the general public through national career conferences and job fairs, local seminars and workshops, and personal advising. The key event on the

ECS calendar is the annual National Environmental Career Conference, which regularly draws hundreds of aspiring environmental workers.

Environmental Career Products (ECP) includes books, articles, conference summaries, reports, and other publications on the environmental fields as well as a regular newsletter, *Connections. The Complete Guide to Environmental Careers* is a key ECP production.

Environmental Research and Consulting Services (ERCS) investigates environmental trends and issues (usually from a human resource perspective) for corporate, foundation, and government clients. ERCS subjects have included environmental salary surveys, employment projections, educational needs in the field, and the role of people of color in the environmental world.

Beginning in 1989, ECO put all four of its programs to work on the latter issue, creating a national Minority Opportunities Program. This program provides summer internships for college students of color pursuing environmental careers, a national Minority Environmental Careers Conference to bring together the growing environmental network of African, Native, Hispanic, and Asian Americans with students of color for learning and networking, a grants program to support internships with nonprofit and small government agencies, and other initiatives.

Through all of this, the Environmental Careers Organization empowers people to protect and improve our environment. Although laws, regulations, funding, and public support are crucial to environmental success, it takes people—individuals such as those featured in this book—to implement solutions, create innovations, enforce the law, and manage funds wisely. ECO is about educating, assisting, advising, and inspiring those people: the volunteers, donors, interns, and professionals of the environmental community, wherever they work.

We hope you will join us.

John R. Cook, Jr.
Founder and President
The Environmental Careers Organization

For more information about ECO programs, events, publications, research, or consulting, contact the office nearest you.

National Headquarters

286 Congress St.
Third Floor
Boston, MA 02210
(617) 426-4375

Great Lakes

50 Public Sq., Suite 628
Cleveland, OH 44113-2203
(216) 861-4545

California

381 Bush St., Suite 700
San Francisco, CA 94104-2807
(415) 362-5552

Pacific Northwest

1218 Third Ave., Suite 1515
Seattle, WA 98101-3021
(206) 625-1750

Northeast

286 Congress St.
Boston, MA 02210
(617) 426-4783

Florida

4902 Eisenhower Blvd., Suite 217
Tampa, FL 33634-6324
(813) 886-4330

Acknowledgments

Hundreds of people have allowed their experiences in environmental careers to be distilled to create the contents of this book. Ultimately, the value of this book is that their knowledge and advice is conveyed to you, the reader. Giving adequate recognition to these people is impossible, but you will meet many of them as you read these pages.

This book is a project of the Environmental Careers Organization (ECO) and is a collective effort by the entire staff. In particular, the responsiveness and expertise of the ECO regional directors have been essential:

- Dee Rollins, Northeast Region
- Lee DeAngelis, Great Lakes Region
- Terry Hove, California Region
- Andrea Halleck, Pacific Northwest Region
- Joni Freedman, Florida Region

All of these people provided ideas and advice, contacts, and feedback in the production of this second edition. The collective knowledge of ECO staff members in environmental career development is staggering, and this book passes along their wisdom to you.

The second edition of *The Complete Guide to Environmental Careers* owes a huge debt to the first edition and the team of professionals that produced it. The George Gund Foundation launched Environmental Career Services with a grant in 1986. The Pew Charitable Trusts funded the original research, which led to the first edition. Lee DeAngelis contributed a great deal to both editions and managed production of the first edition. Stephen C. Basler wrote the first edition—the second edition owes him a debt beyond measure.

Each of the chapters on specific career fields includes Profiles of professionals active in the field and at least one Case Study of an environmental issue specific to that chapter's subject. All of these have been rewritten or replaced for this edition to keep the information current. Many more people have freely given information and advice to make this possible. In addition, several hardy souls reviewed portions of this edition to help ensure its accuracy. The time, energy, and patience of these professionals made this book possible. We thank them for their service to the next generation of environmental professionals.

Kevin Doyle, ECO's national director of program development, orchestrated the planning and completion of this project. He brought to the second edition his special combination of knowledge of the environmental field, enthusiasm for his work, and talent in both writing and editing.

Bill Sharp, free-lance writer and partner in Fresh Air Communications, Newburyport, Massachusetts, wrote or edited much of this edition. More significant assistance came from Bill's wife, Elaine L. Appleton, a professional writer and editor. Jean Anderson conducted research and kept the project under daily control. Catherine Pedersen conducted research, interviewed Profile subjects, and wrote several Profiles.

All of the persons mentioned left their mark on this book. We thank them for their contributions. I dedicate this book to the environmental professionals who daily complete the good work of protecting the environment—often in a low-profile, yet creative, manner. Their dedication and intelligence in finding solutions to the complex problems they encounter in their work inspire us all in our own efforts—present and future.—John R. Cook, Jr.

Last, the authors would like to extend heartfelt thanks to those who suffered patiently through the birthing of this book. Crackers the cat spent long months on top of the computer. Bill's daughter Kate offered encouragement and asked many questions. The long hours, sleepless nights, and lost weekends of writing are not myths. Thank you, Deb Mapes and Elaine—Kevin Doyle and Bill Sharp.

THE *NEW* COMPLETE GUIDE TO ENVIRONMENTAL CAREERS

Introduction to Environmental Careers

Laura DeGuire *is an environmental quality analyst with the Michigan Department of Natural Resources in Lansing, Michigan. She monitors air quality for Clean Air Act compliance and manages safety programs for the office's 130-member inspection staff.*

Victor Furmanec *is an associate planner with Emanuel Associates, a consulting firm in Nyack, New York. His planning work involves advising towns and communities on their growth and helping them to minimize the environmental impact of development.*

Joseph Pavel *is manager of quantitative services for the Northwest Indian Fisheries Commission in Olympia, Washington. He and his staff manage data processing and computer modeling to ensure that annual catches do not endanger salmon fishery stocks.*

Amy Perlmutter *is a recycling coordinator for the city and county of San Francisco. She manages, coordinates, and negotiates to ensure that an increasing percentage of city wastes is diverted from landfills and converted to recycled raw materials.*

Aubrey Smith *is an environmental chemist with British Petroleum America's Research and Development Center in Cleveland, Ohio. He was hired after an ECO internship in which he evaluated drinking water for the Environmental Protection Agency in Cincinnati.*

The careers of these professionals differ greatly from one another, yet all of them concern some aspect of the environment. Environmental professionals are found in all sectors of the economy, all over the globe, using every skill found in the working world.

By choosing to enter the environmental field, you embark on a cutting-edge career, one that is young and evolving every year as new technologies and policies come into play. Perhaps the most exciting element about environmental careers is the people themselves. Even though environmental professionals come from all backgrounds and walks of life, there is a common denominator: most bring a love or passion for the environment to their work and careers. Environmental careers have unlimited potential to be deeply satisfying and creative.

To understand better the nature of environmental careers today, it is useful to know where we have been, both as a nation and as a profession. There are two sides to our nation's relationship to the environment. In our quest for progress and in the name of free enterprise, we have often violated and abused the environment. After a hundred years of building an industrial powerhouse and overlooking or ignoring our environment, we began to reap what we had sown: Our lakes and rivers were dying, our skies had a layer of haze, cities were becoming concrete monstrosities, and wildlife was fading from the picture.

Fortunately, we have another side, one that has been too quiet for too long. Americans do love the land and the waters and the skies, and they place a high priority on their preservation. This is borne out by poll after poll and is clearly revealed in the fabric of our nation's life-styles and heritage. When we can get away from the office, we go outdoors: to play, to exercise, to reflect, to worship. No other park system rivals that of the United States in its scope and diversity.

In the 1960s, this side of the United States sat up and took action. We stood at the brink of ecological disaster, looked down at the future, and made a collective decision to move away from the edge. Citizens' activities culminated with Earth Day in 1970, an event whose popularity among a broad range of participants took even its organizers off guard. The National Environmental Policy Act of 1970 set the tone of new environmental policy by requiring the federal government first to consider the environmental consequences of a proposed action. This instituted what has proved to be a fundamental shift in the priorities of doing business in the United States.

Dozens of landmark legislative packages have followed: major amendments to the Clean Air Act and the Clean Water Act; the Comprehensive Environmental Response, Compensation, and Liability Act of 1980, or Superfund; the Resource Conservation and Recovery Act (1976); and the Forest and Rangeland Renewable Resources Planning Act of 1974, to name a few. To implement these acts, the president's Council on Environmental Quality and, later, the Environmental Protection Agency (EPA) were created. State governments quickly followed with the creation of their own environmental protection agencies.

Many are not satisfied with the results of this legislation, however, and additional, complex environmental problems have arisen. But one thing is certain: The work of the past two and a half decades has begun a process of institutionalizing the strong but sometimes overshadowed environmental ethic of the United States.

A vital part of this institutionalization has been the creation of a broad-based profession for those who wish to make their livelihood by protecting the environment. Before 1960, the environmental field consisted primarily of rangers, foresters, and a handful of public health officials and advocates. Today, environmental professionals work for every municipal government in the nation. Each state has an environmental protection agency, and one would be hard pressed to find a federal agency that did not have a variety of professionals working on environmental issues. A great number and variety of environmental consulting firms have sprung up, offering services ranging from hazardous waste management to development of interpretive programs for nature centers.

Even small companies are likely to have environmental health and safety staffs; large firms may have environmental personnel at every level from headquarters to plant, including engineers, public relations staff members, and laboratory technicians. Nonprofit organizations exist not only in Washington, DC, but also in communities around the country; these organizations engage in public education, research, advocacy, and natural resource stewardship. Universities and technical schools have expanded or created departments to educate these professionals and are engaged in solving a multitude of environmental problems. Finally, the design and production of pollution control equipment is a multibillion-dollar-per-year industry.

Many environmental professionals have scientific and technical backgrounds. One of the strongest messages of this book, however, is that the environmental field also has a critical need for liberal arts graduates, especially those with training in both science and liberal arts. A few of the professions mentioned in this book are not often considered part of the environmental field: accountants, computer specialists, journalists, educators, real estate professionals, lawyers, financiers, entrepreneurs, managers (and more managers), political scientists, and librarians all can contribute to the work of improving the environment.

A remarkable aspect of the environmental field is the pace at which change occurs. Although some subfields remain stable, many aspects of the profession today would have been unrecognizable even a few years ago. If the past two and a half decades are any indication, the pace can only increase. This prompted a wildlife biologist with the state of Michigan to say, "I believe that 80 to 90 percent of the jobs that will exist in the environmental field five years from now haven't been created yet."

John R. Cook, Jr., founder and president of The Environmental Careers Organization, offers an explanation for this rapid evolution: "The development of the environmental profession can be compared with the historical development of other professions. Right now, I believe the field is going through a maturing phase, just as medicine or law did hundreds of years ago. First, everyone is off doing what works best for them. Gradually, knowledge and experience grow and are shared; there is specialization and standardization, accreditation, and development of professional ethics and codes of conduct. It is very exciting to be in a profession during this formative period, and it gives individuals the opportunity to have a profound effect on the field for generations to come."

The modern environmental movement is a quarter century old. Much has been accomplished; enormous challenges lie ahead. Can we continue on the course set by our predecessors? Can we do better? In this increasingly global community, the course we chart, the tone we set, will have a dramatic effect, both direct and indirect, on the environment of the entire world. Charles Odegaard, Pacific Northwest regional director of the National Park Service, while speaking at an ECO annual national environmental career conference in Seattle, stated: "The field in which you are presently engaged is the most important field. What you and I do is going to make a difference as to whether this world exists or does not exist. Whether you're in private enterprise or government, or are a private citizen, the challenge you have is to make sure this world goes on [and remains] a great place in which to live rather than just exist." As to challenge, environmental professionals have found that it also means opportunity.

HOW THIS BOOK CAN HELP YOU

This second edition of *The Complete Guide to Environmental Careers* provides information of several types to help you reach your goals in an environmental career:

• *Career-specific advice.* Each chapter that discusses a particular field of work includes its own Advice section to ensure that the advice conveyed to you is as relevant as possible to your efforts. You will find general

Cuyahoga Department of Health, Cuyahoga, Ohio. Terry Allen collects water samples from used tire lots to track the disease-carrying Asian tiger mosquito.

suggestions about how to approach the field as well as the specific advice that can come only from someone who is out there doing the work.

- *Resources you need.* In chapters 2 through 14 you will find a Resources section that includes a selection of the references we have found most useful in understanding that particular field. Every entry was checked for this edition, and, where possible, telephone numbers were added for your convenience. Many of these listings are themselves lists of resources. Take the time to investigate—exploring these materials will uncover many more listings than we could possibly provide in this book.

- *The real picture.* We are excited about the environmental field and the many careers it includes. However, the chapters in this book make it clear where the growth is—and where it is not. Good training, experience, and determination seem to surmount nearly any obstacle, but those obstacles are higher in some fields than in others. Take a good look through the At a Glance section at the beginning of each of the ten chapters on specific fields and use these facts to make some rough comparisons between fields.

- *Demystified people.* Profiles throughout this book present professionals working in the environmental fields as real people. These are people who explored the Chesapeake Bay, the bayous, the Sierra Nevada, or the Olympic Mountains when they were young. They went to school and earned degrees or did not; volunteered or just got a job; changed their minds several times or went straight to their heart's desire. They represent the public sector, from federal to local positions; private industry and consultants; education; and nonprofit organizations. They represent all parts of the country and many racial and cultural groups. They made the same kinds of decisions you are making, and they want to help you get to where you are going.
- *Job-hunting help.* Beyond receiving inspiration from the superb people who work in the field you are interested in and determining the best mix of courses for the degree you need, you ultimately want to land the right job. *The Complete Guide to Environmental Careers* notes where the jobs are today and how many are expected in the years ahead. Some fields are relatively stable, and others are growing as quickly as competent people can be found to fill the positions; the chapters make it clear which is which. You will also see abundant evidence that practical experience is advisable before applying for a job in any of these fields, and the types of experience that will do the most good are outlined for you. Within these pages you will find more information than is available in any other volume on how to make your environmental job quest successful.

Reading this book will provide you with an overview of the environmental field, its issues, how professionals make the entire range of environmental careers work, and where your place in the field may be. Welcome to your environmental career!

Part I

JOB HUNTING IN THE ENVIRONMENTAL FIELD

1 Careers and Issues

THE 1990s can truly be considered the decade of the environment. We see the evidence in our daily lives: Curbside recycling programs have sprung up around the nation. Household hazardous waste days bring out thousands of people. Billion-dollar initiatives are launched to clean up land, air, and water contaminated by toxic waste accumulated over generations. Schoolchildren come home to tell their parents about the destruction of the rain forest, global warming, and why wetlands are important.

The 1990s can also be seen as the decade of environmental careers. Twenty-five years ago, if a career seeker had any notion of the environmental professions, it was limited to an odd collection of park rangers, game wardens, water and sewer workers, foresters, and science teachers. Today, it is estimated that as many as 3 million Americans are employed in environmental work, many in jobs that were unimaginable even 15 years ago. In fields as varied as law, finance, insurance, real estate, management, and engineering, "environmental" specialists are being hired as quickly as schools and experience can produce them.

This chapter is designed to give you a broad overview of environmental careers today. First, we describe several general trends that characterize the environmental field. Second, we provide a brief introduction to ten environmental career arenas. Each field is detailed more completely in its own chapter. Third, we tell you about some characteristics that differentiate employers in the public, private, and nonprofit sectors based on comments from working professionals. Fourth, we have included a quick overview of the most common job activities for environmental workers.

Fifth, the chapter encapsulates some key advice on how to track down and land your own environmental job. Finally, the role of values and ethics in environmental work is briefly explored.

TRENDS IN THE ENVIRONMENTAL FIELD

A number of forces in the environmental field will influence your opportunities for employment. Some trends represent areas where increased effort on your part may dramatically enhance your value on the job market.

GROWTH

Growth is the dominant theme for environmental careers in the 1990s. Estimates of how much American businesses, government agencies, and individuals are spending on environmental protection and cleanup vary wildly, from more than $100 billion per year to nearly twice that. Even the lowest estimate, however, is equal to 2 percent of the gross national product. In 1992, an estimate of $2 *trillion* over the next ten years was widely accepted. Job growth has been just as dramatic. The *Environmental Business Journal* projects that employment in air and water quality management, solid and hazardous waste management, and related careers will grow at rates as high as 16 percent through 1996, generating nearly 500,000 new jobs in that period.

MATURING INSTITUTIONS AND PROFESSIONALISM

The environmental movement of the late 1960s and early 1970s was often dismissed as a cause for radicals and crackpots. Today, the environmental community is a complex, interwoven collection of federal, state, and local regulatory agencies; industry professionals; consulting firms; legislative bodies; experienced nonprofit research and advocacy groups; and large numbers of college and university degree programs.

As in all emerging professions, there have been growing calls for programs of professional certification and an explosion of professional associations. This growing structure helps the job seeker by creating clear links between school, certifications, and employment. At the same time, however, it puts roadblocks in the way of people who have talent and interest but lack the supposedly "required" qualifications.

PUBLIC SUPPORT FOR ENVIRONMENTAL PROTECTION

Public support for environmental improvement has never been stronger in the United States. Americans do not feel that the desire to preserve natural resources is a fad. It is now an inherent part of our society's value system. Even in the face of economic downturn, public support for environmentally sound policy continues. A national poll in 1991 showed that 80 percent of the public favors protecting the environment over keeping prices down—a percentage up from 51 percent in 1981.

INCREASED NEED FOR ENVIRONMENTAL SCIENTISTS AND ENGINEERS

Environmental work has become dramatically more technical, and the "hottest" careers are overwhelmingly in science and engineering fields. At the same time, environmental issues demand interdisciplinary training, which traditional education is ill equipped to provide. For example, the environmental protection field needs hazardous waste specialists who also understand air and water quality issues. The natural resource management field is calling for wildlife biologists who understand forestry, ecology, and environmental protection issues.

NEED FOR MANAGEMENT AND COMMUNICATION SKILLS

At the same time that employment ads are crying out for more engineers, industrial hygienists, toxicologists, and hydrogeologists, environmental employers are demanding professionals with strong "people" and liberal arts skills: management, mediation, public speaking, education, writing, politics, economics, and clear-headed problem solving. A key trend in the field is that technical skills get you into a job, but communication and management ability determines your rise.

CHANGES IN FEDERAL INVOLVEMENT

Over the past two decades, much of the impetus for environmental protection came from sweeping national legislation and creation of federal authorities such as the Environmental Protection Agency (EPA). In the late 1980s, however, a shift began toward more local initiatives and implementation. Perhaps the most compelling explanation for this phenomenon is that environmental challenges like toxic waste dumps and proposed real estate development occur at the local level. Citizens and units of government respond to local problems with local solutions. This is possible because of the steadily increasing technical competence of state and local governments, many of which act now because they do not want to wait for national legislation.

Reauthorization of major national environmental legislation, such as the Resource Conservation and Recovery Act (RCRA) and the clean air and clean water acts, is structured so that state and local governments are the implementers, the enforcers, and often the designers of the legislated remedies. Private businesses are also moving ahead with protection programs that exceed regulatory requirements.

PUSH FOR POLLUTION PREVENTION

The massive costs, technical problems, and levels of litigation associated with cleaning up past environmental errors have created a consensus that pollution prevention approaches are a much better idea. The federal Superfund program, with its multibillion-dollar price tag and relatively small results, is the prime example. Many environmental professionals believe that pollution prevention represents a revolution in environmental work that will require radical changes in the training and job descriptions of environmental professionals.

INTERNATIONAL OPPORTUNITIES

Environmental problems are global in scope. Solutions to these problems will be global as well. Through the 1990s and beyond, expect an explosion of cooperative actions and increases in funding for international work. Many observers believe that United States companies and consultants, with their technical expertise and experience, will do a great deal of work in Eastern Europe, South America, Asia, and the countries of the former Soviet Union. Whether the United States government is yet prepared to take a leadership role in global environmental and development issues remains an open question.

A GROWING PRIVATE SECTOR

The private environmental industry has grown rapidly because there is a great deal of money to be made in protection and cleanup. It has also begun to consolidate as a few giants increase their share of the market. Companies like Browning Ferris, Waste Management and Chemical Waste Management, Laidlaw, Burlington Environmental, and many others offer comprehensive environmental services, including the construction and operation of facilities. Increasingly, government is "privatizing" environmental work that would otherwise be carried out by public agencies. The day-to-day work of environmental protection is largely carried out by private companies.

A NEW GRASS-ROOTS MOVEMENT

Not everyone is pleased with the growing professionalism and institutionalization of the environmental field. Increasingly, small citizens' groups are being born that are vociferously local, antibureaucratic, activist, and adversarial. These groups are likely to criticize not only private industry and the EPA but the National Wildlife Federation as well. If so much money is being spent and so many intelligent professionals are being employed, they are asking, why are some of the problems getting worse? The new grass-roots movement is also seeking to connect the work of environmentalism to social issues of race, poverty, and power.

ENVIRONMENTAL CAREERS IN THE 1990s

The majority of opportunities for careers in the environment fall into several general categories. Each of the following major areas is treated in a full chapter later in this book.

THE PLANNING PROFESSION

There is wide variety in the planning field, but planners generally focus on either a specific geographic area (neighborhoods, cities, regions) or a specific issue area (air quality, transportation). Environmental planning is making a comeback as policymakers begin to appreciate the integrated nature of environmental issues and the fact that development often has environmental consequences that could have been identified in advance and prevented.

Planning is a process. As such, process skills must be mastered: problem identification and definition, creation of alternative visions, development of action steps to achieve the goal, and coalition building to make it happen. A liberal arts or undergraduate planning degree with a master's degree in planning or landscape architecture is among the more common educational routes prospective planners follow. Aspiring environmental planners might obtain an undergraduate degree in a hard science or natural resource area, work awhile, and go back to earn a master's degree in planning.

ENVIRONMENTAL EDUCATION AND COMMUNICATION

The solution to our environmental problems lies with an informed citizenry that has the information and learning skills it needs to alter its behavior for the better. Nearly everyone agrees with this proposition. In the 1990s, the challenge will be to put money into its implementation.

In addition to teaching school at all levels, jobs in environmental education and communication can include writing for a trade publication, interpreting at a state park, helping firms understand the proper disposal of hazardous wastes, and a hundred others. Although jobs exist and more will be created, plotting such a career requires creativity. Useful preparation includes studying a hard science and developing strong writing, speaking, and teaching skills. Environmental educators are often translators of technical information to the nontechnical public.

SOLID WASTE MANAGEMENT

Some estimates state that solid waste management is the fastest-growing field in the country. Virtually all large cities in the United States, as well as many small towns, face the problem of dwindling landfill space for municipal solid waste. Given environmental concerns, prospects for opening new landfills are slim. Municipalities today scramble to develop recycling programs and environmentally safe incineration systems. This is a field you can enter from almost any discipline, from engineer to accountant. The position of recycling coordinator, for instance, is one of the fastest-growing professions in the nation.

A few particularly useful disciplines for aspiring solid waste managers are engineering, environmental science, urban studies and planning, and a combination of business, management, and finance. Although formal programs are available, volunteer or internship experience often plays a major role in landing a job.

HAZARDOUS WASTE MANAGEMENT

There are as many as 33,000 municipal and industrial hazardous waste sites in the United States and at least 7,000 more on military installations. Cleaning up these sites will cost billions of dollars and employ thousands of environmental workers. And yet these cleanups are not even the largest part of the field. Simply identifying wastes, categorizing them, disposing of them legally, and working to reduce their generation in the first place employ the lion's share of "haz waste" workers.

Opportunities exist for people with expertise in many disciplines, but the shortage of environmental engineers, groundwater scientists, toxicologists, industrial hygienists, and remediation specialists is critical.

AIR QUALITY MANAGEMENT

Many goals set by the first generation of air quality regulations remain unmet even as a whole new set of pollution issues demands attention. Most major urban areas are still out of compliance with carbon monoxide and ozone regulations—some dramatically so. Now concern has been raised over airborne toxins—cadmium, polychlorinated biphenyls (PCBs), dioxins—and indoor air pollution. Furthermore, acid rain, carbon dioxide buildup (the greenhouse effect), and depletion of the protective ozone layer have become issues of international concern.

Local governments, industry, and consultants provide the greatest career opportunities in air quality management. Air pollution control is a technical field in which sophisticated monitoring, chemical analysis, computer modeling, and statistical analysis are the tools of the trade. Technically oriented managers are in high demand.

WATER QUALITY MANAGEMENT

Water quality programs today no longer focus on the gross visible pollutants that so disfigured lakes and rivers at the beginning of the environmental movement. Through the somewhat cleaner waters have emerged newly recognizable toxic pollutants in both surface water and groundwater that will be more difficult to control. Other focuses are nonpoint-source pollution from runoff and erosion and the degradation of coastal waters, wetlands, and estuaries.

Demand in all sectors remains steady for the traditional disciplines of civil, environmental, and mechanical engineering. New fields in demand include chemical engineering, toxicology, hydrology, and water quality planning.

LAND AND WATER CONSERVATION

The field of land and water conservation needs professionals from numerous disciplines, since it involves both environmental protection and natural resource management. Land and water conservation issues include such diverse topics as development pressures in New England, water shortages on the West Coast, and preservation of open space for urban parks. Besides natural resource managers and specialists, the field employs environmental planners, lawyers, land acquisition experts, and advocates.

Outside of the major federal land management agencies, most land and water conservation activity occurs at the state and local levels, using such tools as legislation of development and subdivisions, natural resource inventory programs, and geographic information systems. The flourishing nonprofit sector includes hundreds of local land trusts and numerous national, state, and local organizations. The edge in the job market goes to professionals with a broad base of education and skills along with a range of volunteer or internship experience.

FISHERY AND WILDLIFE MANAGEMENT

The fishery and wildlife management professions, which virtually defined environmental careers for years, maintain and manage fish and wildlife populations for human use and for their own sake. This work involves studying habitat, food supply, habits, and population distribution. Increasingly, the work of fish and wildlife professionals is integrated into broader natural resource management and planning efforts. As a result, these professionals are required to develop an ecological perspective so they can understand and work with other natural resource managers. There is also a shift toward programs that focus on nongame species. There is greater growth in fishery management and aquaculture than on the wildlife side.

Fishery management and wildlife management are two of the toughest environmental fields to enter. New hiring levels have been stagnant. Yet jobs exist for determined and resourceful people. Sound ecological skills and an accompanying major such as forestry aid people seeking employment, as do extensive work experience and relevant technical skills. Consider some of the unique jobs available with utility companies, nonprofit organizations, game preserves, and universities as a starting point for your career in this field.

PARKS AND OUTDOOR RECREATION

Parks and outdoor recreation is one of the most popular environmental fields; many of us dream of becoming a ranger, and the field has a great number of them. Other positions include recreation planner, interpreter, administrator, natural resource manager, and research and maintenance staff member. Despite common misconceptions, only a small percentage of parks and recreation employment is in the National Park Service. Other federal agencies, state and local park systems, and private nature centers provide the majority of jobs.

Demand for outdoor recreation continues to climb, in part because more people live in urban areas and want recreation close to home. Also, an aging population with more free time wants to use recreational areas year-round, not just for hiking but also for many other activities, such as exercising and learning. Consequently, park professionals have to deal with a variety of complicated multiple-use issues. Balancing recreation and preservation tops this list.

The field can be tough to break into, so seasonal or volunteer work is an absolute necessity. Interpersonal skills and some background in hard sciences are the next most important prerequisites. Be prepared to relocate often in your career.

FORESTRY

The days of foresters who spent most of their time in the woods are over. Forestry professionals now have diverse backgrounds and work in a variety of positions. The Society of American Foresters lists more than 700 types of forestry jobs, many of them held by specialists such as forest economists and forest hydrologists. Increasingly, foresters are moving out of the forest and into the office. The fastest-growing demand is for foresters to stem the decline of the nation's urban forests.

Foresters work on issues such as acid rain, smog, and other problems that affect the health of forests. Today, there is increasing emphasis on multiple uses of the forest as a recreational area, a watershed, a habitat for fish and wildlife, and a source of timber.

Nearly half of all foresters work for timber companies or as consultants elsewhere in the private sector, which has grown in its share of the forestry field. An additional quarter of the nation's foresters work for the federal government, and 17 percent work in state or local positions. Overall, forestry employment is stagnant, and many foresters now look for jobs in other, related environmental fields.

Declining admissions to forestry schools and an aging work force will gradually boost employment prospects in the mid- to late 1990s. To compete effectively for scarce traditional forestry jobs as they become available, today's forester needs a higher level of education. Due to increased competition, many more foresters obtain graduate degrees now than was the case in the early 1980s.

WHERE ENVIRONMENTAL PROFESSIONALS WORK

When students decide on the course of study they wish to pursue, their decisions are usually based on interest in a particular issue or subject, whether it is water quality, wildlife biology, politics, or accounting. That is how the educational system is structured in the United States. However, selection of a compatible work environment or series of work environments is at least as important in determining whether your career will ultimately be satisfying. Here are some of the variables to consider in choosing your work environment:

• Will you have contact with large numbers of new people every day, or will your dealings be restricted to several coworkers?
• Will you interact with people in a cooperative way or sometimes in an inherently adversarial manner (for example, will you be dealing with regulators, journalists, and lawyers)?
• What is the pace of the office—will you work on long-term projects or on many day-to-day tasks? Are there seasonal 65-hour weeks with lulls in the winter, or 65-hour weeks year-round?
• How pervasive is the bureaucracy?
• Is it an urban or a rural environment? In an office or out in the field?
• How much traveling will you do?

Different people thrive and wilt in different environments, and your work environment is what you must face every morning. The good news is that even though particular careers have characteristic work environments, you can usually find almost any work environment in any career provided you are resourceful and creative. There are foresters who spend long days in the wilderness and those who sit behind computers, interact with dozens of people daily, work for fast-paced consultants, or do research for universities and foundations.

PUBLIC SECTOR

Public sector jobs in federal, state, and local governments have a broad range in salary, educational requirements, and in type.

Federal government. Virtually any imaginable environmental career exists in government at the federal level, in its dozens of departments, agencies, commissions, and bureaus. The federal government is slowly recasting its environmental role in the direction of developing broad regulatory guidelines, conducting research, providing technical assistance and training to state and local governments, and overseeing state and local governments' environmental enforcement.

Increasingly, federal employees manage consultants who carry out much of the government's research and studies. Some stereotypes of working for the federal government have merit, in particular the image of slow-moving and often incomprehensible bureaucratic requirements. However, there is leeway for creativity. You do not have to search far to find a federal environmental professional with a very dynamic career—several are profiled in this book.

Research not only where the jobs are and how to get them but also the various career tracks and how to take advantage of professional development opportunities within the federal government. The danger in working for a large bureaucracy is getting lost in the shuffle and being pigeonholed in a dead-end job. There are opportunities to transfer within the government, but mobility can be constrained and subject to politics. In many areas, an old-boy network persists. Job benefits are excellent at the federal level, as is job security. Salaries, though generally not at the level of the private sector, are often the highest of any in the public sector.

State government. One theme of this book is the increasing involvement of state governments in environmental matters. Most federal environmental regulations are passed on to state governments, which become responsible for implementation and enforcement. In addition, states go beyond federal regulations and take initiative in matters not covered by federal statutes, such as land-use and growth planning or groundwater protection.

States offer much of the diversity of the federal government, from parks to research laboratories. In general, however, the emphasis is less on broad policy setting and more on carrying out of specific programs, distribution of state funds to municipalities, and implementation of statewide planning projects. Programs vary widely depending on finances, environmental circumstances, and the history of environmental involvement in a given state. Salaries are generally lower than at the federal level and vary significantly by state. The work environment can be fraught with politics, but less so than in the past.

Local government. The capacity to deal with environmental issues is increasing at the local level as well as the state level. The increase in local government capability is partly a result of federal and state regulations but also is due to the demands of local residents, who want responses to environmental problems in their communities. Environmental professionals work in municipal and county government, for regional commissions, at wastewater treatment plants, and with local park systems. The extent of environmental employment in a locality can range from one person who performs environmental inspections among many other duties to departments that rival or even surpass those of state governments in size and complexity.

Local-level environmental work is characterized by hands-on emphasis, whether it consists of inspecting corporate wastewater treatment systems, developing recycling programs, or mediating disputes between developers and residents. There is a lot of laboratory work and fieldwork, program development, management, inspection, and enforcement.

The work environment is more political in local government than at any other level, but as the need for technical capacity increases and urban political reform movements spread, competence rather than connections is becoming the norm. In general, pay is lower than for state and federal employees.

Local government is often an excellent place for professionals to start their environmental careers. Turnover is sometimes high, and, given the hands-on focus, entry-level professionals are quickly given responsibilities and opportunities to learn useful skills.

PRIVATE SECTOR

While the public sector includes many of the most highly prized positions in environmental work, the private sector often provides the highest salaries through jobs in both private industry and consulting firms.

Corporations. Environmental employment in the private sector is of almost infinite variety. Environmental professionals work at the corporate or headquarters level in areas ranging from policy to public relations to overall management of environmental programs. Entry-level professionals may develop, install, and maintain pollution control systems, work with consultants and regulators, and do sampling, laboratory work, and research. The difference between a large company and a small one can be dramatic. A small operation might have one staff person doing everything from collecting samples and doing laboratory work to training employees and designing pollution control systems.

The bureaucratic roadblocks to getting things done and getting promoted are generally not as pervasive in the private sector as in the government. However, the bigger companies are, the more bureaucratic they become. The pace is often quicker and the hours longer than in the public sector. Pay, on the whole, is higher than in the public sector, but job security should not be assumed.

Environmental compliance, even in the most enlightened companies, is a cost of doing business that does not generate revenue or product. Therefore, companies do their best to keep staffing low and costs down. Environmental staff members sometimes feel like outsiders who must work hard for cooperation from other departments. This is typically not the case when environmental professionals work for companies formed for the pur-

BP America Laboratories, Cleveland, Ohio. John Cuzowski (right) and Mike Markelov use laboratory robotics to analyze environmental samples.

pose of protecting the environment or managing natural resources, such as waste management firms or timber companies.

Consulting firms. Consultants work throughout the environmental field. Their projects range from a quick review of an environmental impact statement to the design, siting, and construction of a wastewater treatment plant to the multiyear cleanup of the *Exxon Valdez* oil spill. As a consultant, your meal ticket is your ability to have the answers (or know where to find them), to get things done, and to find people who will pay you for this service.

Consulting is for those who like the fast lane and all that goes with it. Hours tend to be long and the pace is often hectic, although there may be extended lulls (which means you do not have enough business). As one consultant half-complains, "I am either starving or I have three clients— each of whom feels the other two don't rate any of my time." Environmental consulting is broken into a top tier of some 100 full-service firms with large staffs and offices throughout the nation and a second tier made up of hundreds of small shops and independent one-person firms.

A very important feature of consulting, sometimes overlooked, is the sales aspect. You are expected to find new clients, and your salary and survival are often based on the volume of work that you bring to the firm. Professionals generally have strong reactions to work in the consulting field—they either love it or dislike it intensely.

NONPROFIT SECTOR

It is almost impossible to characterize the nonprofit sector. By one estimate, as many as 10,000 nonprofit groups are involved in environmental work in some way. Nonprofit organizations are involved in a range of activities that is wide and getting wider. Offices tend to be small, and the pace, though usually on the fast side, varies. A number of factors—the time it takes to achieve goals; chronic underfunding, understaffing, and overwork; the high level of personal involvement; and frequent encounters with people whose degree of personal involvement can wear you down—easily lead to burnout if you cannot develop patience and take the long view.

There is always too much to do in a nonprofit organization, and for survival one must learn to leave the work at the office. On the positive side, nonprofit organizations encourage, even demand, that staff members stretch their creative potential to the fullest. Usually, you work on a number of projects and it is up to you to guide them to completion. Nonprofit organizations are also known for flexibility, fair treatment of employees, and promulgation of democratic principles in the workplace. If you like to take occasional sabbaticals and are a valued worker, nonprofit organizations are likely to accommodate you.

At some time in your career in a nonprofit organization, you are likely to become involved in fund-raising. In a sense, nonprofit organizations are like consulting firms, soliciting grants or donations to perform services or engaging in fee-for-service activities such as conducting energy audits of housing or helping a public agency establish a recycling operation.

Nonprofit organizations employ a very small percentage of workers in the environmental field. Those people, however, have had an influence far greater than their numbers. Nearly every major environmental victory of the past quarter century can be traced to the leadership or involvement of nonprofit groups.

TYPES OF WORK ACTIVITIES

We have seen that environmental professionals work on a broad array of issues, in many disciplines and for hundreds of employers. Nonetheless, a few constants appear in nearly all environmental fields. These broad types of work define much of the day-to-day activities of environmental positions. What follows is a list of some of the major types of work activities and the fields and sectors in which they commonly come into play.

- *Laboratory work.* Laboratory work resides primarily in the environmental protection fields in the private and public sectors as well as in consulting firms.
- *Fieldwork.* Entry-level jobs in many environmental protection and natural resource professions entail fieldwork. If fieldwork is all you want to do, consider becoming a technician or a research scientist.
- *Planning and design.* Some of the "hot" planning areas include water quality and watershed planning, solid waste planning, land-use planning, and integrated natural resource planning, which includes forestry, fishery and wildlife management, water issues, and recreation.
- *Policy-making.* Nonprofit organizations may be the quickest way to get into policy work, albeit from the outside. Entry-level public sector jobs for those with bachelor's degrees are unlikely to include policy-making responsibility. You are even further away from a policy-making role in your first job in the private sector.
- *Regulatory compliance.* State and local governments are the front-line agencies in enforcement and implementation of environmental regulations. Plant-level private sector employment and many consulting positions will also get you involved in regulatory issues.
- *Public information and education.* Almost all jobs in the nonprofit sector involve a substantial public information and education component. Interpreters for park systems are a large segment of employees in this category, followed by public information and public relations staff members in public agencies and, to a lesser extent, in corporations.
- *Research.* Academia is probably your best bet for research. Besides hiring professors, universities hire many types of environmental researchers. Running a close second is the federal government, followed by the private sector and state governments. Many research outfits are set up as nonprofit organizations by trade associations, foundations, and conservation groups.
- *Information management and computers.* The environmental field lives on data: Billions of water, soil, and air samples. Millions of compliance reports. Reams of laws and regulations. Scientific research studies. Budgets, memos, reports, articles, statistics, maps, aerial and satellite photos, permits, and so on. Gathering data, organizing it into some comprehensible system, entering it, manipulating it, and maintaining it is a huge part of environmental work in all sectors.

- *Working with people.* Working with people is a component of many environmental careers. Some jobs in which you are sure to get your fill are those of interpreter, recreation specialist, consultant, public information officer, lobbyist, environmental manager, and almost any position in the nonprofit sector.

DEVELOPING A CAREER STRATEGY

This book's ten chapters on fields of employment describe present conditions in these areas and outline where they are headed. However, the environmental field is evolving and will continue to change dramatically. Career planners and futurists project that the vast majority of those entering the work force now can expect to change careers, not just jobs, several times over the course of their working years. There will be at least as much, if not more, change in the environmental field.

In the midst of such rapid change, what should job seekers do? The following advice summarizes important points given by environmental professionals with successful careers.

The key word is focus. There are mountains of material on the environmental field and careers. Wading through even a small part of this material will wear you out before you make a decision on a first job, let alone start one. Narrowing the field is crucial to success. Let us assume you are at the starting point and have not yet focused. You think you want to pursue an environmental career, but you are not sure which field you are interested in.

Do not start by asking, "Where are the jobs?" There are already too many unhappy employees in the work force who selected a career path based solely on a forecast of job prospects. Start with yourself—what you enjoy, what your skills are, what you want out of life, where your weaknesses lie.

Go through career-planning and assessment exercises to help you identify your likes and dislikes. *What Color Is Your Parachute?*, by Richard Nelson Bolles (Ten Speed Press, annual), is a classic among career-planning books for good reason, and it also lists numerous other resources.

Read over some general environmental career guides like this one to get the lay of the land. Find issue-oriented overview publications like the annual "State of the World" report from the respected Worldwatch Institute. Talk to people whose work gives them a broad perspective on the field, such as professors, career advisors, federal officials, and environmental affairs directors for major companies. Go to conferences just to chat and look around.

REFERENCE MATERIALS

Once you have narrowed your focus to one or several areas of the environmental field—maybe hazardous or solid waste management, fishery and wildlife management, or forestry—you are ready to get a pulse on these particular fields: What are the growth areas, and what are some of the unique opportunities that might be perfect given your skills and avocations?

There are a couple of elements to this strategy. Know the legislation and regulations that govern the field. Legislation and regulations create many jobs. Do not be caught in the situation of a graduate of a four-year water quality management program who inquired about job opportunities in her field. As our conversation progressed, she acknowledged that she was not aware that the Clean Water Act had been reauthorized, bringing about major changes and new programs in the field.

To research regulations, start with the major federal legislation in a given field. In hazardous waste management, for example, the pertinent legislation would be RCRA and Superfund. The subject chapters of this book discuss major legislation in the various fields. To dig deeper, consult trade association publications or the *Environment Reporter*, published by the Bureau of National Affairs (BNA) and available in most college libraries.

See which level of government is implementing the regulations, what type of programs will be created, and what kinds of expertise or professionals will be required. If you really want to dig, find the economic impact analysis, which must accompany most federal regulations; it specifies the cost to businesses and the government of implementing regulations. The *Federal Register*, available in most major libraries or through the implementing agencies, details expenditures and personnel needs. Congressional Quarterly's *CQ Weekly Reports* provides analysis of upcoming legislative packages.

Do not neglect state and local legislation, which gives rise to a growing proportion of environmental regulations. This information is often available from professional associations and state and municipal environmental protection agencies. For state regulations, also see BNA's *Environment Reporter*. You may be zeroing in on a state or municipality where you want to work, but more likely you will be looking for trends: Are states regulating groundwater in the absence of federal standards? Are state hazardous waste regulations tougher than RCRA? On what environmental issues are large cities focusing? One clue that a major federal legislative package might be on the way is the passage of similar environmental legislation in a number of states.

General environmental publications, which cover the bigger picture, should also be on your reading list. These include *Sierra, Audubon*, the *Amicus Journal, Environmental Action*, and *Environment*. After you have narrowed your search for a field, you can also begin to tap into reams of specialized information. The publications of trade and professional organizations, such as the *Journal of the Air and Waste Management Association* (published by the Air and Waste Management Association), are often useful sources of information.

Another source of information is specialized newsletters, which have sprung up in recent years. Nearly every field and subfield has one or more of these arcane but essential publications. People in the field will tell you which newsletters are important to read. Some of these might be available at college libraries.

Budget a small amount of time each week to stay on top of trends in environmental careers. You will spend years and thousands of dollars getting an environmental education; by comparison, an hour or two a week and $100 for subscriptions is a small investment.

PROFESSIONAL AND TRADE ASSOCIATIONS

Some of the best sources of environmental information are professional and trade associations, which are made up of people working in the field. They sponsor events and conferences, publish magazines and special reports, and often have job-listing services. It is a good idea to join one or several organizations of interest and get involved in the local chapter. Student membership and participation are welcomed and usually sought. The Resources section at the ends of the subject chapters list many of these professional associations. The *Encyclopedia of Associations*, published by Gale Research Company and available at most libraries, provides an exhaustive listing.

ENVIRONMENTAL PROFESSIONALS

Talking to people actually involved in a field is the source of the best and most current information. This includes the often misunderstood process of informational interviewing (see chapter 4 or consult *What Color Is Your Parachute?* for a thorough discussion of informational interviewing). Undoubtedly, it can be more than a little intimidating to call on professionals for information, but if you do it in the right way, the friendliness of their responses might surprise you. After all, most people like to talk about themselves and their life's work as well as help those who show interest in a similar profession.

When planning an informational interview, suggest setting a telephone or personal interview time convenient for the interviewee's schedule, and have your questions prepared ahead of time. During the interview, take less than 20 minutes of the person's time. Informational interviewing is a particularly good method for those looking at the job market and developments in a geographic area or in a particular company. Your first contacts could come from trade associations, authors of articles, or even the telephone book. Ask those you call for more contacts and your list will quickly expand.

Deciding on the career that is right for you is hard work. It involves assessing oneself, conducting detailed research, meeting people in the field, and, finally, taking a risky leap of faith. Once you have set a direction for yourself, however, things will become much clearer. A picture will begin to emerge of which skills you need, where employment opportunities are, how to get experience, and so forth. The remaining chapters of this book provide essential advice on how to proceed in the major environmental fields, once *you* decide where you want to go.

VALUES, ETHICS, AND ENVIRONMENTAL PROFESSIONALISM

An issue that professionals and career counselors too often avoid is that of personal values in one's environmental career. Yet these questions are raised repeatedly by students and job seekers. Many people decide to pursue environmental careers out of a desire to be stewards of the environment.

Is the integration of your values and ethics into your career an area of concern to you? If so, you have already begun to formulate a personal code of professional ethics. Environmental professionals repeatedly state in interviews that much of the satisfaction in an environmental career comes from feeling one has in some way improved the quality of the environment. It is difficult to gain this satisfaction unless certain values serve as benchmarks for your professional conduct and objectives.

Be careful in making blanket assumptions about certain careers or fields, especially those in the private sector. Stereotypes and generalizations have a way of taking on a life of their own, often quite apart from reality. Get your own information. Do not assume you will have no trouble being a purist if you avoid the private sector, for instance, or that all corporate staff members wear black hats.

In the public sector, long-term goals often require short-term compromise. Everyone understands that. When does essential compromise, however, cross the line into lax regulation that threatens the agency's goals? Government workers deal with these issues every day. The nonprofit sector, despite its reputation for promoting advocacy and strict ethics—a reputation that has been earned—has its own ethical challenges. The need for funds to keep the operation going, for instance, can often lead a person away from the work for which the funding is intended.

Some companies and agencies might require you to compromise your personal values significantly. Obviously, you will want to find out about the ethical reputation of a prospective employer. How do you go about this evaluation? In the case of a private company, a great deal of information is available. Read the company's annual report and do a literature search on the company. For a larger company, you can call or write some of the national environmental organizations—such as the Citizen's Clearinghouse for Hazardous Waste, the Natural Resources Defense Council, Environmental Action, and The Wilderness Society—for information on a company's reputation. Greenpeace keeps a detailed record of flagrant corporate polluters. Land trusts may be able to tell you about developers with unsavory environmental reputations.

Talk to local environmental activists and organizations. Consult with public regulatory agencies. Is the company in line with their permit requirements? Do not hesitate to check references and call individuals and companies the firm has worked with. Keep in mind that you will have to do a lot of reading between the lines.

Finally, when you are being interviewed, remember that you should also be interviewing. Employers respect this; it is a plus to ask questions at an interview. Ask for a tour of the plant. Bill Walters, president of the National Association of State Park Directors, advises: "Don't just look for particulars, but try to understand the overall philosophy of any agency, company, or organization. You might dislike working somewhere because of [the organization's] attitude."

Ultimately, choosing an employer will boil down to a judgment call on your part. Armed with as much information as you can find about the company or the agency, ask yourself if you can picture yourself working there, given your values. Focus on the tasks and objectives you would face day to day.

Adherence to personal ethics will not always be easy, regardless of which sector you choose. Charles Odegaard, Pacific Northwest regional director for the National Park Service, puts it this way: "Being and remaining a professional is very difficult. Not to keep your job, but to keep being a professional—those are two entirely different things. For example, every day things will be done that you don't entirely agree with. I guarantee it. Once a decision has been made with everyone's input, however, you have only two choices: You give it 100 percent of your loyalty or you quit. Either way you remain a professional. It takes guts, honesty, and integrity."

2 Education for Your Environmental Career

IF YOU want to be a lawyer, go to law school; a doctor, go to medical school; an accountant, major in accounting; an environmental professional . . . well, take your pick from any number of educational opportunities. The environmental field is diverse, interdisciplinary, and ever changing, encompassing many types of professions and activities. Since the environmental field has evolved rapidly, dozens of new disciplines are being formed, often as combinations of more traditional fields. Frequently, the same job can be approached from numerous directions, since educational preparation is not as formalized as in some other fields.

Your strategy for structuring your education and training for an environmental career should have several stages. For your formal education, you need to choose a field of study and at least one educational institution. But your informal education is equally important and continues long after your formal education is complete. Career changers may need some retraining, and everyone needs to know how to find the educational resources most helpful to them.

It is easy to see the diversity of educational backgrounds among environmental professionals: English majors are working at state parks; botanists are working in wildlife management; business majors are running waste disposal facilities. Some jobs, of course, have more formalized requirements; for your chosen career you might be required to have an engineering degree, plain and simple. However, you might have a degree in civil or mechanical engineering, and your experience in communications or another area might give you the edge over other applicants who have only engineering degrees.

This does not mean that any education will do for an environmental career. But we can broaden the way we view education to include not only degrees but also the relevant skills you will need for your first job and to meet long-term career goals. A focus on acquiring skills is critical for tomorrow's job market. Those who survive and flourish will be individuals who develop and can market transferable skills that will allow them to be flexible and fill many different roles.

In the environmental field, new disciplines are constantly being created in response to demand. Formal training programs do not exist for every job, so employers focus on applicants' relevant skills, experience, and education. For example, there are few, if any, formal recycling education programs. Consequently, recycling employers look for various combinations of skills and experience in business, engineering, communications, and management.

Two kinds of transferable skills are relevant to environmental careers. The first are skills in areas closely related to the particular field you are pursuing; for example, hazardous waste managers should know about water quality issues, and natural resource managers should understand planning issues. A frustrated supervisor for a state department of natural resources comments on the practice of "boxing in" environmental disciplines: "Our wildlife biologists know wildlife, but they can't talk to our foresters. How, then, can they possibly perform the integrated natural resource management that is being called for?" They could if they had taken some forestry courses or held seasonal positions in forestry.

A second type of transferable skills are broader in scope. These are the liberal arts skills, which include interpersonal skills. Writing, speaking, management, problem solving, computer expertise, and analytical thinking are a few of these process skills. Professionals in all disciplines stress the importance of these abilities. A vice president of a large timber company, for example, says: "What separates the forest managers from the technicians is not their knowledge of forestry but the liberal arts skills: Can they work with people, can they communicate, can they see and solve problems?"

Along with the question of what to study comes the query "How long?" Some fieldwork positions require a high school education and hands-on training; most technicians have two-year associate's degrees. Professional positions may require applicants to have a B.A. or B.S., a master's degree, or a Ph.D. As in many fields, however, there has been some "educational bracket creep": jobs that once called for a high school education often require a two-year technician's degree, many technician's jobs are going to college graduates, and so forth.

Environmental professionals hold a wide range of degrees. At one end are broad, interdisciplinary degrees such as environmental studies (hard sciences and liberal arts or social science course work) and environmental sciences (a variety of hard sciences and environmental science course work). The structures of these degrees are as varied as the number of institutions offering them. Other professionals have studied the basic sciences, such as biology, chemistry, or physics, or obtained more specialized degrees, such as in chemical engineering. Finally, many have focused on the liberal arts. But whatever the degree, remember that the diploma is designed to be a key, not a lock. Acquire the skills and then market them and retool as necessary. And keep in mind all of the other factors in an employer's decision on whether to hire you.

It is beyond the scope of this book to list specific schools or programs for your environmental education. Over the past two decades, there has been a tremendous increase in the diversity of programs and the number of colleges offering them at all degree levels. Where to start? Check your public or college library for *Peterson's Guide to Four-Year Colleges* (published annually) or *Peterson's Annual Guides to Graduate Study*.

The undergraduate guide lists colleges under academic majors related to environmental fields. Miniprofiles are given for all colleges; detailed descriptions are given for most. You will have to write to the colleges to obtain program information.

The guides to graduate study come in five volumes. Volume 1 provides an overview. The publication lists colleges under 31 academic majors related to environmental fields. Miniprofiles are given for all colleges; two-page descriptions are given for most.

A real value of both of these guides is that they present miniprofiles and often two-page descriptions of environmental programs, departments, and schools. Included in the descriptions are listings of faculty members and their research interests. This is helpful information in considering graduate programs.

Using these guides and others listed in the Resources section at the end of this chapter, you can find the program that is right for you.

CHOOSING YOUR EDUCATION

You will get the most out of this section if you have already read chapter 1 and, possibly, some of the subject chapters and have some idea of your career goals. Ideally, you would decide on what type of career you want and then select the education that would best prepare you for that career. More often, however, a career decision is made during, and as a result of, your education, and it may be far from solidified when you graduate. This is a bit of a Catch-22. You make an education decision based on a career decision, but your career decision evolves from your education decision.

The best way to resolve this stressful contradiction is to do your homework. Career decisions are easiest when you have as much information and experience as possible. Presumably, you have decided you have some interest in an environmental career. Through reading, experience, reflection, and talking to professionals, you should be able to come up with a general direction for your career. Then you can move forward to your education and adjust or alter your course as you learn more and refine your priorities.

UNDERGRADUATE PROGRAMS

Maybe you are a high school student looking at colleges, a college freshman thinking about transferring, a sophomore agonizing over declaring a major, or a professional thinking about going back to school. In any event, remember that the particular undergraduate degree you obtain is not as important to your career as many would have you think. Most employers consider your degree as one of a number of hiring criteria, and many professionals have careers that are only tangentially related to their undergraduate degrees.

Part of the reason for this is that you generally cannot do very specialized work in college unless you are working toward a narrowly focused degree in, say, wildlife management. For the most part, undergraduate education develops a broad base of skills and teaches you how to learn. After graduation, you build on this information through formal and informal education to determine your career. In other words, five years out of school your view of your career will be related less to your degree than to what you have done in the work force over those five years.

Ideally, the college you select should have a diversity of environmental majors. This gives you the flexibility to try different types of courses and change majors if necessary. If you are interested in environmental protection and have a science and engineering orientation, you might want to attend a college that has undergraduate majors in environmental engineering or environmental health or both. If your interests lie in environmental protection with a communications, education, or policy orientation, you could consider a college that offers a communications, education, or public administration major in addition to environmental engineering or environmental health.

If you are interested in natural resource management with a science orientation, you might want to attend a school with a strong selection of natural resource options. For example, the Ohio State University School of Natural Resources offers 34 options in seven major environmental fields.

Those with a natural resource management focus and an interest in policy should go to a similar school and take communications, public administration, management, and other social science courses.

Such advice would appear to lead you toward a larger university, and, indeed, this is where you are likely to find the largest variety of degrees. However, you can obtain an excellent general undergraduate preparation for an environmental career at a smaller college. One noteworthy benefit of attending smaller institutions is closer contact between students and professors, which can be critical to giving direction to your career. In a smaller school, however, you must take the initiative to get a more diverse education through innovative scheduling, independent studies, and internships. Another alternative is to take some of your prerequisites at a smaller school and transfer to a larger one for specialization later in your education.

If you have the motivation, double majors or a major and a minor are an excellent way to build a strong foundation of liberal arts and analytical skills. Employers love combinations such as chemistry and political science or environmental science and business. Be prepared, however, for resistance from professors and advisors if you express interest in double majors that include hard sciences and the liberal arts—employers tend to like them more than academics do.

Whatever orientation or major you are considering, you should take a very close look at the programs or departments that interest you. Visit the college and talk with faculty and staff members and students. Ask about the graduates of the program: How many go on to jobs or graduate school? What types of jobs and graduate school? What are typical first positions for graduates?

You should look closely at a program's or department's career counseling and job placement activity, especially in the environmental field. Cornell University's Department of City and Regional Planning and the University of Michigan's School of Natural Resources in Ann Arbor are two examples of programs with environmental career placement offices. Some programs or departments have advisors who can guide students in environmental career planning and help with job searches and internship placement. See if there is an environmental career resource center, equipped with directories, newsletters, and books related to environmental career planning and job searching. This not only helps you with your career planning but also says a lot about the program's orientation and commitment to students after they leave the lecture halls.

Finally, write to relevant professional associations (see the Resources sections in the appropriate chapters) to see if the schools you are considering are accredited by these organizations. Many fields, such as fishery and wildlife management, forestry, and planning, have comprehensive accreditation processes established by professional societies.

GRADUATE SCHOOLS

Graduate school is not two more years of college before getting a job. There are key differences in how graduate school is structured and the purpose it serves. Graduate school teaches you a specific discipline and set of skills that allow you to enter a particular profession or job.

Your preparation and motivations for entering graduate school should be quite different from those that went into deciding on your undergraduate education. Unfortunately, many—especially those in academia—do not see it this way. You may experience significant pressure from college

Utah State University, Logan, Utah. Professor Glen Edwards teaches a graduate seminar in forestry.

faculty members, fellow students, and the marketplace to go directly to graduate school. However, although getting a master's degree is almost a prerequisite to being a professional in certain fields, many professionals have established successful careers by the right combination of work experience and undergraduate degrees.

Graduate school requires a lot of work, time, and money. Spend some energy on your decisions involving this investment. The first step is to ask the question "What do I want to do—what type of professional do I want to become?" You should be able to cite the types of work you could do after you receive the degree, including examples of positions.

The types of work you anticipate should be fairly specific, not "I'll work in hazardous waste" or "I can work for a state department of natural resources or a consulting firm." Instead, you might say to yourself, for example, "I am getting a master's degree in environmental engineering with a focus on hazardous waste management because I want to work for an environmental consultant assessing hazardous waste sites and developing remedial action plans. I am looking for hands-on work, and consultants are the ones who go to sites and do the fieldwork and develop site plans. With a master's degree, I will probably start out in the field as part of a site team and gradually progress to managing a team. Eventually, I could head a consulting firm's hazardous waste division or at least a regional office of a national firm involved in this work."

This is a very well thought out plan leading to a decision to attend graduate school. What follows is an overdramatized example of a disaster in the making. "I'm going on to get a master's degree in fishery biology because I majored in fishery biology. I would look for a job now, but my friend said you need a master's degree to get a job in this field. I am not sure what the program will be like, but I figure I'll decide what to focus on after I start. This way when I hit the job market I'll have all my education behind me and I'll be ready to go." Big surprises and frustrations may await this student.

If you are fresh out of college, don't know what to do, and are dreading the thought of looking for a job, the answer is not to go immediately to graduate school but to clarify your interests and strengths through some work experience. This way, you can learn about yourself, work environments, and your field before you specialize. You are not setting your career back by postponing graduate school—despite what classmates, parents, and even professors might tell you.

Many employers like to see candidates approach their graduate degree with some sense of purpose and direction rather than just go immediately to graduate school after obtaining their undergraduate degree. What did you set out to learn? What skills did you pick up? Get some work experience; find out what you like and dislike. Then, armed with this information, head off to graduate school.

Assuming you have done all your homework and have decided to go to graduate school, the first step is to obtain catalogs and additional information from the schools that interest you. Thoroughly research the full range of available programs by looking at the various directories of graduate programs. Ask professionals in your field where they did their graduate work.

A potential graduate student should look not only at the program but also at the department, school, or university that houses the program. Is this program strong compared with the other programs in the department or school? Is it growing or decreasing in importance? Are there other environmental graduate programs at the university besides the one that interests you? A university that has other such programs will present additional opportunities and resources. Another key area to consider is the faculty members and their research and professional interests. Do they fit your goals?

Using this process, you should be able to select five to ten programs that deserve closer scrutiny. If possible, visit these schools to talk with faculty members and students before applying. Also, talk with graduates, especially those who have jobs that interest you. Did their degrees help them

You can choose from diverse environmental educational opportunities in undergraduate and graduate study as well as in continuing education.

obtain their positions? Where do they work? What is the range of starting salaries? Be wary of any program in which faculty members are hazy on this information or will not refer you to graduates.

COMMUNITY COLLEGES AND TECHNICAL SCHOOLS

Some people enter the environmental field primarily because they want to spend a lot of time outdoors. So they get a B.S. and maybe an M.A. to ensure their getting a good job. Much to their chagrin, they find that they are spending a lot of time indoors, doing paperwork, managing staff, overseeing projects, talking on the telephone, and developing budgets. And it gets worse with every promotion.

These people may have been happier obtaining a two-year associate's degree or a technician's certificate, both of which might have taught them skills that would have allowed them to stay in the field and outdoors. If you think you might be such a person, or if a four-year degree is not currently in your plans, read on.

Community colleges offer two-year associate's degrees in a range of environmental subjects: conservation, ecology, environmental studies, environmental engineering technologies, environmental health sciences, forestry, fisheries, wildlife management, landscape architecture, natural resource management, parks management, and pollution control technologies.

You can get a job in the environmental field with a two-year degree. Most of these jobs are for technicians. They are heavily oriented toward fieldwork or laboratory work and hands-on skills. For example, Hocking Technical College in Nelsonville, Ohio, profiled graduates of their two-year programs in recreation and wildlife technology and forestry technology. Graduates' job titles included state game protector, park maintenance supervisor, forestry technician, environmental specialist, and land management technician.

On the environmental protection side, two-year degrees can prepare you to work as an air pollution control technician, wastewater treatment plant operator, and hazardous waste remediation worker. You would also be qualified for a wide variety of field and laboratory positions in the area of environmental health. As these fields become more technical, an increasing number of technician's jobs will become available.

Do some research on the reputation of the school. Is it accredited? What is the placement record of its graduates? Where are they working? Are they really getting the jobs that the school claims to train its graduates for? If, for example, you are told that a two-year degree in fisheries will get you a job doing original research, watch out. Another word of caution: Check with employers beforehand on the employability of those with technician's degrees in that particular field. In some of the more competitive fields, such as fishery and wildlife management, you might be competing during dry spells with graduates of four-year colleges for technician's jobs. Finally, the job placement services of technical schools are very important.

Many environmental programs at community colleges prepare their students for transfer to a four-year college. Often, there are arrangements with four-year colleges whereby the community college serves as a feeder; that is, acceptance to the four-year college is practically guaranteed and all credits earned at the community college are transferred if certain standards are met. Because community colleges are close to home and have lower tuition, they serve as a low-risk testing ground for your interests and abilities.

LOCATIONS OF SCHOOLS

It is often to your advantage to attend school in the region where you would like to work after graduation. In this way, you can begin to seek out potential employers while in school. It will be easy to search for internships and permanent positions, and the chances are good that your school will have alumni working for firms in the region. College faculty members may be researching issues in the region; part-time faculty members may even have full-time jobs in firms or agencies that are potential or current employers of the program's graduates.

EDUCATIONAL OPTIONS FOR CAREER CHANGERS

Not so long ago, changing a career after about the age of 25 was considered a mistake or, at best, a setback. This attitude is changing, albeit more slowly than the reality of the work world. A worker spending a lifetime with one corporation is less and less common: Whole new industries are being created, and others are becoming obsolete. From one angle this is terrifying, but the flip side is that the opportunity to have a diversified and exciting career has never been greater.

The key to successful career changing is the strategy of focusing on the acquisition, packaging, and marketing of skills. You may desire to change fields within the environmental field or to enter the environmental profession from an entirely separate area. In either case, you should not automatically assume that you need to go back to school. Look first at the tools you already possess and see if they can be used to build your new career.

Take Michael Zamm, for example. An elementary school teacher for seven years, he began volunteering at the Council on the Environment of New York City and became its director of environmental education. Lys McLaughlin worked five years for a public relations firm. Using these skills, she became communications director for the Council on the Environment and then executive director. These are people who have transferred into the environmental field using skills developed in other professions. If you are already an environmental professional, it is even easier to find transferable skills. Environmental employers like to hire professionals with broad experience and capabilities.

The first step in this process is to decide what you want to do in the environmental field. Read through the introductory chapters of this book for the bigger picture and hints on making decisions about environmental careers. Read the chapters on specific fields that interest you. Then do your own research: Talk to environmental professionals, read, and do some volunteer work.

Next, you must assess your skills, talents, and interests in the context of the job market. Are there positions that you are qualified for right now? Do not assume that you are not qualified for a job. Ask potential employers and read the job descriptions. For many positions, you may not need to obtain additional education. For some, you may need some additional education to round out your credentials, such as a series of courses on landscape architecture, a two-month urban tree care program, or a one-week course sponsored by a trade association on current regulatory developments in the waste management field. Career changers in particular should look to informal educational opportunities.

For some, the need for further formal education will depend on how dramatic the career change is. For example, if you are a business manager, you can use your skills and experience in an environmental agency, a consulting firm, or a nonprofit organization without additional schooling if you want to manage contracts or budgets. Some demonstrated interest and knowledge of environmental issues will also help you get a job; volunteer work would be useful. If, however, you want to get involved in designing remedial action plans for hazardous waste sites, you may have to go back to school to study engineering and science.

If you do need to go back to school, choose your program carefully. If you already have a bachelor's degree, you should seriously consider obtaining a master's degree rather than a second undergraduate degree; to employers, an undergraduate degree is an educational foundation, while a graduate degree translates to job-related skills. You may need to take a few prerequisites and an entrance exam before being accepted into graduate school, although these are sometimes waived if an older student shows a capacity to succeed in formal education.

THE OTHER HALF OF YOUR EDUCATION

A degree from an educational institution provides a useful foundation and, as one professional says, "proves you are trainable." As far as the success of your career is concerned, however, your informal education is at least as important as your degree.

John R. Cook, Jr., president of The Environmental Careers Organization (ECO), points out that "employers are desperate for employees with a wide range of skills. Often these are skills you just can't develop in the classroom. This brings up the important distinction between education, which occurs at an institution, and learning or training, which is a very personal process and occurs everywhere throughout your career. The key is linking learning with acting. People have gone far in the environmental profession by acting, by going out and doing something—and not always doing it right. This is how learning becomes real."

Every chapter of this book profiles people who took the initiative and responsibility for their informal learning. Consider the following professionals:

- After studying biology for several semesters at the University of Oregon, Al Solonsky moved to Israel and eventually found a position at an aquaculture research station in the Sinai Desert. Armed with his experience, he returned to the United States to obtain a B.S. and an M.S. in fisheries biology, conducting research with professors during the summer. He became an aquatic biologist with a consulting firm in Seattle.
- Jane Armstrong has a B.A. in literature and a master's degree in library science. She started as a librarian at the Environmental Protection Agency (EPA) Motor Vehicle Emission Laboratory in Ann Arbor, Michigan. Dissatisfied with this position, she transferred to a technical position with the laboratory. Having learned largely on the job, she became senior project manager, overseeing technical investigations and studies related to compliance with the motor vehicle emission component of the Clean Air Act.
- When David Miller could not get a job with a nonprofit organization after graduating with a B.A. in environmental science and economics, he moved to Washington, DC, and volunteered full-time with the National Audubon Society. During the day, he delivered information to legislators' offices and wrote action updates. At night, he waited tables. A question he asked at a conference so impressed an employer that he was hired by Scenic Hudson, Inc., a nonprofit agency in New York. Four years later, he became executive director of Great Lakes United in Buffalo, New York.

While you are still in school, there are many ways to begin to obtain informal education. There are a multitude of internship possibilities, some associated with colleges and some not. College credit can be obtained for many of these positions. Summers between school years provide great opportunities to gain volunteer experience, even if only part-time. Another option is to design an independent project to do during the school year.

See chapter 3, Volunteer Programs and Internships, and the Resources section of the appropriate subject chapters for information on organizations for which you might work. Chapter 3 also shows you how to find and structure an internship that is rewarding for both you and the organization. Although this process occurs best while you are attending school so that there is a constant interplay of theory and practice, it does not stop on your graduation.

For professionals who want to grow, or even keep up, continuing education and training programs are ideal ways to expand their base of knowledge and to retool for quickly changing work conditions. Professional associations, consultants, government agencies, nonprofit organizations, colleges, and industries all sponsor short courses, seminars, conferences, and workshops. Many offer scholarships for students; some will waive tuition altogether. If you can demonstrate that you wish to attend to gain information for a paper or, better yet, an article for a newsletter, you can almost always at least stand in the back. Ask if you can help out in exchange for attending the sessions for free.

The professional associations listed in the Resources sections at the ends of subject chapters offer a range of national, state, and regional conferences and seminars. Consultants sponsor seminars, especially for those in business and industry, on environmental compliance and management. Government agencies like the EPA sponsor short courses for professionals to keep them trained on EPA-approved environmental testing methods. Colleges also have short courses for environmental professionals. Some of the best sources of information on these various programs are trade association publications. If you start sending for information on a particular field, you will soon find yourself on numerous mailing lists and will learn of many such events.

Conferences and workshops on environmental policy and technical issues are constantly offered all over the country. For example, one month's *Environmental Events Calendar* from Region 5 of the Environmental Protection Agency (subscription free) included information on such programs as Pond Stabilization Seminar, National Conference on Enhancing State Lake Management, Portable Gas Chromatography, Annual Conference on Great Lakes Research, Waterworks Operators' School, and

Hazardous Materials Managers' Review Course. These programs were sponsored by public, private, and nonprofit organizations.

Lee DeAngelis, director of environmental career services for ECO, says of the importance of ongoing, informal education: "A college degree will provide you with general and some specific skills, but the real education comes from on-the-job experience supplemented by short courses, conferences, seminars, and workshops aimed at your particular profession. The real value of college thus may be whether or not it taught you how to learn. In the environmental field, the learning never stops."

RESOURCES

Where do you start all the necessary research on education for your environmental career? Your first stop should be a public, college, or even high school library. There you will find directories and guides to help you identify the colleges with majors that interest you.

Next, write for college catalogs and ask for any information beyond a description of courses and requirements. College environmental programs and departments often have booklets and brochures that explain their programs in more detail and give examples of the types of careers their graduates have pursued.

Write to the professional associations in the field that interests you and ask for a list of colleges that offer majors related to the field. State, regional, or local chapters of associations may provide useful information on nearby schools. Faculty members of those schools are probably members of the association.

In your research, watch for college programs that are starting, restructuring, or being phased out. More often than not, there is a lag between when a field demands certain types of graduates and when the universities begin to prepare students to meet that demand.

Be sure to check the journals, magazines, and newsletters in the environmental fields that interest you. Sometimes colleges advertise their programs, especially the new ones, in these publications. These publications are also a good source of information on seminars and other informal educational opportunities in your field.

American Geophysical Union, 2000 Florida Ave., NW, Washington, DC 20009. (202) 462–6903.
American Society of Agronomy, 677 South Segoe Rd., Madison, WI 53711. (608) 273–8080.

Conservation Directory (annual). Lists and describes government and nongovernment organizations and personnel engaged in conservation work at state, national, and international levels. Also lists colleges and universities in the United States and Canada that have conservation studies programs. National Wildlife Federation, 1400 16th St., NW, Washington, DC 20036. (202) 797–6800.

Educational Resources Information Center (ERIC). Sponsored by the U.S. Department of Education, ERIC provides access to education-related literature. This includes about 10,000 documents related to environmental education. Computer searches can be done on such topics as careers in environmental education. ERIC also develops special publications. Two examples are *Using Computers for Environmental Education* and *Strategies and Activities for Using Local Communities as Environmental Education Sites*. For more information, write to ERIC/CSMEE (Clearinghouse for Science, Mathematics, and Environmental Education), Ohio State University, 1200 Chambers Rd., Room 310, Columbus, OH 43212–1792. Call ACCESS ERIC at (800) USE-ERIC.

The Environmental Career Guide, by Nicholas Basta (1991). An explanation of environmental jobs and employers and how to prepare for an environmental career. Published by John Wiley & Sons, 605 Third Ave., New York, NY 10158–0012.

National Environmental Health Association, 720 South Colorado Blvd., Suite 970, Denver, CO 80222. (303) 756–9090.

Opportunities in Environmental Careers, by Odom Fanning (1991). Includes a chapter on education for environmental careers. VGM Career Horizons, National Textbook Company, 4255 W. Touhy Ave., Lincolnwood, IL 60646. (708) 679–5500.

Outdoor Careers, by Ellen Shenk. Stackpole Books, P.O. Box 1831, Cameron and Kelker Streets, Harrisburg, PA 17105. (717) 234–5041.

Peterson's Guide to Four-Year Colleges (1992) and *Peterson's Guide to Two-Year Colleges* (1992). Includes lists of colleges under 32 academic majors related to environmental fields. Gives miniprofiles for all colleges; gives two-page descriptions for most colleges.

Soil Science Society of America, 677 South Segoe Rd., Madison, WI 53711. (608) 273–8080.

Your Resource Guide to Environmental Organizations, edited by John Seredich. Includes the purposes, accomplishments, programs, volunteer opportunities, publications, and membership benefits of 150 environmental organizations. Smiling Dolphins Press, 4 Segura, Irvine, CA 92715.

3   Volunteer Programs and Internships

THERE IS no better way to get started in environmental work than with an internship or a volunteer position. There are hundreds of formal and informal opportunities with government agencies, nonprofit organizations, corporations, and consulting firms. The *National Directory of Internships*, for instance, lists more than 100 environmental organizations advertising intern positions. This listing is just a tiny fraction of the total.

Volunteers and interns perform several valuable services for the environmental field. They provide additional person power, helping professionals solve more environmental problems than they could alone. They spread the word about environmental issues beyond professional circles, making environmental protection an activity of the public. Intern and volunteer coordinators also report that enthusiastic, intelligent volunteers and interns provide a continuous infusion of new ideas.

In many organizations, conservation and environmental protection work could not be done without volunteers and interns. The USDA Forest Service, for example, reports that volunteers log more hours of work each year than full-time staff members do. In some nonprofit groups, interns and volunteers *are* the full-time staff. It would be hard to find a field more wide open to interns and volunteers than environmental work.

That is good news for job seekers, because you are going to need this option. Fifteen or twenty years ago, volunteering or interning might have been a nice way for an environmental job seeker to gain an edge in the job search. Today, however, it is almost a requirement because prospective employers are wary of hiring applicants who have no experience. One employer pointedly asks, "If they haven't been able to do some hands-on work in all their years of education, why would they even think I might pick them over the 95 percent who have at least one and usually several such experiences?" A Nature Conservancy director agrees, saying, "There is no excuse for not having work experience as long as there is such a high demand for volunteers in this field."

Career considerations, of course, are not the only reason to become a volunteer or intern, as we shall see. But whether you get involved because of a passion for environmental causes or to strengthen your résumé, you will find that these experiences bring both personal and professional rewards. Take Lois Gibbs, for example.

When Lois Marie Gibbs was a homemaker in a small town near Love Canal in New York, she began to realize that an abnormal number of her friends and neighbors were contracting serious and unusual illnesses. Too many friends were giving birth to babies with birth defects. Angered and scared, Gibbs led her community in a successful volunteer battle against dumping of hazardous wastes into the canal. She later formed the Citizen's Clearinghouse for Hazardous Wastes, which now has four regional offices working with 7,500 grass-roots organizations. Who knows where your experience might lead?

This chapter provides step-by-step advice to help you decide what kind of position you want, find that position, and structure a rewarding internship or volunteer experience.

ENVIRONMENTAL INTERNSHIPS

Internships in their many forms are responsible for bringing to the environmental field some of the most promising professionals we have today. For those entering environmental work, internships provide a pathway into the field that allows them to begin work in their chosen area before their degree is complete.

WHAT IS AN INTERNSHIP?

It is worthwhile to take a moment to think about this question and to define the different types of internships. "Intern" is one of those words that means different things to different people. To some employers, it conjures up a negative image. Some professionals say that interns are people with limited skills who can give only a few hours and who demand a lot of supervisory time for meager results. For others, an intern is a person who does whatever "grunt work" needs to be done so that full-time staff members are relieved of these duties. Finally, there are those who see interns as creative, talented people who are no different from the permanent staff members (and sometimes are better).

Generally speaking, there are four types of internships in the environmental field:

- *Educational internships.* Part of an associate, undergraduate, or graduate degree, educational internships are usually done for college credit. They include some formal learning agenda that must be completed in addition to the work performed for the sponsoring organization.
- *Project internships.* The most common form of internship, project internships are positions in which interns are asked to complete specific duties or sets of tasks based on the skills they have and those they wish to learn. These types of internships are usually built around the current priorities of the sponsoring organization. The organization wants you to help get today's work done, and your success will be measured by whether or not it gets done and how well.
- *Recruitment internships.* These are sponsored by large companies and government agencies to recruit people for future permanent employment. Recruitment internships give employers a chance to test out people in a real-life setting, and they also give prospective hires a chance to check out the organization.
- *Temporary and seasonal employment.* Some work is specifically designed to be completed by interns and, often, by volunteers. In private companies, this may include routine laboratory work; in land management agencies, it may be trail building and maintenance. Every year, hundreds of people carry out such "internships."

How to Develop an Internship

There are two ways to find and develop an internship that is right for you. One is through formal internship programs. The other is to take an informal approach and design a unique experience. Either way, you must do some planning before you begin. Doing a little homework now can save you and your supervisor a lot of pain later. Here is a simple five-step process that may help.

1. *Know what you want from your internship.* What are you hoping to achieve by being an intern? Do you want to learn new skills, find out how a field operates, put your name on a report, give of yourself to make sure an initiative is passed, get a foot in the door with a specific

employer, enjoy a summer outdoors, meet new people, or simply fulfill a course requirement by putting in your time?

2. *Know what you have to offer.* Environmental employers understand that you are at "intern level," that your skills may be limited. Nonetheless, they need to know what you can do for them that will make it worthwhile for them to take you on. Take some time to inventory your skills and abilities so that you can answer this question. This step is especially important if you are competing for an internship through a formal process.

3. *Identify organizations of interest.* If you have completed the first two steps effectively, you have probably begun to develop a clear picture of a possible internship. You may see yourself working in a chemistry laboratory, for instance, because you want to increase your skill level, add some practical experience to your résumé, and find out whether day-to-day life in the laboratory meets your career expectations. Your classwork has given you some basic skills to offer, and you know your enthusiasm is a selling point. Now you need to target organizations that can offer the experience you have in mind. Get directories, talk to teachers and advisors, go to conferences and job fairs, and call prospective employers directly to narrow your list of possible places to intern.

4. *Make your interest known.* Get in touch with people in your targeted organizations. Find out whether the internship you have in mind is a realistic possibility. Ask why the agency or company uses interns. Does the company's need match with your need? If the employer has a formal intern program, get an application and ask for advice on how to be successful in filling it out. Finally, talk to current and past interns if you can to see whether reality matches what you have heard and read.

5. *Land the internship.* The preceding four steps will almost certainly provide you with a variety of choices for internships in which both you and the organization will profit. Select those that seem the best and follow carefully the advice people in the organization have given you. Be sure to communicate clearly that you understand how and why the employer uses interns and that your skills and needs match the profile.

When no formal intern program exists, you may have to carry this process one step further, to the preparation of a formal proposal. If you have found the perfect sponsor for your internship, talked to people in the organization about their work, and identified one or two projects you would enjoy working on and still have not gotten the response you want, try sending a two- or three-page proposal to the hiring authority outlining exactly how you propose to help the organization as an intern.

For example, in researching a local planning agency, you may read a news story stating that the county the agency serves is running out of landfill space and the agency has been designated to develop a solid waste management plan. You might contact the agency's manager and say: "I read in the paper that your agency will be developing a solid waste plan. I would think that one of your initial steps would be to research current solid waste management practices in the country. I gained research experience when I collected information on solid waste management for a case study in an environmental science class. I have prepared an outline of how I could perform this research for you this summer as an intern." The manager may not go ahead with the project you outline, but your approach will get a discussion going and can lead to another mutually beneficial project.

WHERE TO FIND ENVIRONMENTAL INTERNSHIPS

Internships can be found in all sectors and at all levels. They are not always plentiful, but diligent searching will reveal them. The truly inventive can also create them.

PUBLIC SECTOR

Pressures to cut costs and at the same time deliver services of high quality abound in the public sector. Often when budgets are pruned, public agencies turn to internships for professional support.

Federal and state government. Federal and state environmental agencies often have established internship, summer, and part-time programs. Contact these agencies during the fall for summer programs—at least three to six months in advance of when you are available. Consider federal, state, and local opportunities. For example, if you want to work for the Environmental Protection Agency (EPA) or any other federal agency, contact its offices in Washington, DC, but contact regional offices, research laboratories, and other facilities as well. The agencies of the Department of the Interior (National Park Service, U.S. Geological Survey, Bureau of Land Management, U.S. Fish and Wildlife Service, etc.) have detailed requirements for interns, seasonal employees, and volunteers, while other agencies are more informal. Environmental agencies at the state level mirror this distinction, with land management and wildlife agencies usually having more formal programs. Seek out professionals and ask whether their organizations offer internships. If so, query them about the application procedure. Ask which manager makes hiring decisions.

University career placement offices should also know about such opportunities and may have cooperative arrangements with these agencies.

Local government. Some local governments have established internship programs. Usually, however, the process is much more informal, which means it is up to you to take the initiative. A mid-sized or large metropolitan area will have a number of different agencies, and a large municipality will have dozens of municipal and county units of government,

Municipality of Metropolitan Seattle, Seattle, Washington. Tammy Adams collects water samples adjacent to METRO's wastewater treatment plant outlet in Puget Sound.

commissions, and regional agencies. Start at home; local governments like to hire their own citizens. Because local government is so close to the issues, it is an excellent place to gain practical work experience.

PRIVATE SECTOR

Internship programs in private industry or consulting firms will be less common than in the public or nonprofit sectors. There are times, however, when the lack of these opportunities is due to the simple fact that nobody has taken the trouble to suggest and develop them in concert with employers.

Corporations. Although many companies have formal internship programs, few of these programs focus on the environment. Check with the company's human resources department, but do not stop there. If you are interested in a large corporation, seek out local facilities. See whether it has an environmental health and safety staff. At the plant level, you may find that the company has never used an intern and has not even considered the idea; be prepared to assess the company's needs and create your own position. In these cases, specific projects with tangible end products will gain an employer's attention. You might administer a training needs survey that the environmental manager has never found time to do or organize a database. A good question to ask is "What projects have been sitting on your back burner for more than three months that I could take the lead on?"

Consulting firms. Only the largest consulting firms will have formal internship programs, and these programs usually recruit engineers and scientists from disciplines that the firm needs to have represented on its permanent staff. Of the hundreds of smaller firms, few have formal internship programs. Consulting companies are extremely dynamic operations, always looking for business and staffing for projects. If you call them the day after they land a big contract, you may be in luck; if you visit the day they finish that project, you might see laid-off staff members leaving the office. Consultants are accustomed to working with a variety of staffing situations and may be open to part-time and internship arrangements. The downside is that they rarely have a lot of time to train and manage interns. Your task, therefore, is to convince those who have the hiring power that you have a service to offer and are worth a small investment of their time.

A check of the local Yellow Pages under Environmental Conservation and Ecological Services will probably yield 15 or 20 firms in a large metropolitan area. Professors or contacts in professional associations may also know of some opportunities. Also check the *Consultants and Consulting Organizations Directory*, published by Gale Research, which is cross-referenced to list environmental consultants by geographic area and consulting activity.

NONPROFIT SECTOR

Nonprofit organizations are one of your best bets for internships. Literally hundreds of nonprofit organizations offer intern positions in which you will perform challenging work because the professional staff is so small. In major nonprofit groups such as the National Wildlife Federation, the Natural Resources Defense Council, The Nature Conservancy, and so forth, competition for internships is intense. Unpaid internships are common in the nonprofit world, and those that are paid may provide an extremely small stipend. There are many nonprofit environmental organizations at the local level, and if you are a self-starter you can do incredibly substantive work.

Friends of the Earth, Seattle, Washington. Kathy Blume volunteered for the Friends of the Earth campaign to increase media coverage of environmental issues in the Seattle metropolitan area.

NATIONAL ENVIRONMENTAL INTERNSHIP PROGRAMS

In addition to your personal internship search, you may want to enlist the help of an organization that offers environmental internships with many different employers. Two major nonprofit organizations are devoted to developing such positions and finding talented people to fill them. They are the Environmental Careers Organization (ECO) (authors of this book) and the Student Conservation Association.

THE ENVIRONMENTAL CAREERS ORGANIZATION (ECO)

ECO arranges short-term, paid positions in environmental fields for college students, recent graduates, and entry-level job seekers. ECO has

ECO Pacific Northwest Associate Retreat, Seattle, Washington. ECO retreats provide an informal way for associates to meet one another.

branch offices in Boston, Cleveland, San Francisco, Seattle, and Tampa that develop and administer internships in 17 states.

Sponsoring organizations include public agencies at the federal, state, and local levels; corporations; private consulting firms; activist groups; and other nonprofit organizations. ECO's role is largely that of matchmaker, finding the best applicants for positions based on sponsors' needs.

ECO associates, as the interns are called, perform well with minimal training and supervision. A key part of ECO's job is to ensure that an internship is both educational and challenging for the associate and productive for the sponsor.

Applications received at ECO go through a screening process. ECO refers applicants to sponsors for review, and the sponsors decide whom to interview. Three areas are emphasized in the application process:

1. *Direction.* Knowing your career goals and what you want to do now.
2. *Experience.* Volunteer work, research, and class projects.
3. *Strong references.* Favorable review of your work by former supervisors or coworkers.

ECO positions span the entire spectrum of environmental and conservation careers but are more likely to fall in the environmental protection fields than in outdoor conservation areas.

STUDENT CONSERVATION ASSOCIATION (SCA)

A nonprofit organization, the Student Conservation Association has 35 years of experience and develops more than 1,450 resource management positions every year in federal, state, and private parks and natural lands across the country through two programs. One program provides summer internships to about 450 high school students annually. These student volunteers serve in coeducational groups of 6 to 12 participants with one or two adult supervisors. These groups spend three to five weeks working on a project while living in a camp. One week is spent on a backpacking trip or in some other exploratory activity.

In addition, SCA offers about 1,000 positions each year with resource, recreation, forest, wildlife, and fishery management agencies through its Resource Assistant Program, which operates year-round and is open to high school graduates 18 years of age or older. Undergraduate and graduate students find these positions to be great stepping-stones. The program also provides diverse research internships with educational institutions. Positions, which usually last 12 weeks, include a travel grant, free housing, a stipend for food and basic living expenses, and a uniform allowance. The association also publishes *Earth Work*, a monthly publication containing at least 100 job listings ranging from internships to executive positions. Each issue also includes a calendar of events; articles about agencies, issues, and schools; and an advice column for aspiring conservation workers called "Green at Work."

HOW TO MAKE THE MOST OF YOUR INTERNSHIP

Whether you create your own internship, get one through an organization's program, or find a position through ECO or SCA, it is what you accomplish with the opportunity that will determine how useful the experience is for you, your sponsor, and the environment. Here are some pointers to help you make your internship useful and rewarding:

- *Develop goals.* The most successful internships focus on one or two specific projects, are well supervised, run on a schedule, and have an end product. Approach your internship as you would a job: Work with your supervisor to develop a set of goals and a work plan. Be wary of unstructured internships.
- *Get what you need.* Projects for interns are not usually of first priority, and they can often drag on indefinitely while other projects take precedence. Be diplomatic, but try to pin down organizations and supervisors on decision dates.
- *Set regular meetings.* Set up a regularly scheduled meeting with your supervisor, ideally once a week, to evaluate your progress. Insist on sticking to this schedule.
- *Expect some tedium.* Anticipate that you will do some mundane tasks such as photocopying, typing, and running errands. If this takes more than one-third of your time, however, the organization has brought you in as an office assistant, not as a preprofessional intern.
- *Keep records.* Keep records of your accomplishments and copies of your work. Before you leave, request a letter of recommendation that you can use in future job applications. If possible, develop working relationships with more than one staff member so that if your supervisor leaves, there will still be someone who can speak to future employers about your accomplishments.
- *Show enthusiasm.* An unwritten code says that interns should be willing to go the extra mile to get a job done. Many before you have adhered to this code, and your internship will, in part, be evaluated on your willingness to come in on a Saturday or attend an evening meeting. This also allows you to get the most out of your work experience. One reason why

interns are appreciated is that they bring enthusiasm to an organization. Do not be afraid to show some excitement about your work.

- *Get to know people.* Meet people in your company and in related organizations. Ask them about their work and tell them about your professional aspirations. If your work is solid, this networking may take you far.

SALARY

Whether you will be paid for your internship depends on the demand in your field, the organization's resources, and your level of experience and education. A paycheck is nice, but many agencies consider an internship to be part of your education. Thus, your learning, not salary, should be the foremost consideration. A Student Conservation Association worker observes: "We have people who jump at a national park position that pays close to minimum wage for passing out parking stickers. At the end of the summer, what advantage do they have over the individual who took a volunteer position working with a natural resource manager collecting and analyzing data for a resource management plan?"

Although it is true that unpaid internships are more common, paid positions are not at all out of the question. Nearly every state government, for instance, has an "intern" category in its personnel system that carries a stipend roughly comparable to the pay for entry-level jobs. A glance at nonprofit internships listed in career magazines like *Earth Work, Environmental Opportunities, The Job Seeker,* and elsewhere shows weekly intern earnings that range from less than $100 to more than $400 per week. It is not unusual for interns in the private sector (especially engineers and scientists) to earn more than $500 per week. At ECO, where all intern positions are paid, salaries range from $300 to more than $600 per week; the majority are around $400.

VOLUNTEERING FOR THE ENVIRONMENT

We are a nation of volunteers, and nowhere is this more evident than in the environmental world. Nearly everything stated in this chapter about internships is also true of volunteering. The five-step process of securing an internship is virtually identical to that of finding a satisfying way to volunteer. Unpaid internships, in fact, could be considered one form of volunteerism. There are many other ways to volunteer, however, and some special considerations are unique to the volunteer experience.

WHY PEOPLE VOLUNTEER

There are as many reasons for volunteering as there are individuals. A desire to perform community service, personal interest, extension of a career, social interaction, a desire to make a difference, and professional development are a few. Four major reasons for volunteering are worth noting:

1. Many people volunteer to gain work experience, develop skills, explore career options, or find a job. Volunteering allows you to try out different jobs before settling on one. When looking for a job, volunteering can help you get a foot in the door, make contacts, and build a professional reputation.

    Volunteers are the lifeblood of many environmental organizations and agencies. One example is Ron Dodson, president of the Audubon Society of New York state, who recalls, "I spent several years in a capacity that can only be described as professional volunteer before landing my first job with the Audubon Society."
2. Some people volunteer because of a personal interest in an area unrelated to their existing careers. These people often bring valuable professional skills. An example might be a banker who serves on a commission exploring ways to finance options for disposing of solid waste in her community.
3. Often, environmental professionals volunteer as an extension of their careers. Many environmental professionals sit on the boards of local environmental organizations, professional societies, or commissions. Tom Stanley, chief of natural resources for the Cleveland Metroparks, for example, is founder and president of a land trust in his community. One could argue that such "after-hours" participation by environmental professionals is the norm rather than the exception. These people usually say that volunteering is part of their professional as well as personal development.
4. Finally, many people volunteer simply because they are concerned—perhaps even outraged—about the deterioration of our environment. These people ask simply "What can I do?" to improve environmental quality and reverse destructive trends.

HOW TO FIND A VOLUNTEER POSITION

The keys to finding good volunteer positions—as with finding a good job—are knowing what you want from your volunteerism and networking. Take the time you need to find the position you want. Do the legwork of making telephone calls, attending meetings, researching periodicals, and running down a few dead ends. As with internships, if you cannot find an existing position, you can in all likelihood create it.

The Resources section at the end of this chapter will help you get started. To explore local activities, start with the telephone directory. Try the Associations and Environmental categories in the Yellow Pages. Call organizations to discuss issues, or perform informational interviews—and ask for the names of other people you can call. You will quickly wind up with more contacts than you can handle.

Ask for literature from organizations to see what they are about and to get leads on other organizations. Call people who are quoted in the media, and check for meetings listed in local newspapers and magazines.

Other resources include the burgeoning computer-accessed "electronic bulletin boards," which announce organizations and activities in a particular area or field and often serve as forums for discussions. Electronic bulletin boards can be found through local universities, computer user groups, such as the Boston Computer Society, and computer magazines. University bulletin boards and campus newspapers are also good sources of information. Get to know your local reference librarians.

If you are interested in a particular issue, see the Resources sections at the ends of chapters 5–14. Many national associations and environmental organizations have regional, state, and local chapters whose functions you can attend. Environmental agencies and advocacy groups also band together to form cooperative organizations or coalitions; this is true among government agencies as well. Ask about coalitions in the geographic area or field that interests you most.

How to Make the Most of Your Volunteering

In addition to the items listed earlier about effective interning, the following advice from volunteers and environmental staff members should help you in structuring your own volunteer position:

- *Work with your supervisor.* When approaching a volunteer activity, work with a supervisor to develop a goal and several assignments that will help you reach it. Make sure your work plan includes not only your own time line but also one for others whose work interacts with yours. Volunteer projects that go on forever and eventually fade out occur far too frequently and are a bad experience for all concerned. Schedule a regular period of interaction with your supervisor so that he or she may review and respond to your work.

- *Show initiative.* Assume that you will have to manage yourself, and take initiative on your project.
- *Ask for exposure.* Expect that the organization will make some effort to give you exposure to the broader scope of work in the field. But do not assume that this will occur without your asking—maybe more than once.
- *Show confidence.* Have confidence that what you are doing is significant and worthy of the same respect accorded those in paid positions.
- *Meet your commitments.* If you make a volunteer commitment, recognize it as such—just as you would a paid job. People are counting on you. Have some empathy for the staffer who manages volunteers. Show your enthusiasm, energy, and responsibility; these are the best foundation for a good working relationship.
- *Have fun.* You are not going to get rid of all the toxic waste today or finance the recycling center at just one meeting. Enjoy the process.

A NEW WAY TO VOLUNTEER

In her excellent book *Environmental Vacations: Volunteer Projects to Save the Planet,* writer Stephanie Ocko details dozens of organizations that need volunteers for scientific research projects, environmental restoration work, and other opportunities around the world. More and more people are taking advantage of these programs to do something good for the environment while they travel and learn at the same time. Organizations like Earthwatch, the Smithsonian Research Expeditions Program, and many others are outlined in this book (see the Resources sections at the ends of chapters). Most of these programs require you to pay the organization coordinating the trip and pay for your own travel as well. The growing numbers of people enjoying "environmental vacations," however, seem to indicate that many find such trips worthwhile.

SUMMARY

Be persistent. Finding the right volunteer position or internship, like finding the right job or college, usually includes some wild-goose chases. It takes a while to get into the network, but once you, your work, and your interests become known, things will start to fall into place. Work done at the grass-roots level may lead to your participation in regional, state, or national organizations or efforts. As one volunteer says: "At first, I was approaching organizations; now they call and ask me to sit on a board or to help draft a policy statement. I can be much more selective now that I have laid the groundwork."

If you want a volunteer or internship experience that provides you with a valuable jump on your career, you will have to make it happen. You must choose carefully where you want to work. In many cases, you must take the initiative in designing your project. You must even assert your right to adequate supervision; organizations usually seek volunteers because they are short staffed, and professionals are legendary for underestimating the time and energy needed to supervise interns properly. The success of your experience will depend to a large extent on your drive and commitment. Professionals love volunteers and interns who take initiative and risks. These risk takers are the workers who are eventually offered permanent positions.

Finally, volunteering does not end when you have secured the job of your dreams. With experience and knowledge comes responsibility, the responsibility to share with others on boards, commissions, committees, and coalitions or just as another set of hands for the neighborhood cleanup project.

PROFILES

Meredith Savage
Wetlands Biologist
Department of Transportation
Environmental Branch
Olympia, Washington

Wetlands biologists have to be experts in a field that is undergoing increasing scrutiny as the United States struggles to balance the needs of developers with the need for healthy wetlands. Volunteers and interns keep the movement to save the wetlands alive.

For wetlands biologists the hours can be long and the pay low, especially when just starting out, but Meredith Savage says she has gained a tremendous sense of accomplishment from her work and would never trade it for a regular nine-to-five existence. According to Savage, her parents instilled in her a great respect for the outdoors from an early age, so it was only natural that she pursue a career in the environmental field. Savage majored in wildlife ecology at the University of Florida. During the summer after her junior year, she performed fieldwork at a research station in Arizona, studying the breeding habits of the common bushtit, a type of bird.

After graduating, Savage moved to Seattle to work for Greenpeace. The work involved helping to run a toxic waste campaign and testing water from the Cascade Mountains for acid rain. After spending a year with Greenpeace, Savage pursued her master's degree in environmental sciences at the Evergreen State College in Olympia, Washington. One year later, she needed a break, so she worked with a county wetlands program in the Seattle area for a year.

Her present internship as a wetlands biologist in the environmental branch of the Department of Transportation requires that she monitor artificial wetlands that were designed to mitigate the impact of road improvements. Such work requires that she take a census of the birds and other wildlife in the area, identify aquatic insects, take soil and water samples, and do extensive vegetation identification. "Hopefully, you can get some idea of whether you are successful in your endeavor to create wetlands," she says. But she adds, "There is still very little known about the impact of this process."

On a typical workday, Savage arrives by 7 A.M. and leaves by 5:30 P.M. When doing a bird census, she may get started as early as 5 A.M. Since she is still in school, she takes classes three nights a week from 6 P.M. to 10 P.M. "I get about five hours of sleep a night. It's a tough pace, but it keeps me moving," she says.

Savage is interested in making wetlands research and wildlife research, specifically studying birds in wetlands, her areas of expertise. She says that she feels confident that she has a broad background for undertaking any new responsibilities in her field. "You just have to keep plugging away," she advises, "and don't listen to the people who say it's hard to get a job. Focus on the positive." She also advises people to get as much fieldwork as possible under their belts. Savage has done everything from behavioral studies of birds to live mammal trapping and underwater diving to identifying coral reef life. A willingness to work for much less money than most people would find acceptable is also essential, according to Savage. "I have a friend the same age who already owns her own home and works a regular job and does the same thing every day to get the things she wants. For me, it is exactly the opposite. I like a few material things, but what I am doing is the most important thing to me. That is an important attitude to have in this line of work."

—BY CATHERINE PEDERSEN

Ann Blackburn
Environmental Affairs Coordinator
Charles River Watershed Association
Auburndale, Massachusetts

After encouraging her students to volunteer to save parkland, Ann Black-
burn decided to become involved herself and found that she had valuable
skills to use in the environmental field.

Ann Blackburn majored in philosophy at Mount Holyoke College in South
Hadley, Massachusetts, and was working as a teacher in the Washington,
DC, area when she was "snared" by the environmental field. "I have never
recovered," she says. "I was teaching and tutoring a bunch of kids the
schools considered underachievers, but they were among the brightest
children I had ever met. The common theme among them was that they
were all terribly concerned about the rampant development of their favorite wooded places."

Blackburn had lived in the Washington, DC, area in the mid-1950s. She
says that when she returned in the 1970s, she found that the area had
changed drastically. "It seemed so chaotic, but I know that if I had lived
there all along the change might not have made such an impact on me," she
says. As a result of the impact it did make, she encouraged her students to
become involved in saving parklands, advising them that if they dropped
out of school they would be handicapped in pursuing the issue in the
future. Eventually, she started a two-year program in her county that got
young people involved in park development, surveying land, testing water
quality, and laying out trails. "The kids performed so magnificently that
two other programs were started," she says.

Although she enjoyed her 15 years of working with learning-disabled
children, Blackburn says she wanted to apply her "people" skills in an
environmental area. She eventually got a job working for the Interstate
Commission on the Potomac River Basin and from there got her position
with the Charles River Watershed Association. Although it is only 80 miles
long, the Charles River faces a myriad of development pressures. The
association is responsible for analyzing those demands. Some people, for
example, are proposing that a sewer line be run through an aquifer used
for drinking water. "We are trying to get them to shift their approach to
the problem and think about protecting the quality of the aquifer," she
says.

Her work is rewarding, according to Blackburn, because of the opportunity to become directly involved in environmental protection. In addition
to working with the association, Blackburn has helped develop an environmental series for a local television station called Race to Save the Planet

and has coedited an international journal called *The Environmentalist.* "You never know where these things are going to lead. There is no way this could have been planned," she says.

For those wishing to enter the environmental field, Blackburn advises that they volunteer for an organization they have a deep belief in and become immersed. "By volunteering you build your strengths and find out what you're good at. This field can absorb anyone with any temperament or any mix of skills," she says. She knows young people who were on the verge of quitting school who now have master's degrees and Ph.D.s because "they were able to link up with something they cared about." Volunteering gave them the inspiration to push themselves.

—BY CATHERINE PEDERSEN

Jerry Tinianow
Vice President of Regions, Sierra Club
Partner, Hahn Loeser & Parks
Columbus, Ohio

Volunteer work made it possible for Jerry Tinianow to get started in the environmental field while working toward his law degree.

Jerry Tinianow started volunteering in the environmental field while he was still a student at the National Law Center of George Washington University. "During the summer of 1978, when I returned to Cleveland to work between terms, I felt the need to get away from purely academic pursuits, which limited my involvement in outside issues," he explained.

He contacted a friend, who was a volunteer with the Northeast Ohio Group of the Sierra Club, and started to get involved. At the time, the Sierra Club was opposing the construction of a steel mill in Conneaut, Ohio. Tinianow spent most of the summer working on that issue, which included presenting testimony at public hearings on environmental issues related to construction of the mill.

The following fall, he applied for a program that enabled him to receive academic credit for his volunteer work. He chose to work for the Sierra Club Legal Defense Fund in Washington, DC. After graduating from law school, he moved to Cleveland and once again volunteered. Says Tinianow: "I was living downtown in an apartment with a view of Lake Erie in 1981. People didn't even want to go there because it was an industrial dumping ground. It was a disgusting place. By promoting the development of parks, beaches, and hotels, we wanted to get people involved in keeping up the area." As a result, he became a founding member, incorporator, and legal advisor to the Cleveland Waterfront Coalition.

Tinianow has held a variety of local and statewide offices with the Sierra Club. He was a member of the local executive committee and head of the local branch of the Sierra Club Committee on Political Education. He later served as chairman of the Ohio chapter. He became involved at the national level as a member of the Clean Air Campaign steering committee, on which he served for four years, spending two years as chairman. Most recently, he was promoted to vice president of regions for the club, which entails overseeing the club's entire network of regional vice presidents and conservation committee members.

Each level of participation within the organization—local, state, and national—has its advantages and disadvantages. According to Tinianow, "the results of your work are more tangible and visible at the local level; the national level tends to consist a lot more of pushing buttons and pulling strings from afar, but at the same time the effects are more far reaching, and there is, of course, the element of prestige." The local level also tends to be more time-consuming, he says, since meetings and events are held more frequently and the issues are often more pressing. The trade-off at the national level is that "you must accept the organization's philosophy and expound its views rather than pursue your own priorities," Tinianow says. However, he adds, the local level provides the best opportunity to "cut your teeth."

According to Tinianow, he has had the best of both worlds by being both a trial lawyer and an environmental activist. "I've often felt I could do neither one exclusively," he says, "because it would just become work."

—BY CATHERINE PEDERSEN

David Miller
Northeast Regional Vice President
National Audubon Society
Albany, New York

Just out of college, David Miller began his environmental career as a volunteer in Washington, DC, where he waited on tables in order to pay the bills.

David Miller is a good example of someone who resourcefully used a volunteer position to start a career in the environmental field, a tactic that can take considerable effort. After college, Miller moved to Washington, DC, and worked three evenings a week as a waiter to support his full-time volunteer position as a lobbying intern with the National Audubon Society.

His first assignment as an intern required that he collect background information on the Garrison Diversion Project, a water project that would have ruined migratory bird habitats in the Dakotas. The proposal was eventually defeated. Later, he delivered information on issues to congressional offices and made calls to solicit support for upcoming legislation, including a measure urging Congress to act on acid rain and airborne toxic emissions. He also wrote action updates and articles, worked in the society's library, and put together briefing material for Audubon staff members and congressional offices. "I guess you could have called me a jack-of-all-trades," he says of the experience. "As confidence in my abilities grew within the organization, so did my responsibilities as a volunteer intern."

His volunteer work put him in touch with many people in the field. He received his first important job lead while at a conference in Connecticut. During a discussion following a speech given by a member of the House leadership from Connecticut, Miller asked the speaker a question that so impressed a member of the audience from Scenic Hudson, Inc., that Miller was asked to apply for a position with the organization. "Before I knew it, I was their environmental program coordinator," he says. The position put him in charge of monitoring, studying, and finding solutions to air quality and hazardous waste issues in the Hudson Valley; developing case studies to promote and administer public policy; preparing testimony on legislation and regulations; and a host of other duties.

Miller stayed with Scenic Hudson for almost three years. In 1984, he decided to become involved in the presidential election. He became director of voter education programs for the New Jersey Difference in '84, a position that enabled him to present both the Democratic and Republican public policy platforms on the environment. Toward the end of the campaign, he found out about Great Lakes United, an international organization based in Buffalo, New York, dedicated to conserving and protecting the Great Lakes and the Saint Lawrence River. He became the organization's first executive director, a position in which he was responsible for membership recruitment, fund-raising, public policy development, and administration of staff. While working for the organization, he helped build its membership from 95 to 200 members and its budget from $50,000 to more than $300,000. His position required that he monitor acid rain in the lakes, organize letter-writing campaigns, and make recommendations on water diversion and the cleanup of water and air toxins.

After four years at Great Lakes United, Miller is back at Audubon, this time in a senior position as a regional vice president. His job involves working on issues with regard to the Adirondacks, the Northern Forest, and Long Island Sound, along with federal environmental initiatives.

His advice for those who want to try the volunteer route is to be orderly and businesslike, to know what you want, and to develop a rapport with coworkers. "As you slowly gain their confidence, you will get more in-depth projects," he says. "Be diligent and don't give up easily," he added. "The more feelers you have out, the better chance you have of being in the right place at the right time."

—BY CATHERINE PEDERSEN

Aubrey Smith
Environmental Chemist
Environmental Technology Branch
British Petroleum America's Research
** and Development Center**
Cleveland, Ohio

Aubrey Smith highly recommends internships as a way to break into the environmental field and, perhaps more important, as a way to determine what talents and interests a person may have.

Aubrey Smith says that being an intern can be one of the best ways to find out what kind of work you enjoy. Smith was hired in August 1987 as an intern at British Petroleum America's Research and Development Center and after nine months was hired full-time. BP America is involved in the exploration and refinement of crude oil. According to Smith, "too many students choose careers without having enough information on what's available and what they really like doing. For me, internships provided a fantastic opportunity to learn more about myself and my fields of interest."

Smith first worked as an intern during the summer of 1986, after graduating with a degree in biology from Lane College in Jackson, Tennessee. Through a program managed by the Environmental Careers Organization, he was selected to evaluate drinking water for the EPA in Cincinnati. He then spent a year abroad at the University of Edinburgh; when he returned, he again sought out an ECO internship. "The research position at BP America's Environmental Technology Group was perfect for my increasing interest in doing original scientific research," he says. This time, he worked in a laboratory and studied the process of removing sulfur from wastes so that treating the waste stream would be less expensive. The experiments were complex, requiring that he collect data, change parameters, and observe and report the results.

Now Smith's work entails evaluating technologies that will not hinder production at BP America but will allow the company to operate with maximum concern for the environment. "Achieving zero discharge is important," he says. "We want to operate without discharging any waste into the atmosphere or the ground." Reverse osmosis is one such technology, enabling water to be "polished" so that it can be reused by the plant. Another

BP America Laboratories, Cleveland, Ohio. Aubrey Smith's internship experience initiated his career as an environmental chemist.

technology, the aerobic fluid bed bioreactor, treats water with oxygen before it is returned to the environment.

An internship can be a key to finding meaningful work, since it allows people to try different jobs. Smith, however, knew that he wanted to be a research scientist even during his days in high school. "I've always wanted to find out something new that no one knows, produce the unknown. It is exciting."

Smith says he does not regret his decision to accept a full-time position with BP America, even though it means postponing his quest for a Ph.D. "Looking at BP America's program, which allows us to continue our education while working, I decided that it would be best in the long run, even though it meant I would take longer to get my degree. Now when I get my degree, I'll have plenty of work experience to back it up."

—BY CATHERINE PEDERSEN

RESOURCES

DIRECTORIES

Conservation Directory (annual). National Wildlife Federation, 1400 16th St., NW, Washington, DC 20036–2266. (See the Resources section in chapter 2 for a description.)

Directories in Print (annual). Description of every directory (some 14,000 are listed) published in the United States and Canada. Gale Research, 835 Penobscot Bldg., Detroit, MI 48226. (800) 877-GALE.

Directory of Environmental Groups in New England. Environmental Protection Agency, Public Affairs Section, Region 1, JFK Federal Bldg., Boston, MA 02203.

Directory of State Environmental Agencies (1992). Environmental Law Institute, 1616 P St., NW, second floor, Washington, DC 20036. Call (800) 433–5120 to order a copy.

EARTHWATCH Expeditions, Inc. *Earthwatch* (bimonthly magazine). Descriptions of expedition opportunities. 319 Arlington St., Watertown, MA 02272. (617) 926–8200.

Encyclopedia of Associations (annual). Listing of 22,000 associations. Gale Research, 835 Penobscot Bldg., Detroit, MI 48226. (800) 877-GALE.

The Great Lakes Directory of Natural Resource Agencies and Organizations (1984). The Center for the Great Lakes, 35 E. Wacker Dr., Suite 1870, Chicago, IL 60601.

Vacation Work Publications. Send for a listing of publications containing summer job and internship opportunities around the world. 9 Park End St., Oxford, England, OX11HJ.

Volunteer! The Comprehensive Guide to Voluntary Service in the U.S. and Abroad. Council on International Educational Exchange, Publications, 205 E. 42nd St., New York, NY 10017. (212) 616–1414.

Your Resource Guide to Environmental Organizations, edited by John Seredich. Includes the purposes, accomplishments, programs, volunteer opportunities, publications, and membership benefits of 150 environmental organizations. Smiling Dolphins Press, 4 Segura, Irvine, CA 92715.

ORGANIZATIONS

Appalachian Mountain Club, 5 Joy St., Boston, MA 02108. (617) 523–0636.
Friends of the Earth. 218 D St., SE, Washington, DC 20003. (202) 544–2600.
Greenpeace USA. 1436 U St., NW, Washington, DC 20009. (202) 462–1177.
Peace Corps. Recruitment Office, 1555 Wilson Blvd., Suite 701, Arlington, VA 22209. Or call (800) 424–8580 for the Peace Corps office nearest you.
The Points of Light Foundation. Call (800) 879–5400 for information about volunteer opportunities in your area.
Volunteers in Service to America (VISTA). 1400 M St., NW, Washington, DC 20005. (202) 429–1700.

BOOKS

Beyond Success: How Volunteer Service Can Help You Begin Making a Life Instead of Just a Living (1989). Master Media Limited, 17 E. 89th St., New York, NY 10128. (212) 260–5600.
The Experienced Hand: A Student Manual for Making the Most of an Internship (1987). The Carroll Press, 43 Squantum St., Cranston, RI 02920.

MISCELLANEOUS

Independent Sector. A nonprofit coalition of 823 corporations, foundations, and voluntary organizations whose mission is to create a national forum for encouraging donations, volunteering, and not-for-profit initiatives that help the public to serve people, communities, and causes. Publishes *Giving and Volunteering in the USA* (1990), *The Board Member's Book: Making a Difference in Voluntary Organizations* and *Effective Leadership in Voluntary Organizations*, by Brian O'Connell, the organization's president, as well as *Youth Service: A Guidebook for Developing and Operating Effective Programs*. 1828 L St., NW, Washington, DC 20036.
Smithsonian Research Expeditions Program. Provides one- and two-week volunteer expeditions in support of Smithsonian researchers in exchange for contributions of $350 to $1,300. 490 L'Enfant Plaza, SW, Suite 4210, Washington, DC 20560. (202) 287–3210.
Volunteers in Technical Assistance. Private organization providing technical assistance to individuals and organizations in the United States

and developing countries. Emphasizes helping local groups adapt, implement, and market technologies appropriate to their situations. Concerned with restoration, soil conservation, renewable energy, and energy conservation. 1815 N. Lynn St., Suite 200, Arlington, VA 22209. (703) 276–1800.

INTERNSHIPS

Environmental Careers Organization (ECO). (See pages xii–xiii for office nearest you.)

Internships: The Guide to On the Job Training Opportunities for Students and Adults (annual). Peterson's. (800) 338–3282.

The National Directory of Internships (1991–1992). Includes sections on environmental affairs and education, forestry, sciences, horticulture, planning, and recreation. National Society of Internships and Experiential Education, 3509 Haworth Dr., Suite 207, Raleigh, NC 27609. (919) 787–3263.

Directory of Special Programs for Minority Group Members: Career Information Services, Employment Skills Banks, Financial Aid Sources, edited by Willis L. Johnson (5th ed., 1990). Information on more than 2,800 sources of job-training opportunities, scholarships, fellowships, and internships. Garrett Park Press, P.O. Box 190–B, Garrett Park, MD 20896. (301) 946–2553.

Student Conservation Association. Develops internships in natural resource management for students at various levels. See National Environmental Internship Programs earlier in this chapter for a description. P.O. Box 550, Charlestown, NH 03603.

4 Breaking Into the Environmental Field

THERE ARE several stages in developing your career, including reflection, both formal and informal, on your life goals and education. You cheat yourself if you do not give yourself time to dream, explore, and learn. At some point, however, it is time to get a job.

Job hunting is hard work, plain and simple. Yet there are few secrets to job hunting and no really new theories, so starting a career is a skill that can be learned by anyone. Given today's volatile work world, it is a skill that you will probably use many times throughout your career.

If there are no secrets to the career search, however, there are one or two themes that nearly all environmental professionals mention when giving advice to job seekers. These do not involve writing the perfect résumé or finding new ways to uncover "hidden" job markets. Instead, the key to success lies in your attitude about the process. Are you going to approach it with dread and apprehension or with excitement and creativity? Everything about looking for work encourages the first mind-set. After all, in the job hunt we enter the world of sales and must make a lot of cold calls. We are selling ourselves, which makes rejections all the more painful. When an employer says no, what he or she is rejecting is not a used car or a mutual fund but *you*.

Fear of rejection can cause us to delay, to wait for a magic "help wanted" ad to appear, to fantasize about someone doing it for us or knocking on our door with a great job offer. Out of fear, we are tempted to take the first offer that comes our way just to get the job hunt over with. Then all we would have to worry about is being miserable for at least 40 hours a week.

There is an alternative. This is *your* life and *your* career. It really is true that with creativity and persistence you can do anything that you choose. Try to view all the decisions, telephone numbers, and contacts that lie before you not as an impossibly large list to be "gotten through" but as proof of the unlimited possibilities available to you. You have chosen a career in an exciting and diverse field, one in which new options appear with increasingly regularity. What could be more exciting than a job search, than picking and choosing where and how you want to focus your unique creative energy? As for rejection, no one has found an answer to it yet. Getting through it is difficult, but if you allow it to stop you, it certainly will.

Why all this talk about attitude? Because environmental professionals have emphasized it over and over again as a key factor in breaking into the environmental field. To get and keep that winning attitude, they gave the following advice.

Throughout your job search, act as if you *are* an environmental professional, and soon you will be one. Read the publications, participate in the associations, talk to your professional colleagues, and work on projects (by volunteering if necessary). Environmental professionals hire colleagues, not supplicants. Know that the only difference between you and them is that you are not getting paid yet. This sounds simple, but hardly anyone really does it.

Finally, to get through the hard times, lean on a support network of friends, mentors, and fellow job seekers to carry you through.

RESOURCES FOR THE ENVIRONMENTAL JOB SEARCH

You have a considerable array of tools at your disposal, which, when used with foresight and persistence, will yield surprising results.

THE MOST IMPORTANT RESOURCES: SELF-KNOWLEDGE AND SKILLS

Before you begin circling want ads or printing résumés, examine your personal resources—your skills and interests and what you want to do. Let us say that you have already spent some time thinking about what interests you in the environmental field. You have spent some time in education and training to enter the field. You have developed some idea of how you want to be of service. You cannot effectively approach environmental employers, however, until you step back, take some time, and do a thorough inventory of your skills and attributes. In fact, many career counselors instruct job seekers to visualize their next job in terms of skills rather than job title. There are numerous books with exercises to guide you through this personality and skills analysis. Richard Nelson Bolles's legendary *What Color Is Your Parachute?* is one of the best.

The essence of these skills inventory exercises is to list your natural talents, the many skills you have acquired through education and experience, *and* the ways you have used your skills. The next step is to list, in order, those skills you want to use on your next job. These exercises help give you career direction, prepare you to answer tough interview questions such as "What would you bring to this job?," and assist you in identifying gaps in your personal skills bank.

Once you have thoroughly identified your personal resources, you must determine how best to package and market them—how to demonstrate to employers that you have certain skills. For example, you might prove to a prospective employer that you are a talented fund-raiser with excellent organizational skills by telling her: "I chaired the fund-raising committee of our student environmental group. Our fund-raiser netted $3,000 for our recycling project. I was responsible for coordinating the work of five volunteers on this three-month project." Career search books such as those in the Resources section at the end of this chapter also have a wealth of ideas about how best to advertise your skills and accomplishments.

When you know what you want and what you have to offer, it is time to find out about job opportunities that match your interests. Three resources—written material, people, and environmental events—will provide you with plenty of information. Lee DeAngelis, longtime director of the Great Lakes office of the Environmental Careers Organization, tells job seekers "not to focus exclusively on one of these resources at the expense of the other two. Each one has something different to offer that you cannot get through the others."

WRITTEN RESOURCES

If you have not already done so, invest some time and money in written materials that will give you the pulse of the environmental field that interests you, familiarize you with the players, and alert you to job opportunities. This should not be considered a job hunter's burden! You probably already enjoy reading about the field in which you have chosen to start a career. If anything, you may be feeling overwhelmed with all of the written environmental information available to you. Professionals recommend that the environmental job seeker tap into the following sources of information.

Newspapers. Read at least one major metropolitan newspaper, especially the newspaper that covers the geographic area in which you would like to work. This will give you the names of agencies, corporations, and individuals to contact in your job search. The *Wall Street Journal*, the *Washington Post*, and the *New York Times* are excellent sources of information on national environmental issues.

Do not forget the "help wanted" ads, especially those in the Sunday editions. These ads are valuable not only as a source of job leads but as a barometer of who is hiring and what kinds of people are most in demand. Retain any ads that look interesting, even if you could not hope to compete for them. They can help lend clarity to the development of your personal job vision.

Free publications. Many government agencies and nonprofit organizations and some trade associations offer free literature on environmental issues, programs, business developments, and laws. These are often good sources of contacts, job openings, and events. Professionals in the field are resourceful in finding these freebies to stretch their publications budget; ask each person you meet for the names and addresses of their favorite three. Some of the best of these for the job seeker are the internal newsletters of agencies such as the Environmental Protection Agency. Get on the mailing lists for these publications and you will have inside information that may never appear anywhere else. More important, you will have current names of people to talk to about priority projects.

Job listings. There is a growing number of national, regional, and local environmental job listings. Some of these listings are specific to particular employers, and you must go to the agency's personnel department to check them out. You can receive other listings by getting on mailing lists through the employer, who will then send you relevant announcements. Finally, publications like *Earth Work, The Job Seeker, Environmental Opportunities,* and others are filled with current job openings and are available at reasonable subscription rates.

Conference and job fair publications. These little-used resources are invaluable barometers of the times. Even if you are not able to attend events, get copies of conference programs. (See also Events, later in this chapter.) Look over the lists of topics and speakers. Scope out the display ads. People who are chosen to speak at conferences are usually respected leaders in their field or people who hold key positions. It would be advantageous to get to know them.

Magazines, trade journals, and newsletters. There are hundreds of publications on environmental topics. Some, like the *Asbestos Abatement*

Report, are very specialized. Others, like *Sierra*, provide wider coverage of natural resources and environmental protection issues. Read both kinds. The *Directory of Environmental Information Sources*, published by Government Institutes, lists more than 100 U.S. and 50 foreign publications related to environmental protection. *The Conservation Directory*, published annually by the National Wildlife Federation, lists publications related to natural resources. Naturally, these directories and many publications can be found in college or public libraries or are received by college faculty and staff members.

If you have identified an area or discipline of interest, be absolutely sure to join the professional association of that field; this should yield you a professional journal on a regular basis. Ask people in the field to recommend other publications to subscribe to or read at the library.

Annual reports. Virtually all government agencies and nonprofit groups publish some kind of annual report. Public corporations publish annual reports and financial disclosure (10-K) reports, which are required by the Securities and Exchange Commission. You can find both at many university business libraries and some public libraries, or you can request them from the human resources or investor relations department of the organization you are interested in.

Both annual reports and 10-Ks can provide excellent snapshots of an organization. They usually discuss who owns and manages the organization, what the company does, issues the company is facing, strategic plans, and budgetary data. Even if annual reports do not directly discuss a company's environmental work, they identify facilities, plants, and all other company properties as well as the top one or two officials in health, safety, and environmental affairs.

Realize, however, that organizations use annual reports to portray themselves in the best light possible. Although they are usually far drier, 10-Ks are sometimes more useful than annual reports. Reading either or both prior to a job or informational interview will arm you with knowledge that will help you formulate specific, insightful questions. Naturally, your current knowledge about an organization demonstrates initiative and commitment.

Directories. A variety of directories identify companies, consultants, agencies, and individuals as well as publications. Never assume that a directory in your field of interest does not exist, no matter how specialized or even trivial the information might seem. Some environmental directories are listed in the Resources section at the end of this chapter. One massive tome, called *Environmental Industries Marketplace*, includes contacts for 10,000 companies in environmental industries. It is published by Gale Research.

Databases. If you have access to a personal computer, you are in luck. In the past few years, hundreds of environmentally focused electronic bulletin boards have sprung up, and a tremendous amount of information is available on CD-ROM. Not only are environmentally specific job-listing services available via computers; through electronic bulletin boards you can even "meet" professionals and other job seekers on line. Electronic discussion groups provide another way to widen your network and find out about job openings that have not yet been formally advertised. Public and university libraries often provide subsidized access to databases, and career placement offices are sometimes tied to electronic job-listing services. One of the newest directories to such databases is *Ecolinking: Everyone's Guide to Online Environmental Information* (see the Resources section of chapter 6).

PEOPLE

People are your best resource in the job hunt, be they neighbors, professionals, classmates, relatives, friends, experts, writers, or casual acquaintances. One of the cardinal rules of job hunting is to go out of your way to tell *everyone* you know or meet that you are looking for a job—and give them as much specific information as possible on the type of job you want. Most of us love to help others, especially when it is as easy as offering a name or making a telephone call. Each time you tell someone of your job search, your list of potential contacts expands logarithmically. To jog your creativity, the following are a few groups of people who can help.

College faculty and staff members and students. Talk to current or former teachers and advisors and fellow students. Many professors engage in outside research or consulting projects and know professionals in the field. They may be able to provide a recommendation to an employer they know personally. Students from smaller colleges should consider seeking advice from staff members at universities with larger environmentally related programs. Such programs often have at least one career counselor. Time permitting, these counselors will often accommodate nonstudents, especially if you express an interest in graduate study at their university. In addition, many state universities and community colleges employ general career counselors who are paid by the state and thus provide their services free to any state resident.

Alumni. Alumni of your college department or training program can be very helpful. Many graduates of your institution are now working in your field of choice. Because they share with you the bond of having attended the same school, and because many have been through difficult job hunts themselves, they are often willing to help later generations of students. To find alumni, ask whether your school's alumni relations department publishes a directory; some programs actively track alumni careers for the benefit of current students and recent graduates. For example, the Cornell University Department of Agriculture and Biological Engineering has developed the Cornell Alumni Career Advisory Network and an alumni profile sheet with which it links students and alumni. If your school does not conduct such a program, you might suggest that it start one.

Friends, relatives, and neighbors. Do not overlook the obvious. Think of how many successful job-hunting stories you know that started this way: "My uncle put me in touch with my cousin, who knew a consultant who was hiring for a position. I called her, and . . ."

Professional societies. More need not be said about the extreme usefulness of professional groups. The people you meet when you join professional societies can provide advice, furnish leads, and attest to your qualifications.

Volunteering. Working as a volunteer is another way to build up a list of contacts and experience. See chapter 3 for information on where to find volunteer opportunities and internships.

Employment agencies. Should you use an employment agency in your environmental job search? Probably not. Employment agencies specialize in high-demand personnel, such as secretaries and computer programmers. On the other hand, executive recruitment firms—also called headhunters—usually search for experienced specialists and middle and senior managers, culling from the ranks of the employed. A third type of agency is the outplacement firm, which generally works for organizations that are reducing their staff, helping laid-off employees find new jobs. Of these three, employment agencies in particular will seek your business— and some will want your money, too. However, for the environmental job seeker, registering with an employment agency would probably be a bad investment. The exception might be if you are experienced in a high-demand discipline such as environmental engineering, chemistry, hydrogeology, or toxicology. In such cases, executive recruiters may be worth investigating, although you probably will not need much help finding a job.

You may, however, want to consider finding part-time or temporary work through an employment agency while you look for full-time employment. You may be able to arrange placement in an environmental department or corporation, even if the work is not, at first, related to the environment.

EVENTS

In most large cities, aspiring professionals can attend a variety of environmentally oriented conferences. In fact, few professions have so many events—a reflection, perhaps, of the diversity and depth of the environmental field. These events are sponsored by government agencies, consulting firms, corporations, trade and professional associations, and nonprofit organizations.

Attending a conference allows you to meet people in a way that may be less intimidating than making cold calls or visits. If, for example, you are hoping to become a hazardous waste specialist, you could probably benefit greatly from meeting people at an EPA conference on Superfund consulting contracts. Not only would you make personal contacts but you would also discover what kinds of work the EPA is planning to contract out to consultants—and where some jobs might be created as a result. Moreover, simply mentioning to an interviewer something you learned at such a conference makes a good impression.

Students and aspiring professionals attending these conferences have little competition from their peers, since most attendees are seasoned professionals. They are usually impressed when they see students at conferences.

To find out about these events, ask your local or regional EPA office or the state equivalent whether it offers an events newsletter. Naturally, you should also check local newspapers and environmental publications for notices of upcoming events.

INFORMATIONAL INTERVIEWING

You may find it useful to talk with people who are doing the work you think you would like to do. Commonly called informational interviewing, this is an excellent way to try on a job. If you go about informational interviewing in the proper manner, you will usually get a positive response from professionals—after all, most people like to talk about their work.

A word of warning: Do not tell people you want an informational interview when you are actually looking for a job. This will turn off employers; nobody likes to be deceived. So many have abused this type of interview that you probably should not even call it an informational interview. Instead, merely state that you are doing research prior to making a career decision and would like a few minutes of the person's time.

The following are some tips for informational interviewing:

- Talk to people who are doing the work that interests you, not to those who hire them. You are not looking for a job; you are trying to determine what kind of job will suit you.
- Tell your prospective interviewee that you want only 20 to 30 minutes of his or her time, and do not stay any longer.
- Do not waste your interviewee's time by asking questions that you could have answered on your own by researching the company or the profession or by talking to somebody below the person in the organization's hierarchy. For example, ask "What do you like about this work?" rather than "What regulations do you have to deal with?" Do ask the person to describe a typical day or week.
- At the conclusion of each interview, ask for the names of two people doing similar work who might be willing to meet with you. Also ask this question if you are refused an interview.
- Thank your interviewee profusely. Thirty minutes is a big gift for a busy professional to give to a stranger. Always send a thank-you note, and, later, apprise the person of your progress.
- Finally, there is nothing wrong with coming back to the same organization when you *are* looking for a job. Just be forthright about your request. The employer will probably already have a positive impression of you based on the initiative you have shown in your career search.

GETTING THE INTERVIEW AND CLINCHING THE JOB

Hundreds of generic job-hunting and career books crowd the market; some are gems, and others are fluff (see the Resources section at the end of this chapter for some recommendations). Ask career counselors and fellow job seekers what their favorites are.

What follows is the key advice gathered from these publications and from the collective experience of ECO staffers in helping people establish environmental careers over the past two decades.

Take the time you need to find the right job; do not expect it to be a quick process. Career counselors note that the average career-related job hunt takes between six months and one year. One free-lance consultant from Seattle tells students: "You need to look at your career search as a long-term research project that always takes much longer and more effort than you want it to." If you possibly can, try to structure your life so that you are not forced by economics or anxiety to take the first thing that comes along. Lay some groundwork a few months before you actually want to start your job.

Work hard at the search. This sounds obvious, but *What Color Is Your Parachute?* reports that two-thirds of all job seekers spend fewer than five hours a week on the process. At that rate, it takes two months to log just one week of full-time job hunting.

A strategy of blanketing employers with résumés and "To whom it may concern" cover letters takes an enormous amount of time and almost never works. One study found that employers sent out one invitation to interview for every 245 résumés sent cold to their firm. *What Color Is Your Parachute?* outlines an alternative strategy based on networking, discussed previously. In that book, résumés serve to cement a building process that begins with conversations, contacts, and reputations. Although résumés are not useful when sent out in a scattershot approach, they are nevertheless important. Take a look at two good books: the *Damn Good Résumé Guide*, by Yana Parker, which also discusses cover letters, and *Don't Use a Résumé . . . Use a Qualifications Brief*, by Richard Lathrop.

Although employers are usually pressed for time, they do want to know as much about you as possible. Be crisp. Also, become skilled at tailoring résumés to specific jobs so that an employer quickly reading your résumé can easily perceive pertinent experience and interests.

Cover letters are meant to highlight parts of your résumé that especially qualify you for the job, demonstrate that you have done your homework, and convey your enthusiasm for that particular line of work. A carefully written cover letter can go even further than your résumé in getting you an interview.

Never have a misspelling or a typographical error on your résumé, cover letter, or any other correspondence to an employer. He or she will inevitably ask, "If they can't even get it right on a job application, what kind of attention will they pay to important details after we hire them?"

Ask questions at job interviews. This shows your interest and conveys the feeling that you have options, which immediately boosts your stock. Perhaps one of the biggest mistakes job seekers make during interviews is being so determined to come across as cool and professional that they do not show any enthusiasm. Employers like to hire upbeat, excited, and motivated people.

Always send a thank-you note to the interviewer and anyone else you met, including support staff members. Employers often solicit input from everyone who met you, especially future colleagues. Reiterate any points you want to make about your interest and skills.

Very close to the week when the employer will be making a decision, call to express your interest. Many times, a decision on whom to hire is a close call. Once the field is narrowed to a few qualified finalists, gut reactions are important. Showing interest in a professional manner could tip the balance in your favor.

If you do not get the job, send a letter to the lead interviewer expressing interest in future positions. You may want to call and ask about other job leads and ask the interviewer to circulate your résumé if appropriate. In some cases it is appropriate to ask why you were not chosen. The answers may help you solve problems or address issues in later interviews.

ECO's Lee DeAngelis points out: "Employers are practical people. They are interested in what you can do for them, how you can help them solve their problems and make their work lives easier. They want employees who will fit in with their organization, other employees, and the people the organization serves. Finally, they want people who will take on their agenda and be productive and cooperative."

PEOPLE OF COLOR AND ENVIRONMENTAL PROFESSIONS

The environmental field has done a poor job of attracting and retaining people of color. In fact, the entire environmental movement is noticeably undiversified. African Americans, Native Americans, Hispanic Americans, and Asian Americans are few and far between at environmental events, at agencies and companies, and in college classes.

In recent years, this has begun to change, not only because employers are aware that America is becoming more multicultural and that people of color represent the fastest-growing sector of new people entering the labor force but also because of a growing awareness of environmental issues in communities of color.

Some of this increase is attributed to a general rise in environmental knowledge. Children of all races and ethnic groups are exposed to more ecological knowledge in school than ever before, and African American and Asian American children are just as likely as their white friends to harangue their parents about recycling.

Awareness also seems to be growing that environmental careers can offer well-paying jobs with respected employers. Historically black colleges, institutions affiliated with the Hispanic Association of Colleges and Universities, and tribally controlled colleges have a growing interest in preparing students for environmental jobs.

By far the biggest change, however, has been the explosive growth of a grass-roots movement designed to promote "environmental justice" and fight "environmental racism." This movement began in 1987 with the publication of a landmark study by the United Church of Christ that found that, nationally, communities that harbor two or more hazardous waste sites have three times the percentage of minorities than those with no waste site. Additionally, three out of five African Americans and Hispanic Americans live in communities where there are illegal or abandoned dumps. Activists were quick to get the message. Environmental issues were social justice issues.

The movement came of age in 1991 with the First National People of Color Environmental Leadership Summit, which attracted more than 600 African, Hispanic, Asian, and Native Americans from throughout the nation. The people and organizations of this movement are changing and will continue to change the environmental community.

What do all of these trends mean for people of color who want to break into the environmental field? First, there are a growing number of fellowship, scholarship, and internship programs designed to attract students of color to the field. Programs like the Environmental Protection Agency's Minority Fellows Program, the Student Conservation Association's Conservation Career Development Program, ECO's Minority Opportunities Program, and similar programs sponsored by the Environmental Consortium for Minority Outreach, federal and state agencies, private companies, and others are providing opportunities that did not exist even a few years ago. At the Third National Minority Environmental Careers Conference, organized by ECO, twice as many environmental employers were represented as at the first conference.

A second result of the growing environmental awareness among people of color is that the environmental movement must change. The definition of an "environmental" issue is expanding to take in issues of more traditional concern to social justice and civil rights organizations. This expansion will enlarge the circle of environmental professionals to include people working in such fields as housing and public health.

Third, recruiters from private corporations, government agencies, and consulting firms have stepped up their efforts to recruit people of color with environmental backgrounds, especially those with science and engineering skills. In addition, students are beginning to put environmental careers on a par with such professions as law, accounting, medicine, and other engineering fields as a career to be considered.

Finally, the number of nonprofit groups devoted to issues of environmental justice and the scope of their programs will continue to grow, creating both professional and volunteer opportunities to work on these issues.

ENVIRONMENTAL CAREERS FOR THE DISABLED

If you are physically disabled, you may think you have to rule out an environmental career because of limited mobility. However, that is far from true. Environmental jobs are as diverse as the working world itself; you do not have to be a backcountry ranger to do environmental work. Indeed, many people with physical disabilities work to improve human interaction with and access to the environment—for example, by providing access for the physically disabled to outdoor recreational facilities or by designing ecologically sound mass transit systems that are accessible by handicapped citizens.

In January 1992, Congress passed the Americans with Disabilities Act (ADA), which mandates that all public areas be made accessible by disabled people by the use of wheelchair ramps, curb cuts, and so forth. The law outlaws job discrimination against the disabled. The second phase of the ADA, which went into effect in July 1992, mandates that employers provide for the needs of handicapped employees—for instance, by supplying blind staffers with computer-aided voice recognition systems or braille readers. The ADA should not only make it easier for disabled people to find jobs and get their work done but also increase the need for environmental specialists who can help make parks and other public areas universally accessible. For more information on the ADA, see the Resources for Job Seekers with Disabilities section at the end of this chapter.

Consider the following professionals, profiled in the 1984 publication *Able Scientists, Disabled Persons* (J.R. Assocs.), who have not allowed themselves to be passed over and who have aided the environment in the process.

- R. Kent Jones, B.S., who has multiple sclerosis, is a civil engineer with the Metropolitan Sanitary District of Greater Chicago. He directs the activities of his section from his wheelchair.
- Cynthia Dusel-Bacon, B.A., who had an arm amputated, is a geologist with the U.S. Geological Survey. She uses a specially adapted microscope to study geological characteristics of rock slices.
- Odette L. Shotwell, Ph.D., with disabilities that resulted from polio, is an organic chemist at the U.S. Department of Agriculture's Northern Regional Research Center in Peoria, Illinois, where she heads a department of eight specialists.

SUMMARY

Now is a great time to break into the environmental field. Start by understanding your skills, strengths, and weaknesses. Learn about the field through publications, people, and events. Track down the job that is right for you, and get started on a great career.

RESOURCES

ENVIRONMENTAL JOB LISTINGS

Community Jobs: The Employment Newspaper for the Non-Profit Sector. Lists more than 400 jobs each month, many of which are environmentally focused. Individual subscribers: $29 for three months, $39 for six months. Published by ACCESS: Networking for the Public Interest, 50 Beacon St., Boston, MA 02108. (617) 720–5627.

Earth Work (monthly). Contains at least 100 job listings at all levels in environmental fields. Student Conservation Association, P.O. Box 550, Charlestown, NH 03603. (603) 826–4301.

Environmental Job Opportunities. Institute for Environmental Studies, University of Wisconsin–Madison, 550 North Park St., 15 Science Hall, Madison, WI 53706. $10 per year.

EcoNet. International computer network serving the environmental community. Has 100 electronic bulletin boards on environmental topics, issues, services, events, and so forth. One board is a job listing that is constantly updated. 18 De Boom St., San Francisco, CA 94107. (415) 442–0220.

Environmental Opportunities (monthly). Listing of permanent, seasonal, and internship opportunities around the country, primarily in natural resource management, with nonprofit organizations and government agencies. Write for a free sample issue. P.O. Box 4957, Arcata, CA 95521.

The Job Seeker (biweekly). Listing of permanent, seasonal, and internship opportunities around the country in all natural resource and environmental fields with federal, state, local, nonprofit, and private employers. Rte. 2, Box 16, Warrens, WI 54666. (608) 378–4290.

JOBSource. Computer program with a database of current professional job vacancies in the environmental field. Specializes in natural resources, natural sciences, park management, conservation, forestry, and others.

GENERAL CAREER INFORMATION

Damn Good Résumé Guide, by Yana Parker (1990). Ten Speed Press.

Don't Use a Résumé . . . Use a Qualifications Brief, by Richard Lathrop (1990). There are many, many books on résumé writing. It would be difficult to do better than this one. Ten Speed Press. (800) 841–2665.

Ecological Society of America. *Careers in Ecology* brochure lists various job search resources. Center for Environmental Studies, Arizona State University, Tempe, AZ 85287–3211.

The Environmental Career Guide: Job Opportunities with the Earth in Mind, by Nicholas Basta (1991). John Wiley & Sons.

The Way of the Ronin: A Guide to Career Strategy, by Beverly Potter (1984). A discussion of the new work world and the type of employee who will flourish: one who is flexible and willing to make horizontal shifts in career paths, focusing on transferable skills. American Management Association. (800) 538–4761.

What Color Is Your Parachute?, by Richard Nelson Bolles (annual). A guide to career planning and job searches. If you do not own this book, buy it—and read it. Ten Speed Press. (800) 841–2665.

PROFESSIONAL ASSOCIATIONS

American Academy of Environmental Engineers, 130 Holiday Ct., Suite 100, Annapolis, MD 21401. (301) 266–3311.

American Association for the Advancement of Science, 1333 H St., NW, Washington, DC, 20005. (202) 326–6400.

American Bar Association, Member Service Department, 750 North Lake Shore Dr., Chicago, IL 60611. (312) 988–5000.

American Chemical Society, 1155 16th St., NW, Washington, DC 20036. (202) 872–4600.

American Geographical Society, 156 Fifth Ave., Room 600, New York, NY 10010. (212) 242–0214.

American Geological Institute. Publishes *Directory of Geoscience Departments* and *Careers in Geology,* 4220 King St., Alexandria, VA 22302. (703) 379–2480.

American Industrial Hygiene Association, 345 White Pond Dr., Akron, OH 44320. (216) 873–2442.

American Institute of Architects, 1735 New York Ave., NW, Washington, DC 20006. (202) 626–7300.

American Institute of Chemical Engineers, 345 East 47th St., New York, NY 10017–2392. (212) 705–7338.

American Public Health Association, 1015 15th St., NW, Washington, DC, 20005. (202) 789–5600.

American Society of Civil Engineers, 345 East 47th St., New York, NY 10017–2392. (212) 705–7667.

American Society of Limnology and Oceanography, Virginia Institute of Marine Science, 1208 Gloucester Pt., VA 23062. (804) 642–7345.

American Society of Mechanical Engineers, 345 East 47th St., New York, NY 10017–2392. (212) 705–7722.

American Society for Microbiology, Board of Education and Training, 1325 Massachusetts Ave., NW, Washington, DC 20005. (202) 737–3600.

Chronical Guidance Publications, Aurora St., P.O. Box 1190, Moravia, NY 13118–1190.

The Geological Society of America. Publishes *Future Opportunities in the Geological Sciences*, 3300 Penrose Pl., P.O. Box 9140, Boulder, CO 80301. (303) 447–2020.

Health Physics Society, 8000 Westpark Dr., Suite 130, McLean, VA 22102. (703) 790–1745.

Junior Engineering Technical Society, 1420 King St., Suite 405, Alexandria, VA 22314–2715. (703) 548–5387.

National Association of Environmental Professionals. A multidisciplinary professional society dedicated to the promotion of ethical practice in the environmental profession as a distinct career path. Publishes *NAEP Newsletter* (bimonthly) and *The Environmental Professional* (quarterly). P.O. Box 15210, Alexandria, VA 22309–0210. (703) 660–2364.

National Environmental Health Association, 720 South Colorado Blvd., Denver, CO 80222.

National Safety Council, Environmental Health Center, 1019 19th St., NW, Suite 401, Washington, DC 20036. (202) 293–2270.

National Society of Professional Engineers, 1420 King St., Alexandria, VA 22314–2715. (703) 684–2800.

Society of Exploration Geophysicists. Publishes *Careers in Exploration Geophysics*, P.O. Box 702740, Tulsa, OK 74170. (918) 493–3516.

Society of Toxicology. Publishes *Careers in Toxicology*, 1101 14th St., NW, Washington, DC 20005. (202) 371–1393.

Soil Conservation Society of America, 7515 NW Ankeny Rd., Ankeny, IO 50021.

Spill Control Association of America, 400 Renaissance Center, Suite 1900, Detroit, MI 48243. (313) 567–0500.

DIRECTORIES

Consultants and Consulting Organizations Directory (annual). Organized according to consulting activity and geographic location. Gale Research.

Directories in Print (annual). A comprehensive publication whose subtitle explains it all: *An Annotated Guide to Approximately 14,000 Business and Industrial Directories, Professional and Scientific Rosters, [and] Directory Databases.* Gale Research.

Directory of Environmental Information Sources, edited by Thomas Sullivan and Richard Hill (1990). Lists and describes more than 100 environmental databases and data services as well as information on government agencies, professional associations, and periodicals. Government Institutes, 4 Research Pl. Suite 200, Rockville, MD 20850. (301) 921–2300.

Encyclopedia of Associations (1992). In five volumes: volume 1 (three books), *National Organizations of the United States*; volume 2, *Geographic and Executive Indexes*; volume 3, *New Associations and Projects.* Gale Research.

Environmental Information Directory (1991). Tells how to find out what kinds of environmental problems are happening in your area, how you can get involved with a local environmental group, and what kind of legislation is being passed to protect the environment. Provides listings of experts and legislators involved in environmental issues. Gale Research.

Environmental Sourcebook (1992). Covers 8,500 different organizations, associations, agencies, publications, clearinghouses, and library collections associated with the environment. Gale Research.

International Organizations (1992). Focuses on associations that are non-profit, international in scope and membership, and headquartered outside the United States. Gale Research.

Regional, State, and Local Organizations (1992). Lists local, state, and regional nonprofit organizations in the United States and its territories. Gale Research.

World Guide to Environmental Issues and Organizations. Presents significant worldwide environmental problems and their ramifications and nearly 250 international organizations involved in efforts to solve these problems. Also describes "green" parties and their policies and countries of influence and international and regional treaties, conventions, reports, directives and agreements. Gale Research.

RESOURCES FOR MINORITIES

Directory of Special Programs for Minority Group Members: Career Information Services, Employment Skills Banks, Financial Aid Sources, edited by Willis L. Johnson (5th ed., 1990). Information on more than 2,800 sources of job-training opportunities, scholarships, fellowships, and internships. Garrett Park Press, P.O. Box 190-B, Garrett Park, MD 20896. (301) 946–2553.

Minority Organizations: A National Directory. Lists more than 7,700 professional associations, trade groups, and historical-cultural organizations. Garrett Park Press, P.O. Box 190-B, Garrett Park, MD 20896. (301) 946–2553.

The Black Resource Guide (1990–1991). Lists more than 1,500 national resources for black persons. R. Benjamin Johnson and Jacqueline L. Johnson, Black Resource Guide, Inc., 501 Oneida Pl., NW, Washington, DC 20011. (202) 291–4373.

The Human Environment Center. Works to build understanding and form common cause among those advocating greater opportunity for the disadvantaged and minorities and those committed to the protection of natural resources. Special efforts include increasing the number of people of color on the boards and staffs of environmental organizations. 1001 Connecticut Ave., NW, Suite 827, Washington, DC 20036. (202) 331–8387.

RESOURCES FOR JOB SEEKERS WITH DISABILITIES

Project on Science, Technology, and Disability. Founded in 1975 to improve the entry and advancement of people with disabilities in science, mathematics, and engineering. The project is primarily an information center, linking disabled people and their families, professors, teachers, and counselors with disabled scientists, mathematicians, and engineers who can share their coping strategies in education and career advancement in technical fields. American Association for the Advancement of Science, 1333 H St., NW, Washington, DC 20005. (202) 326–6630. (voice/TDD).

Project with Industry. A national industry-based program to assist people with disabilities in obtaining competitive employment. PWI aims to meet the needs of the electronics industry and other businesses by matching qualified disabled candidates with appropriate job openings and to provide support services to facilitate this process. Electronic Industries Foundation, 919 18th St., NW, Suite 900, Washington, DC 20006. (202) 955–5837.

INTERNATIONAL EMPLOYMENT

The Job Seekers Guide to Opportunities in Natural Resource Management for the Developing World (1986). Describes organizations, opportunities, minimum qualifications, and procedures for employment inquiries. World Resources Institute, 1709 New York Ave., NW, Suite 700, Washington, DC 20006. (202) 638–6300.

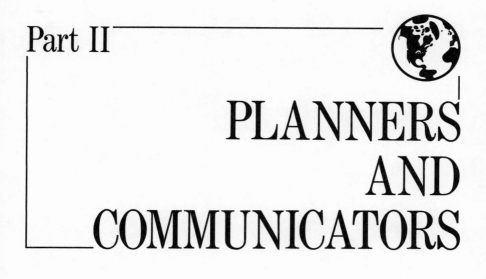

Part II

PLANNERS AND COMMUNICATORS

5 The Planning Profession

AT A GLANCE

Employment:
35,000 professional planners nationwide

Demand:
3 to 9 percent growth per year in the 1990s

Breakdown:
Public sector, 66 percent
Private sector, 15 percent (industry and consulting)
Nonprofit sector, 19 percent (including universities)

Key Job Titles:
Advanced (comprehensive) planner
Air quality planner
Aviation planner
Building or zoning inspector
Current planner
Environmental planner
Growth management planner
Land-use planner
Neighborhood planner
Planning consultant
Planning manager

Recreation planner
Transportation planner
Water resources planner

Influential Organizations:
American Planning Association
Association of American Geographers
Urban Land Institute

Salary:
Entry-level salaries range from $22,000 to $30,000. Average planning salaries are $34,000 to $38,000. Managerial planning positions cover a wide range, from the high 30s to more than $50,000.

While it has a lower profile and less name recognition than some of the other professions in the environmental field, planning work is ubiquitous. Most governmental bodies of any large size have a planner, or in some cases a roomful of planners, to record what is being done where, when, and by whom. Because an environmental occupation is close to a political position, it is a useful training ground for political careers.

WHAT IS PLANNING?

Webster's defines a plan as "a detailed scheme, program, or method worked out beforehand for the accomplishment of an objective." Applied to the environmental field, the definition is an apt one. The objective may be conserving wildlands, reducing air and water pollution, providing recreational access to forests, balancing housing and commercial development with the needs of fish and wildlife, or decreasing automobile use in cities. In every case, the professionals who design the schemes, programs, and methods are planners, and their activity is planning.

As the list of job titles at the beginning of this chapter shows, there are as many types of planners as there are concerns in the environmental world: air quality, water quality, recreation, land use, transportation, solid waste, and other issues can all be used as adjectives for planners. In many ways, planning is a *process* that is incorporated into the jobs of all environmental professionals—a process that involves understanding the key components of interlocking problems and designing sets of meaningful, real-world steps to solve them.

If planning is an integral part of all environmental work, what differentiates the professional planner from any other manager or scientist? "Three things set planners apart," according to one longtime city planning director. "First, our professional responsibility is to design systems which will solve *multiple* problems through *one* solution—a plan. Other environmental professionals tend to have narrower formal responsibilities, such as eliminating a specific discharge, preserving a wetland, or whatever.

"Second, our profession is *inherently* political, social, and economic as well as technical, scientific, and environmental. A plan which cannot be approved by politicians, paid for by existing resources, supported by the public, and carried out with today's technology is no plan at all. Other ecological workers can consider politics and economics as obstacles to their 'real' work. For planners, mastering these 'obstacles' *is* the work.

"Third, planners receive a different training from other professionals. Lawyers often say that their law school education wasn't about the facts of case law. It trained them to *think* like a lawyer. Engineers, scientists, and politicians say the same thing. Planners receive certain tools, skills, and knowledge in their training, but basically we are trained to think like planners—that is, comprehensively, and with a focus on setting up structures that will guide action and results in a desired direction predictably over time."

Planners divide themselves into two broad categories: those whose planning boundaries are defined by geography (towns, cities, counties, states, watersheds, ecosystems, regions, nations) and those who plan within a specific issue or policy area, such as air or water quality issues or hazardous waste management. In both areas, planning follows similar processes and requires similar skills. These processes provide a final definition of planning. In general terms, planners do the following:

- Conduct research to understand the area or problem in question. Development and maintenance of this "baseline" data is a big part of a planner's job. Such information defines "where we are now."
- Develop a vision of the future for the locale or issue.
- Identify activities, laws, and structures that act as barriers to achieving the desired goal and alternative activities that could help promote it.
- Create regulations and incentives to reduce undesirable actions and increase desirable ones.
- Put into place institutional systems to implement these systems and monitor their progress.

HISTORY AND BACKGROUND

Environmental, land-use, and urban planning has been done in the United States for years. Visitors to the well-designed city of Washington, DC,

Cleveland, Ohio. This redevelopment project involves converting a parking lot, once a city dump, into a popular waterfront attraction.

or the greenbelt park systems designed by the Olmstead brothers in Cleveland, Boston, New York, and San Francisco are beneficiaries of visionary early planners and their efforts.

The modern planning profession, however, can probably be traced to the formation of the Regional Planning Association in New York in the 1920s. The planners of the RPA were among the first to think comprehensively about the needs of human beings for transportation, housing, recreation, industry, and communal spaces *and* the protection of forests, water resources, wildlife habitats, scenic areas, and other environmental values. Many of the techniques and approaches to planning pioneered by such people as Lewis Mumford and Patrick Geddes are still used by planners today.

The New Deal programs of Franklin Roosevelt in the 1930s and 1940s brought new prestige to the idea of planning and to planners. Sweeping initiatives such as the act that created the Tennessee Valley Authority in 1933 reinforced the idea that professionals could design and implement comprehensive plans effecting physical development, preservation, and job creation throughout whole regions.

For most of the nation, however, "planning" was a piecemeal effort with little effect on sprawling urban areas and negligible concern given to the protection of the environment. On the contrary, many planners were actively promoting transportation, housing, and industrial patterns such as networks of suburban communities connected by miles of highways that actively destroyed wetlands, open spaces, and wildlife habitats.

"Environmental" planning came of age only in 1970, with the passage of the National Environmental Policy Act (NEPA), a landmark that is almost impossible to overestimate in its impact on planning in this country. NEPA required that environmental impact statements (EISs) be prepared, reviewed, and approved before major federal actions such as building a highway or damming a river could be performed. States quickly followed with their own requirements for EISs on development projects, and many local governments have incorporated the concept as well.

The need to identify environmental impacts and explain their significance, or lack of it, virtually created the field of environmental planning, now a specialization pursued by more and more planners. Dick Booth, a program director in the City and Regional Planning Department of Cornell University, defines the field as "the utilization of the world's resources to ensure human needs are served in a context that allows for long-term stability of the environment." For others, the key that makes a planner "environmental" is simply a greater mastery of environmental science or engineering, which can inform general planning activity. In either case, as more legislation, such as the Coastal Zone Management Act, the Resource Conservation and Recovery Act, Superfund, and the clean air and water acts have mandated planning periods, environmental planners have grown in importance.

Today, urban, land-use, and environmental planning is an integral part of city, state, federal, and business management. Even the smallest communities have a planning department with at least one professional planner. The growth of the field, however, has not reduced the number of problems facing the planners of the 1990s.

ISSUES AND TRENDS

While not a field undergoing rapid expansion, planning is definitely changing, and a clear understanding of the issues and trends shaping this environmental career path is important both to getting a good job and making a useful contribution.

STATEWIDE PLANNING

Until recently, land-use planning was an exclusively local affair, governed by local planning boards with wildly divergent attitudes toward environmental protection. In a growing number of states, however, legislatures have created coordinated land-use planning standards that govern all municipalities. Local planners prepare long-term growth management plans, which must be approved by a state agency. Florida and Oregon are among the leaders in the field. Expect more states to follow, creating planning jobs in state and local government and with consulting firms.

WETLANDS AND FLOODPLAIN PLANNING

The American Planning Association calls wetlands protection "one of the hottest issues in planning today." Increased awareness of the crucial role of wetlands for flood control, wildlife and fish habitat, and water quality has demanded that planners inventory remaining wetlands and design land-use regulations to preserve them.

SUSTAINABLE DEVELOPMENT

In areas with rapidly growing populations, sustainable development means controlling and managing growth to accommodate people while not overtaxing environmental resources. In areas with declining economies, planning for sustainability means economic development that can retain an area's viability while minimizing pollution. Planners who can combine environmental backgrounds with economic development skills are in real demand.

GROWTH MANAGEMENT

In Florida, where more than 900 new residents enter the state each day, planners are struggling simply to keep pace with the need for roads, water, sewer lines, homes, and so forth. Similar situations exist in California, the Pacific Northwest, the Southwest, and the Rocky Mountains. Employment in planning agencies is strongest in these areas.

INTERAGENCY COORDINATION AND AREA PLANNING

The coordination of planning efforts among agencies and areas is an encouraging trend. We have long known that air and water pollution do not respect jurisdictional boundaries, and we have learned that social problems in metropolitan areas are similarly unconfined. Planners are in the forefront of a movement to create appropriately sized planning entities, such as coastal commissions, regional transportation authorities, metropolitan air quality boards, water resource authorities, watershed districts, and even interstate agencies for such massive land areas as the Great

Lakes. People with legal backgrounds are especially needed to sort out the legal ramifications of increased coordination.

FROM NIMBY TO BANANA

Local planners are finding it harder and harder to develop locations for such undesirable facilities as sewage treatment plants, incinerators, landfills, industrial sites, and highways. One EPA official says that we have gone from "not in my backyard" to "build absolutely nothing anywhere near anyone." Planners with strong skills in education, mediation, and public speaking (and listening) are needed to help communities develop consensus on these politically charged issues.

CROSS-MEDIA POLLUTION CONTROL

Early pollution control efforts focused on separate programs for land, water, and air pollution. The result was land pollution control that simply moved pollutants to the air or water, water efforts that transferred waste to the land, and so forth. Environmental planners are leaders in designing programs that reduce pollution to all media.

RESTORATION OF DECAYED AND HISTORIC AREAS

Specialists in historic preservation, architecture, landscape architecture, and economic development are needed to help cities restore "old town" areas and bring back dilapidated waterfront areas for housing and commercial uses.

CONTINUED LACK OF FEDERAL INVOLVEMENT

In the 1960s and 1970s, the federal government was a primary source of financial support and innovation for urban redevelopment and planning efforts. Since 1980, however, local areas have been shouldering an increasing amount of the financial burden. This trend is expected to continue throughout the 1990s.

CHANGING DEMOGRAPHICS

The United States is changing dramatically. Senior citizens comprise a rising percentage of the population. "Minority group" citizens (African Americans, Asian Americans, and Hispanics) are rapidly becoming the majority. Planning agencies will be required to reflect these changes not only in their programming but also in the composition of their staffs. People of color with planning backgrounds will be in strong demand.

GEOGRAPHIC INFORMATION SYSTEMS (GIS)

The computer has revolutionized land-use and environmental planning. Sophisticated geographic information systems (GIS) allow planners to map how natural features, housing and commercial development, transportation networks, legal ownership patterns, and other systems interact. At all levels and in all sectors, there is a high demand for people with GIS and other computer skills.

These are just a few of the trends affecting the planning profession and employment in the 1990s.

CAREER OPPORTUNITIES

Career opportunities in planning are heavily weighted in the direction of lower level public agencies, but they do exist in all sectors and levels.

PUBLIC SECTOR

This sector dominates planning. And while in some areas of environmental work federal positions represent the greatest opportunity, the bulk of planning positions are found in state, regional, and local governmental bodies.

Federal government. Since the large-scale urban renewal efforts of the 1960s, the federal government has had a limited role in urban and land-use planning. That role has grown smaller since 1980. Funding for such programs as Community Development Block Grants and other revenue-sharing initiatives has declined precipitously. In recent years, few have looked to Washington for innovations in planning or for expansion of employment for planners.

Nonetheless, such federal departments as Housing and Urban Development, Labor, Energy, and Defense continue to employ city and regional planners to provide technical assistance, award grants, conduct research, manage contracts, and design military bases and federal installations. The Bureau of the Census also requires planners to make sense of and draw conclusions from its voluminous files of demographic information.

For environmental planners, the federal picture is brighter. All of the federal environmental agencies, and particularly the Environmental Protection Agency, have found that training in environmental planning is a good match for the design and implementation of air and water quality and waste management programs. "Many environmental planners have the mix of technical knowledge, communication skills, political savvy, and regulatory design skills that we are seeking," says an EPA recruiter.

State government. Environmental, land-use, and urban planners work throughout state government agencies. Look for them in the departments of natural resources, forestry, wildlife, fisheries, transportation, social services, public health, and environmental protection. Planners serve two primary functions at the state level. As policy planners, they help research and design the legal and regulatory framework that lawyers, biologists, engineers, and other specialists then work to implement. As line staff members, they often use their training to review and approve permits, conduct inspections, enforce regulations, manage contract work, and educate the public.

In states with statewide land-use planning laws and programs, planners are even more prominent. Planning staff members in such agencies determine what constitutes an "acceptable" plan, provide technical assistance to local communities in preparing their documents, wade through and approve the piles of paper and maps submitted to them, and then monitor progress to ensure that the plans are being fulfilled.

Much of the most innovative planning of the 1990s is being done by states. Jim Bernard, director of the Natural Resources Division of the State Planning Office in Maine, says: "In environmental planning, the state level is where I want to be. At the local level, you don't have as much latitude because you do so much trench fighting and have so many political considerations to contend with. This makes working on environmental issues, while very important, very difficult locally. At the federal level, it's just as bad, but for different reasons. You get locked into regulations and more hierarchy and political volatility." States are seen as far enough from local pressures to see the big picture and close enough to the real world to stay flexible.

Regional government. Regional governments are set up to handle issues that cannot be adequately addressed by a single jurisdiction. They allow for planning to protect air, land, and water around a large natural features, such as the Great Lakes, San Francisco Bay, Puget Sound, Chesapeake Bay, Tampa Bay, Narragansett Bay, or the Colorado River. They may also help coordinate activities in metropolitan areas with many interwoven suburbs; Minneapolis, for instance, has a long history of effective regional government.

Regional governments hire the same kinds of professionals as local planning departments do, but they are much more likely to seek out people with strong skills in research, finance, and policy analysis and computer and technical expertise. Often, these planners provide technical assistance and up-to-date information for local planners who lack time and resources. Rarely, however, do these bodies have strong legal and regulatory authority to realize the plans prepared by professional staff members. In lieu of such powers, political and education skills are at a premium to ensure that good ideas find their way into local laws.

Local government. Town, city, and county planning agencies are far and away the largest employers of planners in the United States. For many people, "environmental planning" is synonymous with the local planning department at City Hall.

These departments are usually divided into advanced and current planning divisions. Advanced planners are involved in writing or revising long-range plans, which outline the broad growth management strategies for the area in transportation, economics, education, parks and recreation, agriculture, water resources, environmental protection, solid waste management, and so forth. The heart of these plans is a zoning map, which allocates land to different types and intensities of uses. Project planners with special skills (transportation, for example) and neighborhood planners are often housed in the advanced planning section. These specialists undertake initiatives such as economic redevelopment efforts in targeted areas, development of low-income housing, creation of bicycle paths, and coordination with citizens' groups.

Current planners govern day-to-day development activities, ensuring compliance with zoning and building regulations, working with developers and the community on approval of permit requests, keeping maps and files up to date, and appearing before elected planning boards to give the department's view when challenges are made by citizens. Current planners may be involved in approving environmental changes as large as a new shopping mall and as small as the installation of a new sign at the local deli.

Inspectors are responsible for ensuring that projects that are permitted for development are carried out in accordance with the law. For instance, inspectors determine that wetlands are not being dredged and filled illegally. Inspectors often have wide authority to stop work that is unpermitted or not being carried out "to code."

Planning supervisors and managers work with elected officials on the strategic future of the area, coordinating with other city departments, such as public works, police, and schools, and representing the city on multijurisdictional agencies and committees. The chief planning director provides overall direction, prepares and manages budgets, and works closely with the mayor or city council on controversial projects.

In addition to professional planners, local planning departments hire biologists, architects, landscape architects, computer mapping specialists, geographers, housing specialists, public administration professionals, lawyers, and engineers.

PRIVATE SECTOR

Corporations, consulting firms, and service companies all provide opportunities for planning careers, though not as many as can be found in the public sector.

Corporations. Environmental and other planners are more prominent in companies with land management responsibilities than anywhere else. Utility companies, forest product firms, railroads, and mining corporations are likely employers. Waste Management, Browning Ferris, and other firms that site incinerators, landfills, and so forth also have a strong need for planners. In general, however, planners are relatively rare in corporate environmental affairs departments.

Consulting firms. Environmental consulting firms, small and large, are much more likely than corporations to employ planners for work with government and business clients. In bad economic times, comprehensive and special project planners are often laid off from government agencies and research studies and long-range thinking is farmed out to consulting and engineering firms. Private developers hire planning consultants to help guide their projects through the maze of environmental and land-use permit approval.

Service companies. Banks, real estate development companies, law firms, architectural firms, and market research outfits all require the services of planners.

NONPROFIT SECTOR

Nonprofit planning jobs do not pay as well as most of the similar positions in other sectors, but they can be an avenue to teaching or working with some of the larger nonprofit environmental organizations.

Colleges and universities. There are roughly 30 undergraduate and 100 graduate planning programs in the United States. Professors, instructors, and researchers at these institutions are a small but influential part of the planning profession. Planners also work as teachers in environmental studies, environmental science, landscape architecture, architecture, public administration, and political science departments. People with an interest in teaching planning will find that a Ph.D. is a prerequisite for all but a few instructor's positions.

Nonprofit groups. Planners are employed by all of the major environmental organizations as well as many state and local ones. Organizations with an agenda that takes in urban and neighborhood issues (housing, small parks, noise, economic development, design transportation, zoning) as well as natural resource issues are more likely to employ planners. Planners are also sought-after members of boards of directors of nonprofit organizations because of their combination of scientific, political, and regulatory skills.

GETTING STARTED

Your first, and perhaps most important, assignment of your entire planning career is to plan that career. Determining the educational route and advice to take to guide your decisions will be crucial factors in your success.

EDUCATION

According to a survey of the American Planning Association's (APA's) membership, the most important credentials in the planning profession are as follows:

- A bachelor's degree in planning.
- An internship position, preferably in planning, before going to work full-time.
- A master's degree in planning.
- Strong interpersonal and communication skills.

The experience of planners who are currently working in the field, however, indicates that only a minority carries the first of these credentials. This is not surprising, since only a small fraction of colleges (about 30) offers a planning major. Any of several undergraduate majors provides a good base for a planning career, including geography, urban studies, political science, environmental studies, environmental science, biology, architecture, landscape architecture, or economics. Some come to planning from even more technical backgrounds in engineering or the earth sciences.

If you do not pursue an undergraduate degree in urban, regional, or city planning, be sure to get some grounding in the natural sciences, economics, government, and the use of computers. Courses that emphasize case study approaches, such as classes in advanced public policy, are strongly recommended. Finally, undergraduate course work that introduces you to environmental law, cartography, urban design, and social science research methods is helpful.

Whatever your undergraduate degree, the third "credential" in the preceding list proves to be fairly important. A master's degree in planning or in a related field is becoming a key credential for those who wish to rise into senior, supervisory, and managerial positions. There are approximately 100 institutions offering advanced degrees in planning disciplines (Peterson's graduate college guide will tell you about them). Public policy, public administration, natural resource management, geography, law, and economics are also good graduate programs to consider for a planning career.

In choosing a college, you may want to consider whether it has been certified by the Planning Accreditation Board (PAB) affiliated with the APA. Seventy-two graduate and undergraduate programs have been accredited by the board, which looks for course work in theory and history; an emphasis on physical planning, economic organization, administration, and government; communications; and a final project that ties the course work together. However, getting a degree from a school not accredited by the PAB does not prevent you from being a practicing planner.

No matter what formal education you receive, planners are unanimous on the crucial importance of practical experience in your education. Evelyn Martin of the APA is emphatic on this point: "The single most important factor in getting your first planning job is to have some practical experience, several internships if possible. In addition to experience, skills, and contacts, this gives you references from people who have seen you do the kind of work you now want to get paid for. Fifteen years ago, that wasn't so common; now it is a virtual prerequisite for the field."

Other planners have said the same thing in different ways, encouraging the use of volunteer positions, cooperative education, course work in college, and participation in advocacy groups such as the many public interest research groups (PIRGs) and independent study research projects that allow you to get involved with real-world problems.

Jim Bernard of the State of Planning Office in Maine sums up the advice of many planners, both environmental and otherwise, when he says: "If you want to be an environmental planner, a strategy that is hard to beat would be to obtain an undergraduate degree in the sciences or environmental studies, find some environmentally related work for a few years, and then get a master's degree in planning from a program that is accredited by the PAB and that has some environmental emphasis that you wish to pursue."

A final note: Adding some weight to your credentials with a certification can be a good idea. The APA administers a day-long battery of tests by which you can earn the American Institute of Certified Planners (AICP) certification, which is the closest thing in the industry to a planning license. You do not need to have a planning degree to take the exam, and passing the test can add credibility to your planning career, especially if you come from an unrelated background.

ADVICE

Here is a collection of advice from experts in the planning field on how to get started and make the most of your opportunities.

Get on planning boards, commissions, and committees. Dr. Margot Garcia, chair of the Department of Urban Studies at Virginia Commonwealth University and past chair of the APA's Division of Environment, Natural Resources, and Energy, points out that there are a myriad of these appointed bodies in every jurisdiction. They include special commissions for environmental planning, roads, solid waste, zoning appeals, and so forth. Some are formal decision-making bodies, and others are advisory in nature. As a member of one of these organizations, you can make a real contribution as a citizen and develop your planning skills at the same time.

Have a specialty to start with. Having a planning specialty, such as transportation, water resources, solid waste, or air quality, is a stronger ticket to an entry-level job than is a general education. See the section on diversifying your skills for a qualifier, however.

Master communication and mediation skills. Planners have emphasized again and again that most of their time is spent in meetings, hearings, and private sessions, where communication and conflict resolution abilities are essential. Gain presentation and public speaking skills. Get involved as a volunteer community mediator.

Learn to write well. Planners are writers. They write memos, permit approvals, letters, reports, research studies, and, of course, plans. Even entry-level job seekers are expected to be good writers and to prove their writing skill with examples from school or internships.

Get in the community network. By the nature of their work, planners are involved with people who care about various issues. Solid waste planners, for instance, know "who's who" in the recycling world of waste haulers, advocates, politicians, agency staff members, interns, volunteers, student researchers, journalists, and so forth. The same group of people meets at conferences, sits together at conference tables, shows up at hearings, and shares job offers. Be part of the network.

Diversify your skills. John McNulty, executive director of the nonprofit group Partners for Livable Places, says: "There is a dearth of creativity in local planning departments today. There are too many report writers and pencil pushers who never take the lead. We need to create a new type of professional who knows how to manage change. This is done not by churning out planners who focus on computer modeling and data crunching but by training planners with a diversity of skills, including law, economics, environmental issues, coalition building, politics, historical preservation, architecture, and more."

SALARY

Starting salaries for planners are in the $22,000 to $30,000 range. Median annual salaries of all planners are around $36,000, and those with ten or more years of experience can easily top $45,000. Large companies tend to pay best, followed by consulting firms, state governments, city governments, and county governments. Federal positions can start as low as $17,000, but many planners earn at the "GS-12/13" level, which can begin as high as $37,000 to $44,000. Planners' salaries have been rising at about 3 to 6 percent since 1987.

SUMMARY

Planning is a diverse profession, and planners come from a variety of backgrounds. Environmental planning is one planning specialty, but the work of nearly all planners requires environmental knowledge and helps determine environmental quality.

The successful planner will have a strong scientific or technical background, perhaps in a planning specialty, coupled with well-developed skills in oral and written communication, mediation, management, and politics and an ability to integrate the work of many different disciplines and the interests of different parts of the community.

The 1990s will see growth in land-use, urban, and environmental planning positions, especially in rapidly growing parts of the country. In addition, the skills and training of planners make them competitive for other kinds of environmental positions as well, especially in government agencies.

CASE STUDY

Turning the Tide in Tampa Bay

Florida's Tampa Bay is a shallow, fragile, and complex body of water now bordered by a nearly unbroken line of dense settlements. Executing an environmental recovery for this ecosystem requires careful planning and cooperation from a number of government bodies.

A casual jaunt out on the bay is as pleasant as ever. The water is blue-green and warm; the sky is clear and untroubled. Pelicans and gulls still wheel overhead. You can still bring home some sea trout and, perhaps, on a good day, a small grouper. But sadly, this is not a healthy body of water. Even though you can still catch fish, they are not available in the size or numbers that were there for the catching even a few years ago. Shrimp, manatees, and many other wildlife species have plummeted in number as well.

Several factors have combined over decades to create today's decline in the bay's ecosystem, but the root of each cause is massive urbanization. Consider the following:

- Human population pressures around the bay have grown enormously. Hillsborough County, which includes most of the bay's coastline (including Tampa), will absorb 20,000 new residents each year and will virtually double in population over the next 20 years.
- Sea grass beds crucial to fish reproduction have been reduced by 85 percent due to shading from floating algae encouraged by wastewater treatment effluent, thermal damage from power plant cooling water, and burial and turbidity from dredging, filling, and port development.
- Powerboat propellers used at high speeds in shallow waters over sea grass beds stir up sediments that cloud the water, blocking sunlight from the grasses and creating turbulence that damages the plants directly. Propellers also kill many manatees each year.

Were powerboats alone responsible for the damage, planning by itself probably would not be much of a solution. But planning can have consider- able effect on wastewater treatment plants, dredging, filling, and port development. It could even help thermal pollution problems. For these reasons, environmental planning has played an important role in the effort to begin the restoration of Tampa Bay.

Another crucial factor in the struggle to help the bay has been the adoption of a consistent set of requirements for statewide planning in Florida. Without such planning coordination, the consistency of action required to make changes would have been very unlikely.

Florida adopted a comprehensive planning process several years ago, and since then state, regional, and local planning authorities have been building their plans and learning how to work more effectively together. Each entity in the state has had to develop plans for roads, sewage, and storm water, along with a 20-year financing plan detailing the sources of their revenues to enable execution of the plan.

But great concepts do not necessarily translate smoothly into effective programs. After setting up some model elements in the planning process, the state of Florida has been unable to provide funding to meet all of its promises to local governments. As a result, many of the state-mandated responsibilities have fallen to local government bodies to implement or enforce, further burdening cities and counties.

In concept, the state of Florida requires local infrastructure to be in place to support development before that development can take place. This would seem to allow easy control over new projects that might damage Tampa Bay or other natural resources. In fact, however, in a seeming perversion of their original intent, the regulations force government bodies to meet the infrastructure needs of developers whenever possible.

Florida's comprehensive planning law has been on the books for only a few years now, not long enough to resolve the problems of Tampa Bay— that will take decades, at minimum. But it has made a start by making possible the kinds of regulations that can prevent further damage and begin to turn back the tides of sewage and sediment that have crippled the ecosystem.

"Now we can coordinate with each other to place limits on dredging and filling operations and limit the amount of effluent flowing into the bay," says Peter Clark, principal environmental planner for the Tampa Bay Regional Planning Council. He acknowledges that the program has so far had little effect on thermal pollution from power plants, but progress has been made.

"We are seeing the water quality improve, and we are starting to see some of the fish and wildlife respond," he says. "It has taken 50 years to wipe out our sea grass, and it will take that long to bring back even half of it."

Further progress will take years of careful work by citizens, planners, and politicians working cooperatively—no easy goal to reach without a focused objective. Negotiation and compromise will be as much a part of the process as good planning. "Some people look at the bay and say, 'Don't allow any development anywhere on the water's edge,' " says Bob Hunter, executive director of the Hillsborough County City-County Planning Commission. "There are a few examples of development there, and we can do it if it is done right, but not everywhere. I am a moderate in my position. The important thing is the bay water quality.

"The environmental planner must realize the agenda and stay as midstream as possible. Many of us would like to be the final authority, but we are not. I have learned that there is an art of compromise. There is a need to get something on the books rather than nothing."

PROFILES

Victor Furmanec
Associate Planner
Emanuel Associates
Nyack, New York

Government agencies and private businesses enlist the services of consulting planners to meet political needs while staying within the boundaries of environmentally appropriate development.

Victor Furmanec has a collection of degrees he earned while deciding on his professional direction. He earned both a bachelor's degree in biology and a master's degree in zoology from Rutgers University. "I thought biology was my choice, and I was interested in graduate work on ecology and habitats," recalls Furmanec. "I was doing research on my doctorate when I stumbled onto landscape architecture. It seemed to emphasize the environment and promote its understanding within development work.

"After two years studying at the State University of New York's College of Environmental Science and Forestry, I realized I was more interested in environmental planning than in design." Furmanec therefore finished up his schooling with a master's degree in city and regional planning from Rutgers.

After working for a time as a research demographer with the New Jersey Department of Labor, Furmanec moved to Emanuel Associates, a

consulting planning firm with a practice that includes work with environmental planning, environmental impact statements, geographic information systems, and waterfront planning, among other areas.

"Essentially, we advise towns and communities on their growth trends
and evaluate various development proposals based on how they will fit into
the town. We help them mitigate the environmental impacts of development." The big mistake communities make in environmental planning is
"not paying attention to detail," says Furmanec. For instance, "they don't
want to get into how drainage will change and the effects that will have on
downstream properties and facilities."

Furmanec's work time is split about evenly between using paper and
using computer-based systems. Word processing accounts for most of his
computer time, followed by spreadsheets, database applications, and geographic information systems (GIS). Because of their ability to integrate
large amounts of data from different sources and allow more flexible use of
that information, GIS are growing in settings ranging from park planning
to fishery futures. "GIS allows you to take time from data collection and
spend more of your time analyzing data and planning alternatives." Everybody in the office now has a dedicated computer system, he reports.

Opportunities for using the latest computer tools of the trade are much
more plentiful these days, and the growth of GIS will ensure that new
entrants will be using them on a regular basis. This is clearly one of the
areas in which new planners would be well advised to get a head start.

Furmanec also recommends a broad education that avoids too heavy an
emphasis on any single specialty. "You need to understand the natural
environment as a whole and the society we live in, including the fiscal
aspects of development." He sees the successful planners of the future as
those who have a broad, holistic training in the essentials of environmental
planning, with knowledge of the techniques and tools that will give them a
competitive edge in the job market.

Linda Saul-Sena
City Council Member
City of Tampa
Tampa, Florida

*Elected officials have a powerful impact on the success of planning work.
As a former planner and current politician, Linda Saul-Sena has strong
views on the limits of planning—and planners.*

"Planners are the intellects driving the process, and the politicians are the
people acting it out," says Linda Saul-Sena, council member for the City

of Tampa and former city planner. "Figure out if your individual strengths make you a planner or some kind of implementer. Don't go into planning thinking of it as implementation."

Saul-Sena is uniquely suited to make the distinction between the expertise of planning and the politics of implementation—she has served in both capacities.

Planners, environmental or otherwise, are the living knowledge base that provides the arguments for change in a community. The ultimate direction of that change is a product of the subtle and convoluted interaction among citizens, planners, and politicians. It is a flexible interaction that can sway influence toward one or another of the three parties at various times and places. Whereas one community may be a tightly run political machine in which planners essentially implement the party line, another may be a free give and take or a location where the influence of planners holds sway.

As a Florida native with a degree in art history and an eye for design, Saul-Sena longed to see urban areas redeveloped and improved while protecting rural areas. Instead, rampant development seemed to her to make a mockery of planning. Rather than remaining just another irritated citizen, she took action.

"I talked my way into a planning job," she says. Considering her training, this may seem incongruous to some, but not to Saul-Sena. "I don't think you need a degree to understand what we need in our environment and what we need to do to protect it. I learned zoning and wrote neighborhood plans for four years."

But even though Saul-Sena embodies what is great about the planning profession—the potential it allows a person to get into the field and make a contribution to one's region—she also points out the frustrations of the field. She found that even her best planning efforts, which she calls "fairly brilliant," sometimes had no effect. "I came to the realization that people do not listen to planners. We need to communicate with the public more effectively. If the public does not pressure officials to move on a plan, it comes to naught."

Saul-Sena is a professional with a strong commitment and deep feelings about the importance of her work. But because of the close proximity of planning to the complex world of politics, pragmatism at times wins out over even the perfect plan. She found that her belief in the relative logic of the planning process gave way to frustration once she was on the job and faced with the reality that a great plan does not always have a great future.

The realities of the profession make the career choices of the would-be planner important ones. "Try to be an intern in the field before pursuing a graduate degree in planning," Saul-Sena says. "It is important for people to get hands-on planning experience before committing to graduate school. The way you think things are going to be and the way they are can be very different." She notes that the money you forgo in a summer of volunteer intern work could be a solid investment when compared with a year spent working on the wrong graduate degree.

Saul-Sena's desire to have a greater voice in the implementation of plans finally took her away from the planning department, first to produce television programs advocating better city planning and historical preservation and finally to public office. As a member of the Tampa city council, Saul-Sena is still very much involved with planning, but from a different perspective. "I wanted to be an advocate, and that is why I am on this side of the fence now."

> ### Dev Vrat
> ### Energy Planning Specialist
> ### Energy Division
> ### Resource Management Department
> ### Santa Barbara County
> ### Santa Barbara, California

Planners with special training in fields such as energy, transportation, water resources, and so forth help bring greater depth to environmental planning and decision making. Diversity in the planning profession, both in the background of its practitioners and in the jobs they do, makes it a field in which enterprising people can create jobs to fit their desires.

Dev Vrat is a man who is in love with the diversity and challenge of his work. "It is everything you could possibly imagine, with every issue that is important to people and the environment," he says. Vrat is an energy planning specialist with the Santa Barbara County Resource Management Department's Energy Division. He combined his undergraduate degree in physics with a graduate degree in urban economics. A college job with the campus architect set his course into planning.

His unique combination of training in physics and planning makes Vrat a natural for dealing with the technical complexities of managing the county's delicate relationship with oil and gas companies. Issues that interweave with Vrat's local planning work include national energy supply efforts, oil and gas development policy, marine resources, air quality, and archæology and geology, to name a few.

In addition to managing complex technical issues, Vrat works with a bewildering array of people from the petrochemical industry; staffers from local, state, and federal agencies; and citizens and lobbyists—all working continuously to further their own particular agendas. For example, a current project involves working with government agencies and a local oil company. The issue is whether to use tankers to transport oil past Santa Barbara or the safer, but more costly and less flexible, solution of land-based pipelines. "The federal government is leasing for petrochemical wells beyond our jurisdiction, and yet we have to plan for it because it will affect us. Right now we are working on an oil-processing plant here that wants to transport oil by tanker ships. We want them to use land-based pipelines to avoid ocean spills and air quality problems. But we do not have sole control over this—other agencies have it, and the feds want the production."

The chaos of conflicting intents is clearly reflected on Vrat's desk. "You come into the office and you have an in-box crammed with all different types of problems, and the answering machine is filled as well. You have developers who want to get something done in a hurry, you are working with attorneys on interpretations of regulations, you are evaluating plans and site visits, you have meetings to inform the public about the planning process, and you are gathering data to prepare reports on the pros and cons of projects. You prioritize what has to be done today and what can be deferred. You have to set deadlines now to allow something to happen at some distance in the future, and you are constantly juggling [those] deadlines."

Yet it is the very chaos and challenge of his schedule that are parts of the allure for Vrat, together with the chance to work with the environment and to have an effect on issues that are personally important to him. The conflicts are those that he cares about and in which he wants to play a role. He has been fortunate enough to find an agency in which his feelings and the agency's mission fit together well.

RESOURCES

American Planning Association. The largest professional organization in the field of urban and regional planning, with 28,000 members and 45 regional chapters. Publishes *Environmental Planning Quarterly*. Student membership in the APA includes the magazine *Planning* (monthly) as well as membership in a state chapter. Other publications and services include *Environment & Development* (monthly), *Planners' Salaries and Employment Trends, 1991, JobMart* (semi-monthly), and a job-listing service. 1776 Massachusetts Ave., NW, Washington, DC 20036. (202) 872–0611.

American Society of Consulting Planners, 1015 15th St., NW, Suite 600, Washington, DC 20005. (202) 789–2211.

American Society of Landscape Architects. Publishes *Landscape Architecture News Digest* (monthly). 4401 Connecticut Ave., NW, Washington, DC 20008. (202) 686–2752.

Association of American Geographers. Publishes *Professional Geographer* (quarterly) and *AAG Newsletter* (monthly). 1710 16th St., NW, Washington, DC 20009. (202) 234–1450.

Guide to Graduate Education in Urban and Regional Planning, by Carl V. Patton and Kathleen Reed (7th ed., 1990). Available through the American Planning Association Bookstore, 1313 E. 60th St., Chicago, IL 60637. (312) 955–9100.

National Geographic Society, Geography Education Program, Washington, DC 20036.

Partners for Livable Places. An international nonprofit coalition of more than 1,000 organizations and individuals committed to improving communities' economic health and quality of life through collaborative resource management. Publishes *Livability* (quarterly newsletter). 1429 21st St., NW, Washington, DC 20036. (202) 887–5990.

Urban Land Institute. Publishes *Land Use Digest* and *Urban Land* (both monthly). 625 Indiana Ave., NW, Suite 400, Washington, DC 20004–2939. (202) 624–7000.

6   Environmental Education and Communication

AT A GLANCE

Employment:
> 150,000 environmental educators and communicators nationwide (includes teachers)

Demand:
> 5 to 10 percent growth per year in the 1990s

Breakdown:
> Public sector, 60 percent
> Private sector, 10 percent
> Nonprofit sector, 30 percent

Key Job Titles:
> Community affairs manager
> Elementary or secondary teacher
> Environmental advocate
> Environmental journalist
> Interpretive naturalist
> Museum educational staff member
> Public information officer
> University or community college faculty member

Influential Organizations:
> Alliance for Environmental Education
> Environmental Protection Agency, Office of Environmental Education
> National Association for Interpretation

National Association of Professional Environmental Communicators
North American Association of Environmental Education

Salary:
Entry-level salaries average $20,000 to $25,000, sometimes lower. Salaries for experienced personnel fall into the $30,000 to $40,000 range. High-end salaries can be as high as $75,000.

WHAT IS ENVIRONMENTAL EDUCATION?

Environmental education is a large discipline with a diversity of opportunities, particularly in the public sector. Salaries are not as high as in some other specialities, but those who work in this area report great satisfaction from their labors.

A naturalist guiding tourists through Yosemite National Park. A journalist writing an article about toxic contamination of local groundwater. Regulators discussing new pollution control requirements with owners of small businesses. Sixth grade students setting up a school recycling program. All of these activities are environmental education.

"Environmental education is not a subject but an interdisciplinary and holistic process for developing awareness of the environment and knowledge of how it works," says Georgia Jeppesen, program specialist with the Office of Environmental Education of the Florida Department of Education. "It is not telling people what to think about the environment, but it is giving them the critical thinking skills they need to gather information and come to their own conclusions." Ed McCrea, executive director of the North American Association for Environmental Education, agrees with Jeppesen. "What we are after is an educational process that gets the public knowledgeable about the basic facts and equipped with the basic tools to step in and take action to preserve environmental quality."

In this chapter, environmental education is defined as including the following:

• Classroom teaching in the schools at all levels.
• Outdoor education at zoos, nature centers, parks, and so forth.
• Environmental journalism, both print and electronic.
• Public information efforts in government and industry.
• Education for advocacy.

Although environmental educators work in a wide range of settings, they all share one objective: to help people appreciate and understand the natural world around them.

HISTORY AND BACKGROUND

In the early 1800s, the United States was still overwhelmingly a rural culture, and "environmental education" was the learning one received from agriculture, hunting, fishing, and other daily activities. Native American communities had built rich stores of environmental knowledge and effective systems for communicating information about the natural world. Already, however, urban areas were growing dramatically, and writers and naturalists such as Henry David Thoreau perceived the need for an education that would incorporate an understanding of nature and raise awareness of ecological degradation.

By 1891, Cornell University was encouraging schools to teach nature study as part of the core curriculum. Early conservation groups, such as the Sierra Club, were forming and undertaking education projects among their first tasks. Visitors to newly formed national parks sought some form of "interpretation," for both education and entertainment.

A dramatic increase in environmental education careers can be traced to the first Earth Day and the first Environmental Education Act in 1970. Earth Day itself was a massive "teach-in," bringing information about pollution and its effects to hundreds of thousands and spotlighting the low level of environmental literacy in our nation. A survey in that year by the National Education Association showed that 78 percent of surveyed teachers felt there was a lack of curriculum for environmental education.

Only in the past few years has environmental education become what could legitimately be called a definable career, according to Stephanie Reith, president of the National Association of Professional Environmental Communicators (NAPEC). "A lot of people have been doing environmental education for several years but not thinking of it as a profession," she says.

In 1990, Congress passed a new Environmental Education Act designed to coordinate educational efforts at federal, state, and local levels, promote the exchange of information, and publicize model programs to encourage their emulation around the country. Many professionals have high hopes that the 1990s will be a decade of strong growth for environmental education.

ISSUES AND TRENDS

It is unlikely that the whole of a discipline will appeal to you. Instead, you will find one or more areas within it that excite you and that are likely to provide employment. Many of the issues and trends listed in this book highlight areas where the chances of your finding that excitement and employment are excellent.

STATE ENVIRONMENTAL EDUCATION PLANS

According to Suzanne Kircos, a public affairs specialist with the Environmental Protection Agency's Chicago regional office, 45 states had adopted environmental education plans by 1989. These plans are important parts of the field, providing curriculum structure for environmental education in local schools.

RAPID GROWTH IN COLLEGE ENVIRONMENTAL OFFERINGS

Environmental classes and majors are exploding in popularity. Classes that a few years ago drew a handful of students are now oversubscribed. Colleges and community colleges are responding by beefing up environmental courses in traditional disciplines, adding new environmental majors, and hiring additional faculty members. Environmental science and engineering classes are growing most rapidly, including environmental technology programs at two-year colleges. Environmental studies offerings in politics, ethics, geography, journalism, and other liberal arts are growing as well.

INCREASES AT THE ELEMENTARY AND SECONDARY LEVELS

The National Science Teachers' Association reports that science teachers of the 1990s should be prepared to teach biology, chemistry, physics, and other fields from an environmental or ecosystem perspective. Although the number of specifically "environmental" teachers will remain limited, environmental concerns will become an integral part of science education.

REGULATORS AS EDUCATORS

Without reducing the rigor of environmental enforcement, regulatory agencies are training staff people to become teachers and coaches to the public, using seminars, workshops, and technical assistance to ensure that the regulated community understands its responsibilities. Small businesses in particular are being targeted as "students" for these environmental educators.

RISE OF ENVIRONMENTAL JOURNALISM

Nearly every major metropolitan newspaper has added an environmental reporter or feature in recent years. The number of magazines devoted to environmental education has grown considerably, with such venerables as *Audubon, Wildlife, National Geographic, Sierra,* and *Environment* being joined by *Buzzworm, Garbage, E, Earth Work, Environmental Careers,* and others. Most major bookstores have added an entire "nature/environment" section to accommodate the growing library of ecological titles. Finally, the past decade has seen an explosion of newsletters, journals, databases, and directories that require research, writing, and maintenance.

COMMUNITY INVOLVEMENT AND ENVIRONMENTAL EDUCATION

Innovative corporations and government agencies are looking for non-adversarial ways to involve the public in decision making on such controversial subjects as incinerator siting, hazardous waste disposal, Superfund cleanups, housing development, and freeway construction. The days of pro forma public hearings followed by years of expensive litigation are beginning to fade. At the heart of this change is a new profession—community relations specialist. In both public and private sector, these people help educate the community about the environmental and scientific aspects of proposed actions *and* educate companies and agencies about community needs, feelings, and proposals.

USE OF NEW EDUCATION TECHNOLOGIES

Some of the same technological innovations that have changed educational capabilities generally will also bring advances in environmental education. Telecommunication, interactive video, and creative new computer software will give teachers tools that can simulate ecological processes and increase understanding.

NEED FOR SHORT-TERM TRAINING PROGRAMS

Requirements for worker safety on environmental projects have created a need for week-long certification workshops (and trainers). New laws generate demand for seminars, short courses, and continuing legal education. Changes in technology require minicourses so that scientists and technicians can keep up. All of these training needs demand talented educators.

USE OF TELEVISION AND RADIO

For many people, interest in the environment began with television. National Geographic specials, Walt Disney nature films, Jacques Cousteau specials, Mutual of Omaha's Wild Kingdom, and public television shows introduced millions to the natural world. In the 1990s, there has been a rapid expansion of television and radio productions devoted to the environment, many at the local level.

NEW HOMES FOR OUTDOOR EDUCATORS

Both adults and families have a growing interest in incorporating active environmental education into travel, recreation, weekend vacations, summer camp experiences, and so forth. Look for a growing market for environmental educators at hiking, camping, skiing, canoeing, and other sites and with firms promoting ecotourism (low-impact vacations to areas like the Brazilian rain forest).

CAREER OPPORTUNITIES

As we have seen, environmental educators and communicators are at work in every part of the environmental community. Each sector, however, requires somewhat different kinds of people and skills.

PUBLIC SECTOR

Environmental education in the public sector ranges from working as a park interpretive ranger at Yellowstone, to directing environmental education programs for state and local agencies, to teaching at a local school.

Federal government. The U.S. Department of the Interior, with its many agencies, including the National Park Service, the U.S. Fish and Wildlife Service, and the Bureau of Land Management, is one of the single largest employers of environmental educators. For many people, in fact, pursuing a career in environmental education is synonymous with becoming an interpretive naturalist at Yellowstone, Yosemite, the Everglades, or the Grand Canyon.

If you are one of these people, do not hold your breath. These jobs are among the most sought after positions in the environmental field, in spite of low pay, poor housing conditions, and limited career paths. Literally thousands of people compete for a handful of positions at the major parks, and some work for years as seasonal or volunteer workers without becoming permanent employees. Educational positions at refuges administered by the U.S. Fish and Wildlife Service are less competitive but still attract huge numbers of applicants. However, if you are not dissuaded by this litany, the Advice section later in this chapter may provide some help.

Competition at agencies that are just beginning to incorporate environmental recreation and education into their agendas is less daunting. These include the Bureau of Land Management and the USDA Forest Service.

Other possibilities are the Environmental Protection Agency's Office of Environmental Education, which offers positions for curriculum developers, trainers, and similar educators; the Department of Energy, with its many laboratories; and the Department of Defense.

State government. State governments are a rising star in the environmental education profession. States play a key role in setting and reviewing curriculum requirements for local schools, creating funding priorities, running grant programs, training teachers, and implementing federal programs and policies. In addition, each state has a collection of environmental and conservation agencies with growing needs for educators and communicators and their skills. These agencies include departments of fish and wildlife, forestry, environmental protection, natural resources, parks and recreation, and public health.

State departments of education are often the focal point for preparation and implementation of environmental education plans under the Environmental Education Act.

Local government. Public schools, from kindergarten to graduate school, hire many times more environmental educators than any other sector. Consider that there are more than 110,000 public and private elementary and secondary schools, more than 2,000 four-year colleges and universities, and more than 1,400 two-year colleges in the United States. *All* of these schools employ environmental educators. They may be called librarians, science teachers, biology professors, or wastewater certification instructors, but they are all environmental educators.

Career opportunities in teaching vary wildly. In some areas, school budgets have been cut for years and schools are looking at continuing bad times. In areas of greater economic and population growth, budgets are better and more teaching positions exist. Over the next few years, however, many schools are expecting large-scale retirements and possible shortages. In many districts, there are already shortages of teachers in science departments, where environmental education is most often housed.

A word about elementary and secondary teaching is in order. Why do it? It requires long training, usually with a master's degree for better positions. Pay is relatively low. Budgets are usually crimped. Facilities are often poor. Success is often frustratingly slow. And yet, in spite of all of this, no single environmental profession needs talented, creative, and enthusiastic people more than teaching does. No career will produce higher rewards in personal satisfaction, and none will create a higher environmental quality return on society's investment. If we are truly serious about environmental change, we must start with the education of our children.

At the community college, undergraduate, graduate, and doctoral levels, there is a strong demand for professors and instructors in environmental areas, as noted in the Issues and Trends section earlier in this chapter. The environmental studies department at San Jose State University in California is representative of the trend. In 1989, 173 students at the college pursued environmental studies. A year later, the number was 241, and by 1992 it was 321 and rising. College administrators seeking students love these kinds of numbers and build faculty employment around them.

King County, Washington. Chuck Dolan, former ECO intern, is a volunteer projects specialist with the King County Surface Water Management Division, Seattle, Washington. The program uses volunteer work to teach environmental concepts to citizens. Here, Dolan instructs volunteers planting saplings along a damaged streambank.

In addition to schools, consider other environmental education and communication positions with local government agencies. Solid waste and recycling programs, storm water management agencies, household hazardous waste initiatives, land-use planning agencies, staff offices for elected officials, neighborhood programs, public works departments, water and air pollution agencies, and other local environmental functions have needs for education and communication professionals and their skills. Look particularly for departments that depend on widespread changes in individual behavior, such as curbside recycling efforts. Education and communication efforts in the form of classes, speeches, brochures, community events, school presentations, public meetings, and so forth are usually a big part of these initiatives.

A final arena for environmental educators in local government is the parks and recreation departments. Many cities, towns, and counties operate zoos, museums, summer education programs, arboretums, botanical gardens, large parks, youth camps, cleanup programs, conservation corps efforts, nature centers, and other places where environmental education is the key service. For the aspiring educator, a significant advantage of the local sector is its willingness to accept, train, and use volunteers and interns.

PRIVATE SECTOR

Private sector jobs in environmental education include community involvement coordinators for private companies, environmental training services, and the environmental media. This is a relatively small area in total employment.

Corporations. Have you been on the receiving end of any of this "environmental education and communication" recently? Your utility company sent you a colorful brochure highlighting ways you can conserve energy and cut your energy bill. The place mat at the fast-food restaurant where you had lunch was covered with the environmental accomplishments of the company. "Printed on Recycled Paper" was prominently noted. The news-weekly you read on the bus carried a two-page ad touting the pollution prevention record of the chemical industry. When you got home, there was a message on your doorknob from the private recycling firm that collects your trash, inviting you to a neighborhood meeting to discuss changes in the system. The notice is signed by the "recycling education staff." Finally, in the evening newspaper, you discover that environmental activists and the area's largest polluter are sitting down together for talks about reducing the use of toxic materials at the firm. The company's representative is referred to a "community involvement coordinator."

"Private companies need to improve their ability to communicate about environmental matters and their ability to listen as well," says a representative of the National Association of Professional Environmental Communicators, an organization that did not even exist until recently but is growing rapidly. "Environmental communication in private companies includes traditional public relations and advertising work but is much more likely to focus on breaking down barriers between environmentalists and the company to get communications flowing."

Federal regulation has helped inspire this kind of need. One example is the "Community Right-to-Know" requirement under the Superfund Amendment and Reauthorization Act (SARA). Under right-to-know laws, reams of data about corporations' use of toxic chemicals are available to the public. It is in a firm's best interest to provide some assistance to the public in interpreting these data. Without such help (and sometimes with it), the likely response is fear of the unknown.

Corporations in the oil, chemical, waste management, manufacturing, and other industries are employing a broad range of environmental communicators with training in public relations, media coordination, graphic arts, government relations, environmental journalism, compliance, law, and technical fields.

Consulting firms. As mentioned earlier, many environmental laws require that workers be certified or receive specialized training before they are allowed to work. A growing number of private firms have sprung up to provide this service. These firms hire instructors, trainers, and workshop leaders to deliver educational services to corporations and agencies. Career opportunities in this field may not require a great deal of specialized training. If you are a quick study and have a winning classroom presence, training firms may be willing to help you learn the material you will teach.

Environmental training specialists will also be needed to work directly for companies employing significant numbers of seasonal or temporary workers.

The media. Print and electronic media outlets such as newspaper, book, and magazine publishers; television and radio stations; audiotape and videotape production companies, and others make up "the media," and all of them have a growing demand for environmental stories, insight, news, and information.

Santa Monica, California. Host Nancy Pearlman and special guest Peter Strauss film the ACE-nominated television special "Gem in the Heart of the City," a documentary on the Santa Monica Mountains National Recreation Area. Photograph courtesy of Nancy Pearlman.

Preparing yourself for a career in the "environmental" sector of this industry is not very different from general preparation. Many of the environmental beat writers for major newspapers, for instance, began in other areas, such as general science, politics, business, or even sports or life-styles. They found that being a superb researcher, interviewer, and writer with an ability to understand science was more important than any special "environmental" training. This is even more true in the electronic media, where technical skills, stage presence, and persistence have proven to be more important than knowledge of a specific field.

In contrast, writing for more exclusively environmental magazines, journals, and newsletters (not to mention books) becomes increasingly more difficult for generalists in proportion to the knowledge base of the readership. Trade, industry, and association publications, for instance, employ and contract with many environmental journalists, and they expect a high level of technical knowledge.

NONPROFIT SECTOR

Nonprofit organizations are a major player in the environmental education field, employing some 30 percent of the education and communication work force. Both the writers and the publishers of this book, for instance, are nonprofit organizations.

Almost all nonprofit environmental organizations, from small neighborhood groups with one staff person to huge international organizations such as Greenpeace and the World Wildlife Fund, engage in some form of environmental education. In 1992, *Buzzworm* magazine printed a *Directory to Environmental Education*, which listed more than 70 nonprofit nature centers, youth programs, camps, publications, classes, and programs. This is just the tip of an extremely large iceberg.

Career opportunities in nonprofit organizations for people skilled in education and communication are greatest with groups in which education is the main activity, such as nature centers that offer field trips for schoolchildren, or with large, well-known groups such as the National Wildlife Federation. Environmental education may also be incorporated into the job descriptions of lobbyists, program and research staff members, administrators, and fund-raisers. Much of this work is seasonal, depending on the school year or on summer vacation activities to provide "customers." Skills in demand include outdoor skills; the ability to teach environmental fieldwork techniques; knowledge of biology, botany, ornithology, and wildlife science; strong oral communication and teaching abilities; and innovative ideas for curriculum design. Schoolteachers seeking summer work, take note!

SALARY

Stephanie Reith of the National Association of Professional Environmental Communicators says that salaries are "all over the place" in this field. "Nonprofit salaries are low, many of them just clearing $20,000," she says. "Government and scientific salaries pay in the middle ranges, and private business and public relations companies are on the high end." Some salaries in the higher ranges of the field are "very good," she reports. Salaries higher than $50,000 are not impossible to achieve with a specialty and an advanced position.

Others have confirmed these estimates. Environmental educators and communicators outside of the classroom share the salary range of their school-based colleagues. Most permanent positions in the field pay a salary of $20,000 to $25,000 to start, sometimes lower. Allison Rasmussen of the Center for Marine Conservation in Washington, DC, reports interpretive salaries as low as $17,000 in North Carolina with a master's degree. Many nonprofit environmental education outfits primarily employ poorly paid seasonal workers or depend highly on interns and volunteers.

In all sectors except the private sector, administrators and directors are the only ones who can expect predictable salaries higher than $40,000. Educators, writers, and other communicators in government agencies and nonprofit groups will level off in the $32,000 to $38,000 range. Salaries for "environmental" positions with magazines, newspapers, television and radio stations, and other media outlets are so varied that an attempt to characterize them would be meaningless.

A bright spot in the salary picture is the pay of college professors in environmental fields. Depending on their institution and field, it is not unusual to find professors earing $40,000 to $75,000, after weathering low-paying positions as graduate assistants and instructors.

Professionals interviewed for this chapter overwhelmingly commented that new entrants should expect relatively low pay and that love of education would be needed to keep motivation alive. Environmental communicators like what they are doing for the world. Choosing a career in environmental education requires that an individual face squarely the fact that some emotionally rewarding jobs are often poorly compensated. If money is a prime motivator, think carefully before choosing this field, and consider educational opportunities and experience that will maximize your value in the job market.

GETTING STARTED

Even for people who have known since reading *Ranger Rick* at age six that they would grow up to become environmental educators, getting started takes careful planning.

EDUCATION

In giving advice on formal education, environmental educators fall into two groups. One group emphasizes scientific and technical knowledge and considers education in teaching and communications to be important secondary training. The second group places teaching and communications abilities first. "You need a fairly solid technical background with a working understanding of biology, chemistry, and zoology," says Nancy Richardson Hansen, senior management assistant for the Storm and Surface Water

Utility of Bellevue, Washington. "To that base is added your communication ability."

In contrast, the National Association of Professional Environmental Communicators' Stephanie Reith picked up her technical knowledge on the job after earning a degree in public relations communication. "The degree is less important than the combination of your knowledge and capabilities," she says. "You have to understand or at least not be intimidated by technical information." Much of what at first appears to be highly technical information is largely jargon.

Ed McCrea of the North American Association for Environmental Education favors a mix of technical and communications training for environmental educators, emphasizing the student's role in monitoring the progress of the degree and making changes along the way. "If you are passive, you will get a very narrow degree that may not help as much later on. Active students can ferret out courses that will help them balance technical background with education and communication skills."

For environmental educators in public and private schools, there will be obvious teacher certification requirements for elementary or secondary opportunities. The vast majority of teachers who consider themselves environmental education specialists have science teaching certifications.

For those who wish to pursue a formal degree in environmental education, there are a growing number of college programs of varying quality. The North American Association for Environmental Education is a good resource for more information about these programs (see the Resources section at the end of this chapter).

Finally, the consensus among environmental journalists is that a combination of strong knowledge of scientific and political processes and superb journalistic skills in research, interviewing, and writing is essential. What seems less important is whether this is obtained by adding science classes to a journalism curriculum or vice versa.

ADVICE

Whatever problem you are likely to encounter, chances are someone has faced it before you. Seek out advice from the veterans. At least they will provide food for thought, and at best they may save you a great deal of wasted effort or needless frustration.

Volunteer. The field of environmental education and communication is wide open to volunteering, and, in fact, many employers expect that volunteer experience and internships will be part of your résumé. Use environmental job listings such as *Earth Work, Environmental Opportunities, The Job Seeker,* and others listed in the Resources section of chapter 4 to identify volunteer opportunities, or contact local schools, environmental groups, zoos, museums, nature centers, aquariums, and so forth. Several organizations have reported hiring exceptional volunteers as paid educators.

Develop some showmanship. In all sectors, there is a need for people who can make learning fun, new, and exciting. At its most basic level, this means mastering public speaking skills. Beyond that, it means imparting a sense of theater to your communications.

Learn experiential education techniques. The field requires knowledge of innovations in participatory learning and community involvement. People learn best by doing, and successful environmental educators will know how to structure that process in the classroom, the meeting room, and at streamside.

Get published. Write for a newsletter or your school newspaper. Write a flier or a brochure. Write a report that is used by a company or agency. Environmental journalists invariably say that people with published articles have a distinct advantage over those without them. Do not wait to be paid. Get started by approaching publications, no matter how small, that seem to be in need of good environmentally oriented copy.

Learn about television and video. For better or worse, more and more training is being done through videotapes, and many people get the bulk of their information from television. Even if you are not considering a production career, learning about these tools and how to use them effectively will be crucial.

Master the legal framework. Environmental communicators on all sides of the regulation equation stress that being up to date on legal requirements is essential to their work. The alphabet soup of RCRA, TOSCA, SARA, CAA, CWA, SDWA, and other environmental laws must become second nature to you. Job seekers who show a familiarity with these requirements and an ability to communicate their essence succinctly will have a distinct leg up.

Think about the future. Do some long-term career planning as you enter your career. What will you want to do in five or ten years? Low-paying positions can be a source of fatigue after several years. If you "burn out," what will you do next, and what can you do now to make such a shift easier?

Pay attention to networking. Get to know your peers on the job. Join professional associations and broaden your horizons to add meaning to your career and develop more long-term alternatives.

SUMMARY

Just as the environmental problems of today have been caused in part by poor environmental education in the past, so the quality of our environment in the years ahead will be a direct result of the environmental education taking place today. Environmental educators have an influence over our environmental future that far exceeds the importance we place on this field with wages or recognition. Demand for environmental educators and communicators appears to be on the upswing for the remainder of the 1990s, which may help to raise average compensation.

Environmental communicators themselves summarize the field with comments that are remarkably similar:

- "It is an opportunity to influence people to protect the environment. I don't have to go home at night wondering if I did something worthwhile during the day." —Jan Ostenson, public involvement manager with the King County Surface Water Management Department in Seattle
- "There is nothing I could do that I would love more. I am one of the very fortunate few people who get paid for doing what [they] love to do." —Nancy Richardson Hansen, senior management assistant for the Storm and Surface Water Utility of Bellevue, Washington
- "I find it tremendously rewarding to speak to a group and feel that I have touched some individuals out there and enlightened them." —Christie Vargo, program officer for the Community Foundation of Greater Lorrain County, Ohio
- "I want to know that I have helped someone when I go home each night." —Suzanne Kircos, public affairs specialist, Environmental Protection Agency

That says it all.

CASE STUDIES

Don't Mess with Texas

Teams of environmental educators and communicators often pool their efforts to create innovative methods for getting an environmental message across to the general public. Texas's state program is one example.

In the rural Texas hill country outside Austin, a pickup truck roars down a back road through the handsome rolling grasslands. The young male driver of the pickup, a "Bubba" in local parlance, takes the last swig of beer from a 12-ounce can and flings it casually out his window. It joins other cans, bottles, hamburger wrappers, and miscellaneous litter at the side of the road.

Texas experienced a plague of littering in the 1970s and early 1980s, particularly by young rural men, that sent trash cleanup costs for rural highways soaring. Cleanup costs along highways increased by 15 to 20 percent annually by the middle of the decade. As locals would put it, it got to the point where the typical nearsighted armadillo could hardly forage at the side of a Texas road without getting a nasty bump on the head from a beer can or pop bottle.

But that was before "Don't Mess with Texas."

The Texas State Department of Highways and Public Transportation decided that enough was enough when the annual cleanup cost for roadside debris soared to $24 million in 1985. They reasoned that a $2 million advertising campaign would be worth the investment if it simply halted the rapid rise in cleanup costs. The challenge was to communicate effectively with Bubba the idea that tossing trash onto roadways was messing up his beloved state and that a lot of Texans he admired wanted it to stop. This would be environmental education translated into language that would hit home with the intended audience.

First, surveys determined without a doubt that Bubba was the culprit. Then an innovative advertising campaign was devised to appeal to young Texas males' powerful sense of pride and appreciation of blunt talk. "Don't Mess with Texas" came at Bubba from every angle, in the form of sincere messages from Texas performers like Stevie Ray Vaughan and Willie Nelson and Dallas Cowboy football stars "Too Tall" Jones and Randy White and in songs from the Fabulous Thunderbirds and many other Texas musical groups.

"Don't Mess with Texas" appeared in bright red, white, and blue letters on Texas-sized litter bags for cars and pickups; on bumper stickers, grocery bags, and soft drink cans; and in numerous other places. Bubba could not help but get the message.

Although "Pitch In" and other antilittering slogans of the past had failed miserably, "Don't Mess with Texas" generated Texas-sized results. Between 1985 and 1991, visible roadside litter in Texas decreased by more than 72 percent and was projected to improve further. Rural litter in fact decreased by 75 percent. The litter reduction translates to millions of dollars of savings in trash cleanup costs for the Texas treasury. In addition, at least ten national awards have been presented to the program. A follow-up program to reduce urban littering further was planned for 1992.

Program organizers in the highway department worked to expand the program to other areas while retaining the "Don't Mess with Texas" slogan. Companion programs now include the following:

- "Adopt-A-Highway," in which local groups get together to clean up a specific two-mile stretch of roadway on a regular basis.
- "The Great Texas Trash-Off," a once-a-year effort in which thousands of volunteers clean up roadside trash.
- "The Great Texas Cleanup-Greenup," an effort that combines roadside trash pickup with planting of wildflower seeds in the same areas.
- "Spread the Word . . . Not the Waste," an environmental education program for grade-school children that teaches citizenship attitudes, values, and skills.

And just in case there are a few Bubbettes out there who do not already know where to put their trash, the Texas Girl Scouts can now earn a "Don't Mess with Texas" patch by helping with cleanup efforts.

Beach Cleanup in Hampton, Virginia

The best environmental education and communication efforts get valuable information across to a wide spectrum of people, inspire them to action, provide a mechanism for that action, and bring people into a network for future environmental work. This project meets all the criteria.

Ocean dumping got the headlines and the blame when startling numbers of syringes and "beach whistles" (tampon applicators) began floating onto New Jersey's beaches in the late 1980s and early 1990s. In fact, however, analysis of beach debris around the United States shows that industry is far from being the sole perpetrator. Beachgoers, shippers, streamside campers, classy ocean cruise lines, and the U.S. Navy also contribute to marine pollution.

All over the world, beach lovers are the aesthetic losers as beaches are trashed by ocean debris dumped by every nation with some ocean frontage. But marine wildlife pays an even heavier price for human trash. Plastic fishnets and strapping bands kill 30,000 northern fur seals per year in the Pribilof Islands alone. Sea turtles die trying to eat plastic bags and balloons, which closely resemble their favorite food, the jellyfish. Huge numbers of seabirds meet similar fates each year as well.

Before she became director of the Pollution Prevention Program for the Center for Marine Conservation's field office in Virginia, Kathryn O'Hara already had a great love of the ocean and its coastline. "I have always known I wanted to be involved in marine science," she says, "ever since I was three or four years old [and] my grandfather took me fishing. When we came home with our fish, we dissected them and saw what they were eating. I spent all my summers on the coastline and was exposed to the marine environment and relatives explaining things to me."

Years later, after finishing her master's degree in marine biology with a thesis on oyster reef ecology in the Carolinas, Kathryn joined the Center for Marine Conservation—at a fortuitous moment, as it turned out. The year was 1985, and the nonprofit organization had just received a contract to conduct a study and compile data to answer the question "Is garbage in the ocean a problem?"

"I was there at the right place and the right time, before [ocean dumping] became a national issue," O'Hara recalls. "We started that study with just me, and now I have a staff of 12 and we are the nonprofit experts in marine debris." But O'Hara's team includes far more than just the 12 full-time employees in her office. Her team, in fact, includes many thousands of volunteers around the United States and in other countries as well, all working to help resolve the problem of beach debris.

At first, O'Hara focused her efforts on lobbying for legislation to prohibit ocean dumping, which remained "perfectly legal until 1988," she says. The center helped lobby for the international law that now prohibits ocean dumping, and it followed up by studying the sources of ocean debris.

"People are the source of ocean debris, and that's why education is so critical," O'Hara says. The focus of her department's work is environmental education and outreach work to explain what ocean debris is, why it is dangerous, and what must be done to stop it. O'Hara's approach has been to identify polluters and go directly to them for help in resolving the problem. In working with industry and even the U.S. Navy, this has been an effective approach.

But working with the public has required a larger educational effort—a beach cleanup. The center's first beach cleanup took place in Texas in 1986. In the fall beach cleanup of 1991, more than 145,000 volunteers in U.S. coastal and inland states, as well as in 12 other countries, helped collect more than 3.7 million pounds of trash from 4,290 miles of beaches. Beach cleanups now take place in a large number of countries around the world, including Japan, the British Virgin Islands, the United Kingdom, Canada, Cuba, Greece, Mexico, the Netherlands Antilles, Guatemala, Guam, Israel, Greece, Norway, Venezuela, and Barbados. O'Hara's office is a major organizing force for all of these efforts.

O'Hara's job now includes considerable work with beach cleanup efforts outside the United States. On a trip to Japan, she worked with concerned Japanese citizens who wanted a formula for protecting their beaches from debris. She now spends as much as half of her time traveling to keep programs moving around the country and giving presentations.

The center's "Beach Cleanup Report" lists the types of debris found and traces plastic items back to their sources whenever possible, publishing manufacturers' names in the report. Nervous companies then call her office to get advice on what they can do to ensure that their products do not turn up in ocean debris.

Aircraft carriers in the U.S. Navy fleet can produce 15,000 pounds of trash each day, which they will soon be prohibited from dumping. To help its ships meet these tightening requirements, the navy flew O'Hara to a carrier stationed off Puerto Rico to get her advice on reducing the amount of waste it produced.

As more and more people receive the message, the levels of beach debris may begin a gradual decline. That is what motivates O'Hara. "When you are educating people about the marine environment, there is a feeling of power that you can make a difference."

PROFILES

Susan Amtower
Instructor and Public Relations
Director
Pocono Environmental Education
Center
Dingman's Ferry, Pennsylvania

Environmental educators come from a wide variety of backgrounds and serve many job functions. Working with schoolchildren encourages environmentally sound habits in the next generation and provides richly rewarding careers for a large number of environmental professionals.

Each year, 20,000 students, teachers, parents, and children arrive in carloads and busloads at the Delaware Water Gap National Recreation

Area to visit the park and come to the Pocono Environmental Education Center. The nonprofit center uses a site within the park grounds. Visitors may come just to visit, to attend an environmental educational program, or to learn how to be a better environmental educator.

The center's staff of 25 includes Susan Amtower, instructor and public relations director. Her dual role allows her to manage communications projects and get outside and teach schoolchildren as well.

"Spring and fall are our busiest times of the year," says Amtower. "During the week, student groups come here from New York, New Jersey, and Pennsylvania for programs on canoeing, orienteering, and wildlife, forest, and pond studies. On the weekends, we have similar programs for scouts and church groups and workshops for teachers. We have more than 74 weekend workshops planned for 1993, and we instruct about 5,000 teachers each year." Other educational events at the center include field trips, workshops, and special youth-at-risk programs for urban youngsters.

Amtower's role varies substantially depending on the time of year. During the busy spring and fall periods, as much as half of her time is spent teaching, but during the slowest parts of the year, instruction takes as little as 10 percent of her time. Amtower divides the rest of her time between communications and fund-raising activities. She spends 40 to 60 percent of this time supervising the planning, design, and production of communications materials, such as a newsletter and brochures for the center. The remainder goes to helping the center raise money through direct mail and grant applications.

As in any up-to-date office, computers play a role in Amtower's work, and she notes that between word-processing, graphics layout, and database management applications, most of her time in the office is spent in front of a computer. She has been working in front of computers at the center since joining the organization several years ago as a temporary instructor, a position that was to last six months. She later progressed to administrative assistant and then director of public relations. She spotted the job in *Earth Work* magazine's monthly listing of environmental jobs.

Amtower's bachelor's degree in wildlife and fisheries biology came from North Carolina State University, not far from the North Carolina mountains where she grew up. While working at a summer environmental job, Amtower met a fellow North Carolinian, who became her husband. The following summer, they toured the country, working together on a 4-H wildlife and fishery program, then both landed temporary jobs at the center. Her husband is now a biological technician with the National Park Service.

"Be flexible enough to take temporary positions to get the experience,"

Amtower says. "Use cooperative education, internships, and volunteering. Very few people are lucky enough to go right from school into a full-time position."

David Orr
Professor
Department of Environmental Studies
Oberlin College
Oberlin, Ohio

Educators at the college level often debate how environmental issues, science, and politics should be taught. When the subject arises, David Orr's is a voice to be reckoned with.

When David Orr, professor with the Department of Environmental Studies at Oberlin College, asked an assemblage of notable environmentalists *why* they became environmentalists, he got an interesting response:

1. The environmentalists all had a difficult time answering the question because they had not thought about it before.
2. Their eventual answers to the question traced their environmental interest back to childhood experiences, not schooling.

Orr has a gift for posing interesting questions, challenging assumptions, and thinking about environmental issues in new ways. He is the author of *Ecological Literacy*, a collection of his articles and essays intended to foster ecological literacy. Orr is also one of the environmental thinkers sought out for an EPA panel to help determine how colleges and universities might reorganize their environmental programs to educate new environmental professionals and those in other fields.

"When an instructor asked a group of business MBAs several questions about environmental issues, such as 'What is the ultimate source of all our energy?' most of them did not know the answers," says Orr. "This represents a massive failure in environmental education. Much of what we do in higher education about the environment involves undoing the mistakes of earlier education, even among the so-called environmentally aware crowd. We have to learn how to educate in different ways so people understand how environmental systems work."

Asked to define environmental education, Orr comes up with five distinct levels of environmental awareness, all of which, he says, are necessary for a person to be an effective environmental citizen:

1. Knowledge of current events in the world.
2. Knowledge of global ecology and the interrelatedness of the world's physical systems.
3. Awareness of the causes of environmental problems—why the world is not working well as a physical system.
4. Knowledge about solutions to our environmental problems.
5. A willingness to make the mental transition from "I know" to "I care, and I am ready to roll up my sleeves and get into the fight."

Orr's own journey to environmentalism began in the countryside of western Pennsylvania. His parents had a cabin in the Allegheny National Forest amid a forest of virgin hemlock in an area inhabited mostly by deer and bears. Both of his parents were interested in natural history. "Nature was on my mind," he recalls. Orr says that when he read some of the works of the late René Dubos and Aldo Leopold during graduate school, "their ideas resonated with something in my mind, a sense of wonder about the natural world that my parents fostered."

Orr earned his bachelor's degree in history at Westminster College, his master's degree in history at Michigan State University, and his Ph.D. in international relations at the University of Pennsylvania. Before taking his present position at Oberlin, Orr worked for 11 years creating an environmental education center called Meadow Creek, Inc. in the Ozarks and taught at the University of North Carolina.

Orr gives three bits of advice to those who want a career in environmental education:

• Learn everything.
• Develop a wide-ranging curiosity.
• Develop a specific focal point for your expertise.

Orr worries that parents today are much more interested in creating "little geniuses of calculation than inculcating a sense of wonder and mystery about the natural world." Without that kind of guidance, he warns, we are unlikely to create a new generation of planetary stewards.

RESOURCES

Alliance for Environmental Education. Publishes *Network Exchange*. 10751 Ambassador Dr., Suite 201, Manassas, VA 22110.
Ecolinking: Everyone's Guide to Online Environmental Information, by Don Rittner (1992). Has a section on education. Peachpit Press, 1085 Keith Ave., Berkeley, CA 94708. (510) 548–4393.

Educational Resources Information Center (ERIC). See the Resources section of chapter 2 for a description.

Heldref Publications. Publishes *Environment* and *Journal of Environmental Education*. 4000 Albemarle St., NW, Suite 504, Washington, DC 20016.

National Association for Interpretation. The consolidated Association of Interpretive Naturalists and the Western Interpreters Association, which merged in 1988. Sponsors an annual conference and the Interpretation Management Institute, has regional chapters, and publishes *Legacy* (bimonthly). Employment services include Dial-a-Job ([303] 491–7410) and Dial-an-Intern ([303] 491–6784), which are updated weekly. A printout of the week's listings costs $3. P.O. Box 1892, Fort Collins, CO 80522. (303) 491–6434.

National Association of Professional Environmental Communicators, P.O. Box 06 8352, Chicago, IL 60611. (312) 661–1700.

National Environmental Training Association, 2930 East Camelback Rd., Suite 185, Phoenix, AZ 85016. (602) 956–6099.

Natural Science for Youth Foundation. Works to help localities establish and maintain nature centers. Also the professional organization for personnel of nature centers and small nature museums. Provides training for nature center management at its annual conference; publishes a job opportunities bulletin (bimonthly) and *Natural Science Center News* (quarterly), as well as a directory of natural science centers. 130 Azalea Dr., Roswell, GA 30075. (404) 594–9367.

North American Association for Environmental Education. A support group for those involved in environmental education. Membership sections include elementary and secondary education, university environmental education, conservation education, and government and private sector personnel involved in environmental education and communications. Sponsors annual conference and workshops, lists internship and employment opportunities in *The Environmental Communicator* (bimonthly), and otherwise works to promote environmental education. P.O. Box 400, Troy, OH 45373.

Outdoor Writers Association of America, 2017 Cato Ave., Suite 101, State College, PA 16801. (814) 234–1011.

Part III

ENVIRONMENTAL PROTECTION

7   Solid Waste Management

AT A GLANCE

Employment:
More than 300,000 professionals in all sectors nationwide

Demand:
13 percent average growth per year, producing more than 150,000 new jobs by 1995

Breakdown:
Public sector, 40 percent
Private sector, 45 percent
Nonprofit sector, 15 percent

Key Job Titles:
Chemist
Civil engineer
Economist
Environmental engineer
Hydrologist
Logistics expert
Mechanical engineer
Planner
Recycling coordinator
Solid waste manager
Transportation specialist

Influential Organizations:
  Air and Waste Management Association
  Environmental Protection Agency
  National Recycling Coalition
  National Solid Wastes Management Association

Salary:
  Entry-level salaries range from $15,000 to $30,000. Federal entry-level engineers earn $23,000 to $28,000. Salaries for more experienced positions range from $40,000 to $70,000, with some higher.

Solid waste management is by far the largest of the environmental fields, and it is the fastest growing as well. In the 1990s, solid waste managers are experiencing fundamental change as landfills are closed, incinerators are blocked, and communities demand recycling, reduction, and reuse of waste products.

WHAT IS SOLID WASTE MANAGEMENT?

Solid waste management, as defined by Allen Blakey of the National Solid Wastes Management Association, is the use of proven, effective tools to reduce the volume and toxicity of solid wastes and manage the recycling and disposal of remaining waste material. In practice, these tools fall into four primary categories.

SOURCE REDUCTION

Source reduction means keeping things out of the waste stream to begin with—using less packaging material on products, for instance. This is a relatively new area that receives limited attention from those working in the solid waste industry because, by definition, they never see the problem—waste reduction is something that takes place before waste disposal. Source waste reduction may ultimately be the most important means of control over our solid waste problem.

RECYCLING

Recycling means reusing materials from the waste stream and, whenever possible, separating them at the source to control costs. Currently, paper, glass, and aluminum are the materials most often recycled. The total amount of recycled materials, however, still represents a fraction of all solid wastes. Recycling has gained a great deal of attention in recent years, but in fact it is still in its infancy.

CLEAN WASTE COMBUSTION

Combustion of clean wastes for energy production, also called waste-to-energy combustion or resource recovery, is an offspring of incineration. In facilities that carry out clean waste combustion, combustible portions of the waste stream serve as fuel for generating steam or electricity—with dramatically reduced emissions compared with those from old-style incinerators.

SANITARY LANDFILLS

Landfills are still the eventual end point for the majority of municipal solid wastes. Even though we have come a very long way from the days of "the dump," an uncontrolled place for the disposal of just about anything, the majority of solid waste still ends up underground.

HISTORY AND BACKGROUND

Dumps are a time-honored tradition in human society. Archaeological digs show lots of bones, stone tool chips, pottery shards, and other debris, sometimes in concentrated points around early human settlements. The first written records of a dump date back to at least 500 B.C. in ancient Greece, and dumps have been springing up across the landscape ever since.

Open-air dumps, coupled with the burning of trash, have been part of our own culture since its foundation. As American cities grew, crude incineration became a larger component of waste management efforts, converting mounds of wastes into clouds of air pollutants. These methods came to a halt with the enforcement of the Clean Air Act in the late 1960s. Chicago, for example, was forced to shut down three of its four incinerators, necessitating a major reorganization of its waste disposal methods.

Landfills were the next answer, and the shift was rapid. In 1960, when crude forms of incineration were still accepted, landfills received only 62 percent of all municipal solid waste. By 1980, the decline in incineration had brought the total to 81 percent. By 1988, development of cleaner waste-to-energy combustion systems brought the landfill portion of the total waste stream back down to 73 percent.

The landfills that received this huge increase in solid waste, particularly those built before 1970, did little but shift pollutants from the air to the water table. Leaking municipal landfills have become hazardous waste disasters, with dangerous chemicals leaching into wells, lakes, streams, and rivers. The ominously named Fresh Kills landfill on Staten Island once leaked as much as 4 million gallons per day. Of the more than 30,000 identified hazardous waste sites in the nation, a huge number are former landfills.

And we are running out of room at those landfills that remain. Fully half of the nation's 15,000 landfills will be closed by 1995. The need to find a place to put our wastes has driven some municipalities to seek desperate measures. In 1987, the infamous garbage barge from Islip, New York, roamed the eastern seaboard for weeks after Islip ran out of space in its landfill and sought to ship the problem away. The barge became a potent metaphor, teaching us that there *is* no "away."

As landfills have filled up across the country and both clean air and clean water regulations have made new landfills tougher to operate, options have begun to recede and costs to rise. This new level of financial pain creates opportunities to reexamine how we dispose of our wastes. Source reduction and recycling have gradually grown as a result of the garbage glut, and new landfill and cleaner incineration methods have developed as well.

The problem, however, continues to get worse. According to a 1990 Environmental Protection Agency report:

- We are generating more trash than ever before.
- Americans generate more than 180 million tons of trash per year, or 4 pounds per person per day, of which 156 million tons are either burned or sent to landfills.
- Without source reduction, waste generation will reach 200 million tons per year, or 4.2 pounds per person per day, by 1995.
- Paper remains by far the largest part of the waste stream, at 40 percent. The rest includes yard waste (17.6 percent), metal (8.5 percent), glass (7 percent), plastic (8 percent), food waste (7.4 percent), and other wastes (11.5 percent).

Without fundamental change, our solid waste crisis will continue to deepen.

Two fundamental laws define the structure of the solid waste management industry.

Resource Conservation and Recovery Act (1976). This act defines categories of wastes and sets standards for their disposal. As this book was being completed, the act was in the midst of reauthorization, according to Steven

Levy, special assistant in the Municipal and Industrial Solid Waste Division of the EPA. A new version of the act was expected to be passed sometime in 1992. "Expect an increased emphasis on recycling," Levy notes.

Clean Air Act amendments (1990). The 1990 modifications to the Clean Air Act will gradually affect the solid waste industry, requiring significant changes in landfill emission provisions, incineration, and other areas. The act helps ensure that problems of solid waste pollution are not transferred from the land to the air.

ISSUES AND TRENDS

The following are some of the larger concerns that will affect the solid waste management industry in the 1990s.

SITING OF LANDFILLS AND INCINERATORS

Even if recycling and source reduction efforts reach the levels predicted (15 percent by skeptics, 25 to 30 percent by many government agencies, and 40 to 50 percent or more by activists), industrial and municipal landfills and incinerators will still be needed. Most communities reasonably agree that such facilities are necessary yet expect them to meet the NIMBY requirement ("not in my backyard"). As a result, it is nearly impossible to find sites for new landfills and resource recovery plants. Siting efforts are a major environmental battleground of the 1990s. A new twist is the growing environmental justice movement, which has provided powerful evidence that people of color are actively discriminated against in the siting of these facilities. Grass-roots organizations have sprung up to stop what are seen as racist practices. People with legal, planning, transportation, management, community relations, mediation, and related skills are needed to create agreements on siting facilities when they are necessary.

LANDFILL TECHNOLOGY AND OPERATIONS

Assuming that a landfill can be sited, new technologies are needed to ensure that it does not pollute land, air, water, and groundwater resources. Solid waste experts say that they can build new landfill sites that are safe and effective. With new designs that can be sealed at top and bottom and methods for gathering both leachates and air emissions, waste disposal managers feel that they have good solutions. More professionals are needed with the expertise to design, build, and operate such facilities and to help educate the public about them. Landfills are now high-technology devices, and there is demand for people who can work with multiple liners, leachate collection systems, emissions systems, coverings, and groundwater monitoring equipment.

Toxic Materials

A significant reason why safer landfills are essential stems from the toxicity of materials that find their way into these repositories. Finding new techniques for reducing the toxicity of landfill wastes could help make them less dangerous to the environment and reduce the cost of landfills. This will increase demand for chemical engineers, toxicologists, and civil engineers.

Waste-to-Energy Combustion

Concern about air pollution, airborne toxic emissions, and waste ash dogs this alternative, in which old-fashioned incinerators have been redesigned in recent years to burn more cleanly and generate steam or electric power as a by-product. In addition to the pollution concerns, these facilities (termed "combustors" by the EPA) are enormously expensive to start up, and construction usually takes more than five years. Nonetheless, there will probably be a lot more of them in the future. The total share of solid waste sent to incinerators has climbed slowly from a low of 10 percent in 1980. New combustors designed to meet air pollution requirements increased this share to 14 percent by 1988. The EPA estimates that combustion of solid waste will increase further—to 25 percent—by the end of the 1990s. This increase will produce a demand for qualified professionals to design, build, and operate combustion plants, and there is a shortage of people with the requisite skills.

Ash

Once waste-to-energy facilities have burned municipal solid wastes, the 10 percent left over in the form of ash must be disposed of—in a landfill. Because this concentrated form of waste can itself be quite toxic when materials it contains, such as heavy metals, enter the waste stream, many landfills refuse to accept ash. Further, if waste ash is designated a "hazardous waste," it can be many times more expensive to dispose of. Ash is a huge problem in search of bright ideas from scientists, engineers, planners, economists, and others.

SLUDGE MANAGEMENT

When municipal and industrial sewage plants have done their work, the water they produce is clean enough to discharge into rivers, bays, and lakes. Left behind, however, is the equivalent of the incinerator's ash— sludge. If heavy metals, toxic chemicals, and other hazardous wastes are represented in high enough concentrations, sludge, like ash, can become an official hazardous waste. Where should we dispose of it, and how? Water quality planners in most metropolitan areas are working with solid waste planners to solve this problem.

COMPOSTING

Nearly a quarter of all solid waste is organic matter, such as yard clippings and food waste. Rather than delegating this material to landfills or burning it, innovative solid waste managers are developing community composting programs. Look for these programs to become a bigger part of solid waste strategies.

MAKING RECYCLING WORK

The following four trends are those most often highlighted by professionals who are on the cutting edge of the recycling world.

Rapid growth. The EPA estimates that recovery of materials from municipal solid wastes will reach 20 to 28 percent in 1995, with considerably higher numbers possible by the end of the decade. Some municipalities are already well ahead of this timetable, such as San Francisco, where 35 percent of municipal solid wastes are currently recycled. "There has been a huge shift in the use of recycling during the past five years," says Peter L. Grogan, director of materials recovery for R. W. Beck & Associates in Seattle. "More than 3,500 cities are now doing curbside recycling," he says. Bringing these and higher goals into reality will require many new recycling coordinators and facility managers for municipal systems around the country.

Improved technology. Better technologies are essential to making the most of recycling. Paper is a key example. Once paper is collected, we must have technologies that can effectively reuse it over and over again to produce a quality product. Civil, mechanical, and process engineers are designing more effective systems at private companies and in university laboratories.

West Coast Salvage and Recycling, San Francisco, California. WCSR's "can line" separates and weighs aluminum cans.

Long-range cost accounting. "Large cities, like San Jose and Seattle, have demonstrated by their implementation of recycling programs that they can reduce total solid waste costs," says Grogan. However, in many locations, recycling involves front-end costs that make it appear more expensive than landfill. Only by calculating the long-term costs of other solutions can municipalities justify recycling on a strict financial basis. Economists and government finance specialists can help by using such long-range accounting and by more accurately reflecting the total cost of disposal methods in setting dumping fees and charges.

Increased demand for recycled goods. Perhaps the most discouraging problem with recycling is a lack of predictable demand for recycled raw materials. This depresses the prices paid to municipalities for these materials, which increases the cost of recycling. Even at today's rates of recycling (around 14 percent), some markets for recycled materials are glutted. Says Jeff Solomon-Hess of *Recycling Today*, "There is a tremendous amount of work to be done in finding manufacturers to buy [recycled materials], treat them as raw materials, and make new products with them." One example of creative solid waste management in this area is laws that define and specify the standards for end products containing recycled materials. If paper goods must have higher percentages of recycled material to be called "made from recycled paper," demand for collected material will rise and investment in expensive machinery will have a more predictable payoff. Economists, logistics experts, materials scientists, business managers, and activists are needed to create demand through product design or by propping up the market legislatively.

RETHINKING WASTE MANAGEMENT

The EPA predicts that by 1995, some 20 to 28 percent of municipal solid wastes will be recovered and reused. However, notes an agency report, "exceeding this projected range will require fundamental changes in government programs, technology, and corporate and consumer behavior." Peter Grogan calls for a new specialty in this field, which he dubs "social reengineering." "We must communicate a message to the public that we want them to rethink waste management at home and on the job," he says. "There is a tremendous task ahead of us in educating 250 million people on the value of recycling." The majority of this work in raising people's awareness about waste reduction will take place at the state and local levels. Employment opportunities exist here for environmental communication professionals and teachers.

CAREER OPPORTUNITIES

PUBLIC SECTOR

Public sector jobs in waste management account for 40 percent of the total jobs in the industry. While federal positions are minimal, there is work for state governments in managing programs and providing guidance for local efforts, and a broad range of local positions, where most of the real work in solid waste management takes place.

Federal government. Washington has long left primary responsibility for solid wastes with state and municipal governments, limiting its activities to data collection, analysis, and technology transfer. This is changing somewhat.

New minimum standards for landfills are the first in what may be a series of new controls on the municipal solid waste industry. Siting, design, operation, and closing of landfills now are subject to these regulations, which serve to force lax states to improve the safety of their landfills. Many expect that the EPA will get more involved in promoting recycling and waste reduction as these activities become politically popular. More federal jobs in solid waste management will be available than in the past as new measures take effect.

State government. States are extremely active in legislation and planning for solid waste management and offer some of the most exciting opportunities for environmental professionals.

Many state governments are engaged in some form of statewide solid waste planning, including mandated levels of recycling and requirements for local solid waste management plans, usually with a mandated focus on recycling. The number of curbside programs would be much smaller if not for state action. Many states also operate regional siting authorities, require recycling of beverage containers through bottle deposit laws, restrict wastes coming into the state, and work to stimulate new markets for recyclable materials.

Municipal landfills are often a state concern. Many states set environmental criteria for landfills specifying, for example, what materials can and cannot be placed in them. Fully half of the states have special regulations on the disposal of incinerator ash. With new EPA minimum standards for landfill siting, design, construction, and closure, all but a handful of states will find their existing landfills in need of improvement. This will generate new state needs for sanitary landfill experts who can work with the EPA's more stringent requirements.

State positions in solid waste management include planners, communications and education specialists, lobbyists, program managers, recycling experts, enforcement personnel, hydrologists, geologists, materials specialists, engineers, planners, and generalists.

Local government. Waste management activity is inherently local. It is in the neighborhoods and industrial parks that waste is collected, separated, and recycled or sent to landfills and incinerators. However, for many municipalities, contracting these services out to private firms is the preferred way to go because it holds down local government employment.

Local government, on the other hand, is overwhelmingly the home of the recycling coordinator—one of the environmental profession's "hottest"

careers. This position is particularly appealing to environmental generalists because, so far, at least, it can be entered from almost any educational
background. The nation will need thousands of these people, who design
and manage recycling programs, find markets for collected goods, educate
the public, and push to keep ever higher levels of waste out of the landfills.

Finally, local government bears the brunt of most landfill and incinerator siting battles and must handle landfill closures as well. This activity
may be handled as much by the planning and legal departments as by the
solid waste department.

Depending on the size of the population served and whether contracting
is done, the solid waste department may be very small or quite large. Small
departments are composed primarily of those doing or managing the
actual waste management work. Larger departments in metropolitan
areas include the full range of professionals listed earlier in the description
of state government and may include waste pickup, landfill management,
and combustion operation staff.

PRIVATE SECTOR

Waste management companies and consulting firms make up the bulk of
the private sector of waste management. Together, they account for nearly
half of the employment in this environmental discipline.

Private waste management firms. The National Solid Wastes Management Association (NSWMA) estimates that in 1990, private waste management companies moved 75 percent of the nation's total wastes,
collecting from 60 percent of all homes and handling 95 percent of all
commercial and industrial wastes.

Private sector firms are also the largest employer in solid waste management, accounting for 45 percent of the work force. This is an astounding
change in a short period of time. In 1970, the NSWMA estimated that the
municipal solid waste industry included 10,000 very small firms with total
revenues of less than $1 billion. By 1990, revenues were estimated at $25
billion, and several large companies had begun to dominate the business,
accounting for more than $8 billion of the total. The NSWMA expects that
having doubled its revenue from 1980 to 1990, the industry will double
again to $50 billion by 1995 and there will be even greater dominance on the
part of industry giants like Waste Management, Browning Ferris, and
Laidlaw.

There are a number of reasons for the consolidation of the solid waste
management industry around fewer and fewer companies, but financial
pressures are part of all of them. Environmental regulations place the cost

of a modern, environmentally safe landfill beyond the means of the small family businesses that once dominated waste disposal. Small businesses are being replaced by companies that can make the investments in plant and equipment now required by law. In addition, insurance liabilities for hazardous wastes in landfills have created financial and legal barriers that only a well-heeled company can overcome. Finally, communities are requiring comprehensive services from their solid waste vendors, and the cost in staff, benefits, and financing is more than many smaller outfits can afford.

Comprehensive solid waste firms hire a wide range of people, starting with plant operators, laborers, truck drivers, technicians, and others and including a wide range of engineers, regulatory compliance specialists, lawyers, environmental scientists, and community relations staff members.

The smallest segment of private sector employment involves professional waste managers working directly for large corporations. One such program, at McDonald's Corporation, is profiled in this chapter.

Consulting firms. Private sector waste management also includes consulting firms that design and construct landfills and combustors, assist communities in the design of waste strategies, and help private companies run their own waste management programs. This last area is fertile ground for entrepreneurs. Matthew Costello, president of Corporate Conservation in Massachusetts, helps firms in the Boston area run office paper recycling programs. He says that currently only a fraction of companies are recycling, in spite of the huge cost-saving potential (one client saved $27,000 of a $70,000 trash bill, paying for the program in four months). Costello estimates that "only a third of white office paper is recycled today in the Boston area." Other cities have similar opportunities.

NONPROFIT SECTOR

Nonprofit organizations employ the fewest solid waste management workers of the three sectors, accounting for some 15 percent. Nonprofit groups are involved in solid waste management in three ways: as providers of recycling services, as advocates for new legislation to reduce waste and improve recycling, and as activists to restrict the siting of landfills and incinerators or ensure their safety.

Small, nonprofit, community-based recycling efforts have been a mainstay in the recycling world until recently, when local governments and private industry began to take over the field. In many communities, recycling remains a community initiative, often run by volunteers or activist staff people who have provided the service because government would not.

Local, state, and national advocacy groups are credited with pushing government into innovations such as bottle deposit legislation, statewide solid waste planning, packaging limitations, community composting programs, mandatory recycling goals, and other initiatives. Through lobbying, initiative petitions, and public education, organizations such as the public interest research groups help raise the standard of success each time a new benchmark is achieved.

Finally, nearly every proposed siting of landfills and combustors has provoked the creation of neighborhood and city groups to fight back. Often working in cooperation with better-known state and national groups, these groups (often unstaffed and unincorporated) have been successful in many cases.

Solid waste management professionals in the nonprofit sector include lobbyists, planners, environmental scientists, lawyers, fund-raisers, public education specialists, and recycling service providers, such as truck drivers and collection and separation technicians.

SALARY

Salaries in solid waste management vary according to sector, academic degree, level of experience, and region of the country. The private sector pays the highest salaries, followed by the public and nonprofit sectors. Advanced technical degrees and multiple degrees can result in higher salaries, as do applicable years of experience and jobs in large cities. Regions with traditions of higher pay, such as California, New York, and Washington, DC, follow the typical patterns, generally accompanied by a higher cost of living.

Private sector jobs for individuals with B.A. or B.S. degrees bring starting salaries ranging from slightly less than $20,000 to perhaps $30,000. Engineers and individuals with desirable multiple degrees will be at the high end of the pay scale.

State government salaries tend to be a bit lower than their private sector counterparts and may not vary much according to your degree. Expect a range of $20,000 to $25,000 to start. Local government and nonprofit positions may start a bit lower yet, paying anywhere from $15,000 to $22,000, except in the larger programs. However, a management spot in a large city may bring $50,000 to $60,000 or more, and salaries for private sector or consulting managers can be higher still.

GETTING STARTED

Solid waste management has been transformed during the past two decades by a combination of economic and political forces. As a profession, it is still sorting itself out. So, although specific fields of study will lend credibility to the newcomer and ease the pathway to a new job, failure to have the "right" degree will not prevent an interested person from getting into solid waste management. Hands-on experience, enthusiasm, and an ability to get things done are just as important.

EDUCATION

"People are coming to this field from every walk of life," says Jeff Solomon-Hess of *Recycling Today*. "Twenty years ago, when I started, it was hard to even find an *environmental* program. The closest thing I found was forestry. Now there are degree programs in solid waste management at many universities in the country." The students who come out on top, he says, will be the ones who have multidisciplinary educations that include some scientific or engineering course work. He also cites business training with a focus on environmental issues as a good pathway into the field.

A graduate degree of some sort is essential to building a lasting career in many environmental fields. But at least for now, it is possible to succeed in solid waste management without an advanced degree. Many professionals argue for getting into the field with a basic degree and gaining several years of real-world experience. Then, they say, take that experience back into graduate school once you know what you want to get out of that advanced degree.

For people with an interest in the waste-to-energy field, a background in engineering (civil, mechanical, or electrical) or environmental science is useful. Degrees in planning, economics, business, chemistry, and air-related sciences are good tools as well.

Landfill professionals point to environmental engineering and public health as key backgrounds. Planning, hydrology, earth sciences, and community relations are also needed disciplines.

A number of leading universities are developing an integrated waste management minor that could augment many different fields of study to produce an individual ready to participate meaningfully in the solid waste management field. The proposed minor includes seven courses:

- Introduction to Integrated Waste Management
- Resource Stewardship (public policy issues)

- Source Reduction (source reduction and public education)
- Recycling
- Transformation Technology (composting and waste energy)
- Sanitary Landfill
- Internship (required)

Everyone in the field who was interviewed for this book, however, emphasized that the best education comes from practical experience. It is virtually a prerequisite to show proven ability through internships, volunteering, cooperative education, summer employment, or research projects.

ADVICE

Additional advice and tips to those starting careers in solid waste management include the following.

Start from anywhere. Starting with an unusual degree is not an impediment in this field. Peter Grogan of R. W. Beck & Associates in Seattle earned his degree in psychology; while working with troubled adolescents, he organized recycling efforts to raise money for the programs. He then split off an organization devoted to recycling, which grew. Now he journeys around the world as a "hot" consultant for a leading environmental consulting firm—but he started in psychology.

Women and minorities are wanted. Under the management of Diane Gale, employment of women in Seattle's Solid Waste Utility has gone from 20 percent to nearly 50 percent. (The Solid Waste Utility's story is told in this chapter's Case Study.) Gale likes female employees because of what she sees as their "broader view." Women and minorities with training and interest will find great opportunities in the solid waste management field.

Take some risks. Corporate Conservation's Matthew Costello sees a need for people who will take risks and find ways to recycle and reuse materials that typically are ignored and sent to landfills. "Most people, when thinking of entering the field, think immediately of recycling paper," he says. "If anybody can really get wild and master an unusual material, they could answer a real need. Master a niche. Know more about the insides of appliances than anybody. I still don't see anybody doing anything creative and unusual with, say, old stoves."

SUMMARY

Solid waste management is a field that is growing rapidly and will continue to grow for the foreseeable future. It is among the most wide-open fields for people with a variety of backgrounds, although some areas are becoming more technical and may soon require specialized training, which is being developed. The private sector employs nearly half of all solid waste management professionals, and that sector is increasingly dominated by a few large firms.

A first job in this field may be anything from helping to publicize a pilot waste project to entering data into a computer system for waste facility planning at a consulting firm to fielding consumer calls at a local agency or checking regulatory paperwork for a disposal firm. Remember the importance of real-world experience in this field and the need for practical solutions to real problems.

CASE STUDY
City of Seattle's Solid Waste Utility

Seattle's Solid Waste Utility was in a shambles; an embarrassment to the city, it was ridden with crisis and running low on morale. When the mayor's office created a new top position as director of the utility and talked to appropriate people about taking the job, few were interested.

One of the few was Diane Gale, who was then director of Seattle's legislative and public policy analysis staff. Gale had a good knowledge of city government and how it works, grass-roots organizing experience, and a stint on the city council in her past. She got the job—and the massive problems that went with it.

Gale called on her training in education and her experience in school finance reform gained during an earlier career. The core problem, she says, was creating change in a public sector work environment, something that is historically very difficult to accomplish.

"What I did was recognize that I needed a very diverse team that could manage environmental issues that were controversial. I brought in new kinds of people that are important to understanding environmental issues." That team included four economists to help the department understand economics and econometric forecasting, skills that previously had not been considered important to the department. She brought in engineers with technical skills to deal with landfills more effectively and project managers who could understand multidisciplinary environmental data and had strong scientific backgrounds.

Gale also added two people with experience in rate setting and public finance. She added another six people with experience in solid waste management, including recycling and source reduction. Some of her new hires also had experience in public information, community development, and outreach programs to help get information out to the public. "These sets of skills are important in all environmental programs," she says. "The issues are complex and interdisciplinary, so people need to be able to work together, have good communications skills, and understand the importance of outreach to the public."

With her team in place, Gale's department proceeded to close two landfills that had been designated as Superfund sites, locations where hazardous waste accumulations constituted a danger to health. For each landfill, she assigned a project manager with a strong science background, an engineer, and an environmental analyst.

The department initiated curbside recycling programs and "pay as you throw" inverted rate charges that cost residents less when they reduced their trash output. "With a proper set of programs and a strong outreach effort, you can generate significant change in the environmental field," Gale says.

"Significant change" meant that 82 percent of Seattle residents voluntarily signed up and participated in curbside recycling and 68 percent took part in a yard waste composting program. "We have 89 percent of the people on one can or less of weekly trash," she reports, compared with Seattle's 1981 average of 3.5 cans, which is the national average.

"Overall, we are recycling or otherwise diverting 40 percent of our waste stream," says Gale. "Residential tonnage went down by 22 percent in 1989 alone." The department has won a number of awards, including best civic program for two years running, a 1990 award from the Kennedy School of Government and The Ford Foundation, and a national recycling award.

"We set cities moving in a new direction. New waste management programs are coming on line now in Minneapolis, Newark, San Francisco, and Los Angeles, as well as in smaller cities such as Olympia, Washington. EPA now publishes a decision maker's guide on waste management, and other books are available as well."

Each location must tailor a program to its individual needs. Whereas Seattle's is voluntary, with incentive-based rates, Newark has a noteworthy program that is mandatory. Wellesley, Massachusetts, has a voluntary program in which residents bring both trash and recyclable materials to a central site—there is no pickup. Palm Beach and Rhode Island also have award-winning programs.

But Gale's award-winning programs in Seattle are worth attention for more than trail-blazing work in waste management. She regards her accomplishments as important proof of what women can accomplish in government—and proof that a woman does not have to be a spring chicken to do it.

"As a woman, I hate to admit this, but I am 50," Gale says. "It is important for young people to see that you can grow older and survive in the working world. The pieces of my career came together in this program. All the little pieces that make up me are called upon in this job."

And she has called upon women and minorities to help as well, both now represented in her department approximately in proportion to their percentage in the city. The department was 20 percent female when she took over and is now 50 percent female. Gale calls on the Environmental Careers Organization regularly for help in locating women and minority group members qualified to work on her staff and has a steady stream of volunteers, a number of whom have become full-time employees.

"We started as a utility in crisis with no direction, no disposal option, and no functioning programs," says Gale. "In three and a half years, we became a model for the nation. We started with a plan and implemented comprehensive recycling and waste reduction, resetting the rates to encourage the kinds of public behavior we wanted to see.

"What is exciting is taking what was viewed as the worst-managed division in the city and making it a national model. It is a real statement about how the public sector can perform, and the key is getting the right people into the right places."

Gale found her way into her current position managing a large solid waste utility via a circuitous route that began with a double major in history and political science and a stint in the foreign service. After realizing that the foreign service in the 1960s was male dominated, she moved to local government and school financing. When she identified environmental issues as growing in importance, she moved to solid waste management. Her most effective tool was volunteer work.

"I highly recommend volunteer work, especially if you are trying to change fields," Gale advises. She did a lot of volunteer work herself at the start of her career. "Volunteer activity gave me tricks in my skill bag that I would not have gotten otherwise."

PROFILES

Amy Perlmutter
Recycling Coordinator
City and County of San Francisco
San Francisco, California

The position of municipal recycling coordinator is one of the fastest-growing professions in any field, not just in the environmental professions. The profile that follows is of a recycling coordinator with one of the most respected programs in the country.

Serendipity smiles on Amy Perlmutter. While in college, wandering from major to major, she realized during a class in anthropology systems theory that she could connect her environmental interests with political science, with her love of nature, with economics, and with social sciences. The blend she discovered is called public service.

Perlmutter has a secure future in solid waste management because she was late to a student meeting. By the time she got to the session to sign up for part of a grant on alternative energy sources, Perlmutter recalls, "garbage was the only thing left on the list." For her part of the project, Perlmutter did a waste stream analysis for Orange County, New Jersey, and recommended recycling rather than a waste-to-energy plant.

When New Jersey passed laws on solid waste disposal, Perlmutter took action. "I kept attending conferences there and passing my résumé around." Passaic County, New Jersey, was impressed, and hired her to set up a solid waste department. She stayed there for four years, until she was wooed away to become recycling coordinator for San Francisco.

"I love my job," she says. "It is a great job. There are things about it I don't like, but most days I just think, 'I love my job.' San Francisco is a great place to work."

Hers is a job in which results appear very quickly, Perlmutter says. "Last month, we recycled 4,500 tons of bottles, cans, and paper from our curbside program. We recycled about 35 percent of our total waste in 1990. We have programs for recycling phone books and Christmas trees and a very active school education program."

Like others who are trying to communicate with the elusive American family, Perlmutter has found that children are one of the most influential conduits for information. Environmental education begun young is the most effective, and the enthusiasm of youngsters frequently brings the rest of the family along. She finds San Franciscans to be more committed than most citizens to recycling and the work it requires.

"The city has made a commitment that recycling is important. It is easy, but it costs money. On the other hand, you are keeping materials out of the landfill that would eventually require the cost of a new landfill, which is a much greater expense than the recycling. And in terms of the long-term health of the economy, recycling is a much cheaper way to get raw materials than mining." And that cost differential will grow as subsidies for timber and mining disappear, she adds. San Francisco voted not to develop a waste-to-energy facility, opting instead to work solely with source reduction, recycling, and composting to avoid the environmental impact of incineration.

"I like to think that in the near future, recycling will have a more level playing field in competing with virgin materials and will make even more economic sense." In the meantime, Perlmutter uses her considerable skills to keep everything possible out of the landfill. And she makes it clear that in essence, her job is not what one would expect.

"This is not a recycling job. It is an administrative job that happens to deal with recycling. Basically, I do a lot of paperwork." Her notes on a typical day make this clear. About 60 percent of her average day is spent on administrative tasks, 19 percent goes to telephone calls, another 19 percent is spent on managing staff and staff projects, and the remaining 2 percent is taken up by fieldwork. She manages a staff of nine, including two interns.

Work in the recycling department requires communicating and working with politicians, the public, nonprofit groups, and private businesses and understanding each group's expectations. Employees must have strong "people" skills and analytical skills and must be able to make decisions and understand solid waste issues.

Perlmutter says that over the next several years, as waste management issues become more important, privately owned businesses will be looking for in-house people to manage recycling programs and take on other environmental issues. "Garbage costs are going to continue to rise, and companies need to save money. Start a recycling program in your company and make a case for employing you to work on environmental problems full-time. You don't have to leave your current job to get into recycling."

Perlmutter advises job seekers who call people in positions like hers not just to say that they are fresh out of school and willing to learn. Instead, she says, tell her what there is in your background and training that will enable you to help her get the job done. If you are a career changer with some unique background and experience, this is even more important—sell your strengths.

And perhaps most important, Perlmutter says, is to get out and do some volunteer work in the field. You will pick up lots of information about the field that will help you land a job later and will demonstrate your commitment. "Work at a recycling center, go to workshops and conferences, learn about the issues in your local area, and find the local recycling organizations and work with them." When Perlmutter was looking for a position, it was her volunteer work that made the difference in her getting her first job in the field.

Jodie Bernstein
Vice president of Environmental
Policy and Ethical Standards
Waste Management, Inc.
Oak Brook, Illinois

Waste management is a rapidly expanding field—and one that has given Jodie Bernstein an opportunity to utilize fully her legal and management skills.

After graduating from Yale Law School in 1951, Jodie Bernstein began her legal career as a generalist. Following a family-rearing period, she decided to specialize on returning to work because that was where the action was going to be. "As far as a career opportunity, I knew that I would have a better shot in a specialty than in a well-developed field where people of my generation were already well established," she says.

Bernstein got a job in consumer protection at the Federal Trade Commission, where for six years she was able to observe the regulatory structure and internal workings of other government agencies, such as the Environmental Protection Agency. She says she became "intrigued" with the EPA due to her own interest in the environmental movement. However, she did not become directly involved with EPA issues until she joined a private law firm and became a specialist in legal issues concerning the newly enacted Toxic Substances Control Act.

Under President Jimmy Carter, she became general counsel of the Environmental Protection Agency. "I was among the first female general counsel of a major government agency and was the first woman general counsel at EPA," she says. Eventually she left that position and worked for a law firm with a large environmental practice. However, Bernstein soon found private practice constricting. "I found practice limited my involvement in how things got done." In 1983, she began representing Waste Management, Inc. (WMI) as outside general counsel. Soon she accepted a promotion to vice president and general counsel, and in 1990 she was appointed as the corporation's vice president of environmental policy and ethical standards. Bernstein says it is her practical experience as a lawyer in an up and coming field that is largely responsible for her success. "Others knew more but hadn't done the practical things, such as drafting subpoenas and marching into court," she says.

Her job at WMI involves, among other things, directing internal audit teams that inspect company facilities, developing new training programs, maintaining a customer information HelpLine, and representing the company at environment, ethical, and related forums. Even though she no longer works as a lawyer, Bernstein says that her background is still useful, since WMI must always be aware of any potential liability.

The decommissioning of U.S. military bases, where there are often large volumes of hazardous wastes, is an important area for future growth. "In the years to come, there will be a tremendous amount of pressure to get that work done and for Congress to find the money to pay for it," Bernstein says.

However, she notes that hazardous waste is not as great an environmental risk as some might think. "Waste in general is much more of a public perception," she says. As a result, much of her position requires that she communicate her company's environmental efforts to the public. "We maintain an 'open door' policy for people who want to come and visit and see what we do. We also publish information about the management of waste, including recycling and waste reduction programs. We're always looking for ways to enhance grass-roots understanding," she says. In addition, Bernstein says, WMI runs seminars for its own people, "so they know they are the ambassadors to the community."

Ari Smith
Field Operations Manager
Tri Ace
Hinsdale, Illinois

Fast-food restaurants have long been a vivid symbol of our throwaway culture. For those who care about reducing solid waste, a good way to start is by recycling or reducing the small mountain of paper, plastic, and Styrofoam produced by every burger and pizza outlet. Solid waste management professionals are working with convenience-food chains to bring about such change.

Ari Smith puts it very simply. "My background is in logistics, transportation, distribution, warehousing, and information systems. You don't need to have an environmental background to get involved with the environment." And, sure enough, he is part of a team working to make the most of recycling at McDonald's restaurants, with a goal of nothing less than recycling 100 percent of the waste stream from the thousands of "golden arches" locations around the United States and abroad.

McDonald's believes in small, efficient operations, so it regularly spins off specialized tasks by forming new companies. Tri Ace of Hinsdale, Illinois, was formed expressly to help McDonald's build an effective recycling program.

"We look at the waste materials generated in the restaurants, what kinds of materials they buy, if they are recyclable or not, and what happens to these materials after they are thrown away," says Smith. "We cannot do much about the materials people take out of the store, except make sure these are nonhazardous materials that are easily recycled. We concentrate on the materials that stay in the store, whether inside or out in our parking lot. Our mission is to divert 100 percent of our wastes out of the landfills and into recycling."

The crux of the McDonald's recycling program is building what Smith calls a "distribution system in reverse." Whereas the company's front-end distribution system brings many different products from many suppliers and coordinates their transportation to restaurants according to their varying demands, its new waste stream system will take the materials left in the restaurants, break them down into separate recyclable products, and get them to vendors who can use these materials in their own products. And, Smith says, much as with the front-end distribution system, the vendors receiving the materials for recycling are different for each waste and are spread all over the nation.

Tri Ace's burden is minimizing the cost of this system while maximizing its efficiency and timeliness—a classic logistics problem. The toughest part is keeping the costs down. "You can empty a garbage truck at a landfill for about one-quarter the cost of recycling that material," he says.

Skills that are crucial to make the process work include analysis, attention to detail, mathematics, and the ability to negotiate, as well as marketing and sales know-how. And at times, the job gets bigger than expected. In some malls where McDonald's finds its waste materials mixed in with everybody else's, the effort has extended to getting the entire mall to recycle its wastes.

Smith offers the following advice to those who would work in solid waste management:

- "Get the lay of the land. Learn about environmental jargon in the field, what is low-density and high-density poly, and why one material or another is used for this or that.
- "Unless you are working for a nonprofit, if you don't make a profit, you will cease to exist. Pay attention to basic business skills.

- "Computers are important. All businesses have seasonality and other variables, and computers are the best way to analyze data of this kind and take it into account on a daily basis."

To Smith, Tri Ace and its venture "looked like a promising industry for the nineties, and socially redeeming," he says. "This is something that is going to be around for awhile; there is value in it. It's nice to be able to go to work and help people."

RESOURCES

Air and Waste Management Association. P.O. Box 2861, Pittsburgh, PA 15230. (412) 232–3444.

BioCycle, Box 351, Emmaus, PA 18049.

Fibre Market News, 156 Fifth Ave., New York, NY 10010.

Garbage: The Practical Journal for the Environment (bimonthly magazine). Old House Journal Corporation, 2 Main St., Gloucester, MA 01930. (508) 283–3200.

Greenpeace USA. 1436 U St., NW, Washington, DC 20009. (202) 462–1177.

INFORM, Inc. 381 Park Ave. South, New York, NY 10016. (212) 689–4040.

Institute of Scrap Recycling Industries, 1325 G St., NW, Suite 1000, Washington, DC 20005. (202) 466–4050.

National Recycling Coalition. Provides technical education on recycling and source reduction, fosters public awareness of and support for effective recycling and conservation programs, promotes market development for recyclable content products, and encourages the implementation of sound laws and regulations. 1101 30th St., NW, Suite 305, Washington, DC 20007. (202) 625–6406.

National Solid Wastes Management Association. A trade group representing the entire private waste services industry. Publishes *Waste Age* (monthly) and *Recycling Times* (bimonthly); has local chapters, conferences, and seminars; offers internships. 1730 Rhode Island Ave., NW, Suite 1000, Washington, DC 20036. (202) 659–4613.

Recycling Today (monthly). GIE Publishing, 4012 Bridge Ave., Cleveland, OH 44113. (216) 961–4130.

Resource Recovery Report (monthly). 5313 38th St., NW, Washington, DC 20015. (202) 298–6344.

Resource Recycling (monthly); *Bottle & Can Recycling Update* (monthly);

Plastic Recycling Update (monthly). P.O. Box 10540, Portland, OR 97210. (503) 227–1319.

Scrap Age, 3615-111 Woodhead Dr., Northbrook, IL 60062.

Scrap Tire News, Recycling Research, Inc., 133 Mountain Rd., Suffield, CT 06078.

Solid Waste & Power (bimonthly). HCI Publications, 410 Archibald St., Kansas City, MO 64111. (816) 931–1311.

Solid Waste Report (weekly). Business Publishers, 951 Pershing Dr., Silver Spring, MD 20910. (301) 587–6300.

The Management of World Wastes (monthly). Communications Channels, Inc., 6255 Barfield Rd., Atlanta, GA 30328. (404) 256–9800.

Waste Watch. P.O. Box 39185, Washington, DC 20016. (202) 895–2601.

8   Hazardous Waste Management

AT A GLANCE

Employment:
  90,000 to 120,000 professionals in all sectors nationwide

Demand:
  18 percent growth per year, creating 75,000 new jobs by 1995

Breakdown:
  Public sector, 24 percent
  Private sector, 75 percent
  Nonprofit sector, 1 percent

Key Job Titles:
  Biologist
  Chemical engineer
  Chemist
  Civil engineer
  Environmental engineer
  Environmental planner
  Geologist
  Geotechnical engineer
  Hazardous materials specialist
  Hazardous waste engineer
  Hazardous waste technician
  Hydrogeologist

Industrial hygienist
Lawyer
Process engineer
Project manager
Radioactive waste engineer

Influential Organizations:
Air and Waste Management Association
American Chemical Society
Citizen's Clearinghouse for Hazardous Waste
Environmental Protection Agency, Office of Solid Waste and Emergency
    Response
Hazardous Materials Control Research Institute

Salary:
Starting salaries range from $23,000 to $35,000; salaries for experienced personnel range from $40,000 to $65,000; and top management
salaries can reach $85,000 or more.

Hazardous waste is everywhere. An estimated 41 million Americans live
within 4 miles of a Superfund hazardous waste site. Former dumping sites
in Love Canal, New York, and Times Beach, Missouri, are infamous, and
thousands of equally important, if less sensational, environmental disasters have been identified. The cleanup task is huge and seems to grow
larger; the more we look, the more we find. Consider the following:

• In 1980, there were 400 major abandoned hazardous waste sites nationwide. The Office of Technology Assessment now identifies 4,000 and says
  that many thousands more may be discovered in the coming decades.
• The Environmental Protection Agency estimated in 1970 that the
  United States produces about 9 million metric tons of hazardous wastes
  per year. That estimate has increased every few years and currently
  stands at 550 million tons per year, more than 60 times the original
  estimate.
• Of 1,200 sites identified as priorities for cleanup since 1980, only 63 had
  been cleaned up by 1992.

As the scope and seriousness of our hazardous waste problems grow, a
huge industry and profession have arisen to implement solutions. Hazardous waste management is one of the fastest-growing environmental
professions.

WHAT IS HAZARDOUS WASTE MANAGEMENT?

We might start by asking, "What are hazardous wastes"? Hazardous wastes can range from the most toxic manufacturing by-products to used battery acid and household cleaning materials. The Environmental Protection Agency defines a hazardous waste as any substance that is ignitable, corrosive, reactive, or toxic. This broad definition covers millions of tons of material produced annually.

Although hazardous wastes are produced everywhere, a few sources account for high percentages of the problem. The chemical industry accounts for about 68 percent of all industrial hazardous waste, with metals and related industries such as electroplating and metal finishing contributing another 22 percent. Other large sources include the military and the cumulative waste of millions of households and small businesses. Hazardous waste managers must find ways to deal with it all.

The following are key activities in hazardous waste management:

- Identifying hazardous wastes.
- Permitting (requiring and issuing permits) to control production, transportation, and storage.
- Tracking to ensure safe waste handling.
- Disposing of hazardous wastes according to strict regulations.
- Monitoring disposal sites to ensure their safety.
- Reducing use of hazardous materials wherever possible.
- Cleaning up hazardous spills and contaminated sites.
- Communicating with the public about the problem.

HISTORY AND BACKGROUND

The concept of handling hazardous material carefully and disposing of it properly sounds like good common sense today, but it is markedly at odds with our history. For decades, we were simply ignorant of hazards accompanying our more dangerous wastes. Until recently, most industrial waste was simply dumped on the site where it was generated, often into a stream, pond, or lake or simply onto the ground. New England's waterways from Connecticut to Maine are just beginning to recover from accumulations of hazardous wastes thoughtlessly dumped over two centuries. Individuals have followed suit, pouring motor oil, paint thinner, pesticides, and other wastes onto the ground and into storm drains.

Although hazardous wastes are now subject to legal requirements that differentiate them from solid, or nonhazardous, wastes, these materials were commonly mixed with municipal solid wastes until just the past few years. Most older landfills contain significant amounts of hazardous wastes along with the typical garbage. In thousands of communities across the country, household products that qualify as hazardous wastes are *still* being disposed of along with more innocuous trash.

Early environmental legislation may have contributed to the problem. A significant portion of waste was diverted to landfills to avoid releasing it into the air or water because of pollution control requirements in the clean water and clean air acts. Technologies developed to clean air and water produced unexpected new hazardous wastes: Air pollution abatement devices such as scrubbers produce large amounts of wastes. Wastewater treatment facilities also produce sludges that can be hazardous. Municipal waste incinerators produce significant volumes of ash containing heavy metals, considered by some federal and state regulations to be a hazardous waste. For years, these products of "environmental protection" went straight to the landfill.

These dumps now leak hazardous wastes into groundwater and generate toxic airborne emissions as well. The history of hazardous waste management until just a few years ago is a perfect example of cross-media pollution, an environmental shell game in which changing regulations shift pollutants from one area to another without eliminating the problem. As we will see, dealing with the legacy of these dumps and preventing future such occurrences are the key challenges faced by hazardous waste managers.

Three major federal laws constitute the core of federal hazardous waste regulation.

RESOURCE CONSERVATION AND RECOVERY ACT (RCRA)

RCRA applies to current operations of private businesses and other hazardous waste generators. Passage of RCRA in 1976 signaled the federal government's entry into the business of regulating both solid and hazardous wastes. RCRA regulations establish a "cradle-to-grave" system for tracking and permitting of hazardous wastes from their point of origin to their disposal time and location—and 30 years beyond.

The Hazardous and Solid Waste amendments of 1984 significantly amended RCRA. Changes include the following:

- A severalfold increase in the number of hazardous waste generators under regulation.
- A schedule to ban land disposal of hazardous chemicals.

- Encouragement of source reduction efforts.
- Development of a process for classifying wastes.
- Formulation of regulations involving underground storage tanks.

If a contest were held for the most controversial of all federal environmental regulations, RCRA would be near the top of the list. Its sweeping provisions automatically labeled more than 360 million tons of waste as hazardous and brought anyone who produced more than 100 pounds of such waste per month under regulation. Dry cleaners, photo development shops, auto repair outfits, and other small businesses are examples.

More important, RCRA has proven to be difficult to comply with, even for environmental professionals who want to do so, if only to avoid stiff fines or prison terms. The main catch is that under RCRA, hazardous waste must be properly treated and disposed of. For this to happen, treatment and disposal facilities must be available, either on site or close enough that the waste can be transported without public hazard. Unfortunately, very few such sites are approved, and no one wants a hazardous waste disposal facility anywhere near his or her neighborhood.

The need for complying with and enforcing RCRA virtually created the hazardous waste profession; anyone with an interest in the field will need to get acquainted with its provisions as the very first step.

COMPREHENSIVE ENVIRONMENTAL RESPONSE, COMPENSATION, AND LIABILITY ACT (CERCLA)

Hardly anyone calls this law by its full name. Most people know it by the huge amount of money it authorized to fulfill its mission—Superfund. Whereas RCRA regulates the ways in which existing businesses dispose of hazardous waste, Superfund is aimed at cleaning up abandoned, inoperative contaminated sites. There is little disagreement that the original CERCLA legislation of 1980 was woefully inadequate, considering the scope of the problem. In response to criticism, the Superfund Amendments and Reauthorization Act of 1986 (SARA) reauthorized Superfund for another five years, including provisions for the following:

- Expanding and strengthening the cleanup program.
- Increasing the cleanup trust fund from the $1.6 billion level of the first five years to $8.5 billion for the second five years.
- Establishing a new trust fund to clean up leaking underground petroleum storage tanks.
- Requiring disclosure of hazardous waste sites under community and worker "right-to-know" regulations.

By general agreement, Superfund has not yet been particularly effective in cleaning up contaminated sites. More than 1,200 sites have been placed on the National Priority List, and several times that many are being considered, but only a handful have actually been cleaned up. Nonetheless, the federal Superfund program and its state counterparts have created a great deal of environmental employment. Lengthy technical, legal, scientific, and financial processes must be gone through simply to get a site *considered* for the national list, and this involves many types of environmental professionals. Actual cleanup activity involves even more field, laboratory, and managerial workers.

TOXIC SUBSTANCES CONTROL ACT OF 1976 (TOSCA)

TOSCA was designed to give regulators and the general public some advance warning that manufacturers are considering commercial production of a substance that may be toxic. Manufacturers submit a notification to the government along with detailed data and must win approval before proceeding.

RESULTS OF HAZARDOUS WASTE LEGISLATION

Since passage of these and other laws, there has been a wholesale change in how we deal with hazardous waste issues. Methods for dealing effectively with hazardous wastes now fall into two categories: devising more effective ways to treat and store hazardous waste, and finding methods to reduce the use of toxic chemicals in the first place.

Advances in treatment and disposal. Research scientists and engineers are devoting a great deal of time to developing treatment options, which include the following:

• Biological treatment
• Carbon absorption
• Dechlorination
• Incineration at high temperature
• Neutralization
• Oxidation
• Precipitation
• Solidification and stabilization

Even after the most sophisticated treatment, however, the resulting material remains at least somewhat hazardous. Thus, the final resting place for fully 80 percent of hazardous wastes is some form of land disposal. These sites include hazardous waste landfills that have lined and sealed trenches or cells to isolate the wastes; open ponds, pits, or basins for liquid wastes; and underground injection wells, where wastes are pumped into steel- and concrete-encased shafts deep underground. These wells account for 60 percent of hazardous waste land disposal; an additional 35 percent is in surface impoundments.

Reduced use of toxic chemicals; pollution prevention. The problems of RCRA and Superfund, including high costs, long delays, unproductive time spent on lawsuits rather than in the field, and extensive paperwork, have had one invaluable effect. They have helped turn the focus of hazardous waste programs for the 1990s to reducing hazardous wastes by avoiding their generation in the first place. The EPA, state agencies, and, not surprisingly, the chemical industry are adopting new measures to limit hazardous waste production. If pursued vigorously, this effort could be a major success. In 1987, the congressional Office of Technology Assessment estimated that within a few years, half of the hazardous wastes in the United States could be eliminated using existing technology.

Although individual companies and, in some cases, industries have made progress toward this goal, progress to date has been slow. Conceptually, however, the shift has been made. "Once there is pollution, I have failed," says Manik Roy, pollution prevention specialist with the Environmental Defense Fund, Washington, DC. Roy feels that in addition to cleanup, future hazardous waste professionals will focus on minimizing hazardous waste production and reducing the use of toxic substances.

ISSUES AND TRENDS

Beyond the reduction in use of toxic chemicals and pollution prevention, a number of other trends in hazardous waste management are generating employment.

SIZE OF THE PROBLEM

The sheer number of hazardous waste disposal sites and the length of time it takes to clean up even one ensure that there will be billions of dollars' worth of work to be done in this field for decades. It is not an exaggeration to say that hazardous waste professionals have their job security almost guaranteed if they keep up with technological changes.

FEDERAL SITES

As the federal government moves to force hazardous waste cleanups around the country, it finds that some of the most difficult sites exist on its own property. The Office of Technology Assessment estimates that 5,000 to 10,000 federal sites require cleanups that may cost as much as $250 billion. And the wastes continue to accumulate. Each year, domestic military bases generate more hazardous waste than the top five U.S. chemical companies combined. Federal cleanup sites require professionals in all of the key job titles listed at the beginning of this chapter, and the need is growing.

SPEEDING UP THE PROCESS

The EPA seeks ways to speed up the process of cleaning up Superfund sites, a process that currently averages seven to ten years per site from listing to completed cleanup. Chemical engineers, hydrologists, geologists, and others will speed the process of characterization—that is, determining what wastes are present and how best to separate and dispose of them.

IMPACT OF "RIGHT-TO-KNOW" LAWS

Under SARA, as noted earlier, companies must now provide detailed information on thousands of chemicals and compounds to local authorities and the general public. Simply preparing the paperwork for this requirement and tracking the status and location of hazardous materials are generating a large number of entry-level jobs. An additional impact, however, is in the creation of positions in local government to prepare emergency plans and in nonprofit organizations, which are using the data to develop advocacy strategies directed at local companies.

SMALL PRODUCERS

Hazardous waste reduction requires creativity in many places that seem far removed from large-scale Superfund sites. Small laboratories, schools, colleges, and universities search for ways to teach chemistry without generating hazardous wastes, reports the American Chemical Society. Some schools are turning to microscale chemistry, in which traditional experiments are conducted on a smaller scale, and others are switching to video demonstrations entirely. These schools work with consultants who help them deal with the regulations. Work in this area requires training in chemistry, occupational safety, and health or chemical engineering.

MATERIALS SUBSTITUTION

Finding less dangerous replacement materials reduces hazardous waste. Research work is needed in many industries to devise materials and methods to substitute for those that today generate hazardous waste. Chemists, chemical engineers, materials scientists, and systems specialists, apply here. Expect this area to grow explosively in the future.

HOUSEHOLD HAZARDOUS WASTES

Every household uses hazardous wastes in quantities that are large enough to be a problem if the wastes are not disposed of properly. Local governments across the nation are adding a new position—household hazardous waste coordinator—to deal with the problem through education, waste disposal networks, collection days, and promotion of nontoxic household products.

CROSS-MEDIA POLLUTION

Efforts to eliminate hazardous waste must increasingly address the problems of crossover pollutants. Incineration methods that avoid creating airborne toxic emissions and land disposal methods that protect groundwater and surface water supplies need further development. This stimulates research in the private sector, at universities and in federal agencies by toxicologists, chemists, hydrologists, and air pollution scientists.

LONG-TERM ECONOMICS

In this time of government deficits and weak private economies, no one likes a program that is a multibillion-dollar blank check. Expect growing financial pressure to create demand for experts in finance and economics who can find ways to cut costs. Risk assessment professionals will also be in demand to help determine just how much protection and cleanup is necessary to protect the public and the environment. Lesser levels, if accepted, could save billions. Expect a growing demand for government finance specialists to devise appropriate permit fees, dumping fees, fines, and penalties to pay for all of the cleanup.

COOPERATION AMONG ACTIVISTS, BUSINESS, AND GOVERNMENT

The "trend" toward cooperation among diverse interests may be more a wish by practitioners than a social reality. However, many professionals in the field believe that the relatively ineffective and cumbersome system of hazardous waste management will become so infuriating that all parties to the equation in local areas will work together to create something better within the law. Pollution prevention will probably be at the heart of such efforts.

EXPORTATION OF EXPERTISE

Hazardous waste management is a field in which the United States is well ahead of most of the world. Consulting services and hazardous waste disposal companies are already looking to expand their markets outside the United States, and with good reason. "Americans who have [worked] with hazardous wastes can bring their experience to the work that is just beginning in Eastern Europe," says Jodie Bernstein, vice president of environmental policy and ethical standards for Waste Management, Inc., of Oak Brook, Illinois. "This could be a huge market. Underdeveloped countries such as Mexico could be even more of an opportunity than Europe."

POLITICAL EXCLUSIONS

Some materials that qualify as hazardous under the EPA's tests are currently excluded from regulation for political reasons. These materials include some oil and gas industry wastes and used motor oil. Safe and effective methods to reuse, recycle, or reduce the hazards of these wastes are needed from chemists and chemical engineers, and political and non-profit lobbying opportunities exist here as well.

LOW-PRIORITY SITES

Some "low-priority" hazardous waste sources now receive greater attention. These include underground storage tanks, state-mandated cleanups, inactive mining sites where hazardous minerals are leaching into surface water and groundwater supplies, and inactive uranium tailings that are releasing radioactive wastes. Agencies and consulting firms need geologists, chemical engineers, and hydrologists to work on these issues before they explode politically.

SPENT NUCLEAR FUEL

As of 1990, the United States had some 20,000 tons of spent nuclear fuel. According to "Nuclear Waste: The Problem That Won't Go Away," a publication from the Worldwatch Institute, commercial nuclear power plants account for "less than one percent of the volume of all radioactive wastes in the United States, but for 95 percent of the radioactivity from all civilian and military sources combined." Permanent storage of expired nuclear fuel is a field in which uncertainties abound, along with the need for further study by physical scientists, materials experts, geologists, hydrologists, and geotechnical, thermal process, and radioactive waste engineers.

RISK ASSESSMENT

Companies in the hazardous waste disposal field work to understand better the likelihood that hazardous materials will escape storage and what the damage and economic repercussions of such an event would be. Starr Dehn, division manager of the Hazardous Waste and Industrial Processes Division for the CH2M Hill consulting firm in Sacramento, California, defines risk assessment as "using scientific methods to quantify uncertainty so you can employ levels of safety factors." It is a field that requires knowledge of hazardous waste technology as well as economic and, at times, political factors.

CAREER OPPORTUNITIES

Employers in every sector of this field are scrambling to find employees who can help them solve hazardous waste problems. Although many types of professionals are needed for these efforts, the following specialists are most in demand:

- Hydrogeologists, to trace pathways of contaminants in groundwater.
- Quality control and quality assurance professionals with chemistry and systems backgrounds, to evaluate and manage projects.
- Risk assessment workers, to determine the likelihood and severity of future problems.
- Public and environmental health professionals, to manage and execute programs to protect the public.
- Environmental engineers, to design systems and processes to reduce, recycle, and treat hazardous waste streams.

- Environmental chemists and toxicologists, to determine the chemical breakdowns and pathways of wastes.
- Lawyers with experience in hazardous waste issues.

PUBLIC SECTOR

Public sector positions at federal, state, and local levels drive the policy of hazardous waste management. From the Washington, DC, offices of the EPA to the state and local bodies that add management labor of their own, this is a field controlled by public officials.

Federal government. Although the private sector dominates employment in the hazardous waste management field, federal legislation is the impetus behind regulation and cleanup activity. Each of the Environmental Protection Agency's ten regional divisions administers and enforces Superfund and RCRA regulations. As these two programs have expanded, so has the EPA staff charged with executing them. EPA employment in hazardous waste management is expanding by about 10 percent per year.

Although the federal government's hazardous waste activity centers on the EPA, positions related to hazardous waste management in both research and cleanup exist throughout the federal government. In future years, in fact, cleanup efforts at the thousands of military bases with hazardous waste dumps and at Department of Energy laboratories will create programs involving large numbers of professionals.

In addition to the key scientists and engineers already mentioned, these federal agencies have a need for project managers, contract administrators, inspectors, and budget specialists.

State government. States increasingly regulate hazardous wastes as the principal implementers and enforcers of federal environmental statutes. States are the first line of RCRA enforcement, and many states have hazardous waste legislation that goes beyond RCRA. Illinois, for example, is one of a number of states phasing in a ban on land disposal of liquid hazardous wastes, the largest category of hazardous waste. Most state legislatures fund their own "superfund" programs to supplement federal activities and to clean up sites not on the National Priority List.

States are involved in and often have final authority over the thorny issue of siting hazardous waste facilities. They lead in developing emergency response plans for use in the event of toxic releases. Many states go beyond the federal focus on cleanup and work to prevent the production of future Superfund sites. More than 33 states now have waste minimization efforts. Minnesota, for example, provides on-site and telephone waste

Michigan Department of Natural Resources, Lansing, Michigan. Trina Swygert analyzes organic waste compounds taken from water samples to be tested in the department's environmental laboratory.

reduction consultation, a waste reduction resource bank, and research grants for waste reduction projects.

Hazardous waste management is usually housed in the state department of environmental protection or environmental regulation and requires all of the professionals listed earlier in this section and in the section on federal government.

Local government. All hazardous waste is generated and finally disposed of in some municipality or county. Thus, despite a complicated web of federal and state regulations, hazardous waste is a local issue. The result of this is increasing amounts of local activity and local awareness of hazardous waste issues.

Hazardous waste management jobs in local governments are located in many places. Fire departments, police and emergency response sections, planning departments, public health divisions, sewer and water outfits, and solid waste departments are all places in which hazardous waste professionals are housed.

County governments are involved as well. Dozens of counties now have community "right-to-know" ordinances forcing disclosure of hazardous waste locations, emergency response teams to protect the community in the event of a hazardous waste accident, household hazardous waste collection programs, a groundwater mapping project, and waste reduction assistance for area businesses.

Hazardous waste professionals in government tend to have health and safety backgrounds. Safety engineers, hazardous materials specialists, industrial hygienists, and those with similar backgrounds are in demand. As local governments get more involved in preventing pollution instead of preventing or responding to accidents, this may change.

PRIVATE SECTOR

Hazardous waste management is big business. A study by the Freedonia Group projects that the U.S. hazardous waste market will top $24 billion in sales by 1995 and exceed $41 billion by the year 2000. The projections, broken down by treatment type, indicate that more than 80 percent of treatment sales will be in the chemical, petroleum, and metals industries, with nuclear, medical, and other industries splitting the remainder. Broken down by type of service, some 60 percent of sales will be for management, with transportation, land disposal, and other segments each accounting for 17 percent or less of sales.

The private sector dominates the hazardous waste industry, accounting for 75 percent of employment. This sector can be divided into three broad categories: companies that generate hazardous wastes when manufacturing their products; firms that transport, treat, or dispose of the waste that other companies produce; and consulting firms that supply expertise, management, or on-the-job labor to either the private sector or the public sector.

Hazardous waste generators. At the generation end of the spectrum, companies need personnel who can help them comply with environmental regulations in a cost-effective manner. For larger firms, this translates into an entire environmental affairs department, complete with lobbyists, lawyers, engineers, hazardous materials managers, industrial hygienists, regulatory compliance analysts, chemists, and technicians. Mid-sized companies have significantly smaller staffs. Smaller companies use all-purpose "environmental" staff members or consultants to fill their needs, although the likelihood of a company's hiring in-house staff has increased with the complexity of regulations.

Hazardous waste management firms. Driven primarily by hazardous waste regulations, the transport, treatment, and disposal segment of the private sector has evolved rapidly into an entire industry. Some of these firms are new companies; many have evolved from and are part of the solid waste management business. They range from mammoth international companies such as Chemical Waste Management, Inc., with $1.2 billion in sales during 1990, to local firms specializing in the treatment of a waste stream from a particular industry, such as metal finishing. Many of these firms continue to orient their operations toward land disposal of hazardous wastes. Others are developing new treatment and detoxification methods and moving into areas such as waste reduction and recycling.

There are many opportunities with these firms, including testing of companies' waste streams; regulatory analysis; research on waste treatment technologies; design, construction, and operation of landfills and other waste treatment facilities; and marketing of these companies' services. Engineers of all types are in high demand at these firms.

Consulting firms. Consulting firms comprise the third component of the private sector. They do business with both government agencies and the industries that generate wastes. The federal government hires consultants to do most of its hazardous waste work. This includes initial feasibility studies, testing, laboratory analysis, designing of solutions, actual cleanup, and even coordination of public participation.

Companies hire consultants to help them understand and comply with federal, state, and local hazardous waste regulations. There are some Superfund-related activities, including compliance with community reporting requirements and emergency response planning provisions. Large companies need assistance in complying with evolving RCRA regulations, and many smaller companies that were brought under regulation by the 1984 RCRA amendments turn to consultants rather than hiring staff.

Consulting firms are hired for their technical expertise, so engineering and scientific degrees are most in demand. See the Profile in this chapter on CH2M Hill's Starr Dehn for more details.

Finally, a growing part of the private hazardous waste management field deals with the labeling, packing, and disposal of medical wastes. Professionals in this field work in hospitals, laboratories, health care facilities, and pharmaceutical firms or with consulting firms that serve them.

Chemical Waste Management, Inc., Pompano Beach, Florida. Lisa Spivey (right), technical services field analyst and laboratory manager for CWM, works with Terry Heilman conducting on-site hazardous waste management.

NONPROFIT SECTOR

It was neither the government nor the private sector that brought the problem of toxic hazards to the public's attention. Rather, public awareness of hazardous waste issues is the result of efforts by local nonprofit environmental organizations. Lois Marie Gibbs, a resident of Love Canal in New York, led the fight in her community when toxins from an abandoned dump began leaking into basements and appearing in school yards. This was the nation's first widely publicized toxic disaster. Gibbs went on to form the Citizen's Clearinghouse for Hazardous Wastes (CCHW), with five offices nationwide. She attributes the success of her effort to organizing, not lawsuits, and CCHW operates under a philosophy that environmental public policy is 90 percent politics and 10 percent science.

National organizations such as the Natural Resources Defense Council, the Sierra Club, Environmental Action, the Environmental Defense Fund, the National Toxics Campaign, Greenpeace, and the National Wildlife

Federation work extensively on hazardous waste issues. As the environmental movement matures, these organizations are hiring more technical staff members such as scientists and economists to bolster their arguments.

In the past decade, there has been a huge increase in the number of small, grass-roots nonprofit groups that have sprung up around the issue of siting local hazardous waste facilities. Many of these groups have no paid staff at all, but as they mature, more positions will become available.

Nonprofit organizations look for people who understand how public policy is formulated, who can communicate, who know how to organize people into action, and who can raise money. Although a technical background is extremely useful, it is probably of secondary importance. The jobs are there, even though the competition is tough.

SALARY

Starting salaries in hazardous waste management are generally comparable to those in the solid waste management field, ranging from $23,000 to $35,000. Salaries are higher for consultants, starting closer to $25,000. A graduate degree may bring $25,000 to $35,000 to start. This reflects both higher demand and the more stringent credentials required in this field. Consulting firms often use the credentials of employees as part of their marketing effort, so appropriate degrees are often a requirement and bring higher compensation. The salary for the manager of a consulting team with several years of experience could rise to $75,000.

Starting salaries in established hazardous waste management companies or companies that generate hazardous waste tend to be a little higher, ranging in the high 20s and into the 30s. Graduate degrees bring higher starting rates.

Federal and state agencies vary widely in hazardous waste management pay. Generally, however, people with undergraduate degrees in scientific fields can start at around $24,000 and rise quickly to the mid-30s. Engineers earn slightly higher entry-level salaries, as do those with graduate degrees.

GETTING STARTED

If the preceding material helps you determine at what level you might like to work in this field, the following material will guide you on how to get from where you are to where you want to be.

EDUCATION

You can get a good job in hazardous waste management with an associate's or undergraduate degree. Because of the technical nature of the better jobs, however, graduate and technical degrees are more important than in the solid waste management field. Chemistry, biology, geology, engineering, and health technology are undergraduate degrees of value. Environmental studies, environmental science, and liberal arts majors should take as many hard science and engineering courses as possible. Learn about hydrology, toxicology, public health, economics, public policy, and statistics.

After you work for a while, you will see the range of specialties available to you and will be able to target further study accordingly. The more popular areas of graduate study include engineering (especially chemical and environmental), public health, toxicology, public and business administration, chemistry, groundwater science, planning, and industrial hygiene.

If you have a B.A. or B.S., in your first job you will probably be doing a lot of fieldwork and laboratory work, tracking down data, performing data entry tasks, helping out on various projects, and possibly doing some writing. You will be a technician of sorts, learning some basic and important skills.

After being in the field for some time, you may wish to take an examination to become a certified hazardous materials manager. The Institute for Hazardous Materials Management administers this exam and tests for theoretical and practical knowledge of hazardous materials management. Hazardous waste specialists are certified by the National Environmental Health Association in Denver.

A growing number of two-year and four-year colleges have degree programs specifically designed to train you as a hazardous materials specialist or technician. You can get a list of many of these schools from the Hazardous Materials Control Research Institute (see the Resources section at the end of this chapter).

ADVICE

Many of the professionals interviewed for this book offered encouragement and advice. The following are some of their comments.

Attend public meetings. Volunteers, students, and retired people can play a role in hazardous waste management, says consultant George Wetzel. "Legal provisions allow local representation at many public meetings. In that process, volunteers have the opportunity to interact and take part in formal processes, keep track of proposals, and interact on behalf of the community." These meetings are great places to find out "who's who" in your local community of hazardous waste workers.

Get some experience. Hazardous waste management professionals like people with some experience because much of the knowledge base needed is best learned on the job. Obtain experience while still in school through internships, independent projects, volunteer work, and research. Good experience for the hazardous waste field includes demonstrated laboratory and field skills; projects that show a grasp of relevant legislation and the workings of federal, state, and local regulatory processes; computer projects; technical writing; and any work in a government office or regulatory agency. "Students need to go out and work on internships whether they get credit or not," says David Galvin of the Municipality of Metropolitan Seattle (METRO). "Too many people are coming out of school with master's degrees who have never worked a single day and do not have a clue what is going on in the outside world. Work part-time, or at least do related summer work. Get an internship through an organization like ECO, of which I am a big fan. Get your hands dirty."

Hanover, Massachusetts. Mike Szerlog reviews new regulations governing the disposal of hazardous wastes with local print shop owner Bob Parmenter.

Think ahead. Today's jobs are primarily focused on complying with RCRA and cleaning up past messes. Hazardous waste management positions of the future, however, will require pollution prevention skills. Training for the two areas is often quite different. Talk to people in both camps to determine what kind of education and experience will take you where you wish to go.

SUMMARY

Hazardous waste management is a "hot" environmental career in the United States and will remain so for at least the next decade. The field needs creative individuals from all backgrounds—people who have specific technical skills and, just as important, those who see the larger picture. How can we cost-effectively mitigate the environmental hazards from thousands of uncontrolled waste sites? How do we address cross-media issues so that solving a groundwater pollution problem does not create an airborne toxic emissions dilemma? How does a country, and the world for that matter, continue to progress economically yet not threaten the health and very existence of its environment with toxic by-products? People with the skills to answer these questions will have no problem finding a satisfying career.

CASE STUDY

Superfund

Nearly 41 million Americans live within 4 miles of a hazardous waste site. The Superfund program, established to clean up abandoned or uncontrolled hazardous wastes, has affected both cleanup and controversy. It is also producing many jobs for scientists and engineers.

On a 440-acre manufacturing site in northern Virginia, a succession of several owners made rayon, polyester, and polypropylene from 1940 until 1989. Manufacturing waste, by-products, and fly ash were routinely dumped into a series of 23 unlined, open impoundments on the property, some lying along the shore of the Shenandoah River directly across from a housing development. In addition to producing synthetics, the plant's operation had the following results:

- Carbon disulfide contamination in nearby residential wells was discovered in 1982.

- Groundwater contamination was detected across the Shenandoah River from the site in 1983.
- A permit to release effluents into the Shenandoah was revoked in 1989, after repeated permit violations.
- Primary groundwater contaminants at the site include carbon disulfide, phenol, sodium, lead, arsenic, and cadmium.
- Chief soil contaminants include carbon disulfide, phenol, arsenic, and lead.
- Health threats at the site include exposure to contaminated soil, water, and dust.
- Under the EPA's direction, groundwater treatment began in 1988 under the agency's Potentially Responsible Party (PRP) regulations. Site owner Avtex Fibers, Inc., and former owner FMC Corporation may be required to pay for part or all of the cleanup effort.

The environmental degradation at the Avtex site presents a compelling argument for Superfund regulations, but it is far from a singular case. The EPA's National Priority List (NPL) of serious Superfund sites includes 1,245 locations around the country, says Don Clay, EPA assistant administrator for the Office of Solid Waste and Emergency Response, which manages the Superfund program.

"Avtex was in financially marginal condition," says Clay. "They walked away from [the plant] and left the chemicals on site. We sent down a crew on an emergency basis, and we're still there. We go in and take care of the immediate threat right away. Around the country, we are current with serious threats."

The Comprehensive Environmental Response, Compensation, and Liability Act (CERCLA), known as Superfund, became law in 1980 in an effort to force cleanup of abandoned or uncontrolled hazardous waste sites. As the Superfund program approaches reauthorization, its effectiveness is being questioned. Critics charge that the vast majority of funding for the program goes into the salaries of managers at consulting firms, not cleanup activities. At the same time, even though the cost of Superfund is high, Clay is moving rapidly to show results in the program.

Of the 1,245 NPL sites, Clay said in early 1992: "We have completed 65. We will double that by the end of the year and triple it by the end of 1993. It takes eight to ten years to complete many of these sites, so we can expect the pace of completions to increase." The EPA reports that there are Superfund sites in every state, and some 41 million people in the United States live within 4 miles of a hazardous waste site.

People expect to see rusted 50-gallon drums and pools of murky liquids at hazardous waste sites, envisioning them as places from which waste must be removed for safe disposal. However, as Clay points out, this mental picture is not always appropriate. "Those removal sites are the most spectacular, but a lot of the hazardous waste sites look more like a parking lot. They don't present as much of a visual image as the 'valley of the drums' that people imagine."

The hazard at these "parking lot" sites is not what you can see but what lies invisibly beneath your feet—groundwater contamination. "A lot of what we do is groundwater remediation," says Clay. "It's just a physical fact that water is very difficult to clean up." Long after the surface of a hazardous waste site is considered clean, groundwater treatment may continue.

Clay argues that although serious political and scientific questions remain in the hazardous waste field, the crisis mentality is gone. "Most of the waste generators are regulated now, even overregulated in some areas," he says. Hazardous waste management is a field in which processes have been developed and are applied each day. Research continues on new technology to apply to the problems, but the shock days of Love Canal are over. The exception to this, however, may be federal lands.

The largest single focus of hazardous waste attention will be, ironically, federal government facilities. Nuclear weapons sites such as the one in Hanford, Washington, still contain some nightmares, such as "large tanks full of bubbling radioactive wastes," Clay says. For the most part, though, the picture of a parking lot requiring groundwater treatment is far more accurate.

Even though this image makes the hazardous waste problem seem less threatening, the hazards are still there, and the business of cleaning them up is growing. The Department of Defense alone will spend close to $5 billion per year on cleanup activities, mostly with consulting firms. And now that the focus of hazardous waste work is shifting to cleanup rather than studies, many new professionals will be needed on-site to direct cleanup activities, says Clay. The EPA will need more help as well.

"EPA looks for people who believe in what we are doing," says Clay. "EPA is unique in our government in that way. Most new employees will have scientific or technical backgrounds, particularly in the EPA regional offices." Clay notes that EPA regional offices have a difficult time keeping people, as they often slip away into more lucrative private sector jobs once they have been trained in the EPA.

Many opportunities are available in state and local hazardous waste programs as well, says Clay. New Jersey, Michigan, and other states with active hazardous waste programs work closely with their federal counterparts, turning over to the EPA the most serious and expensive cleanup sites and managing many of the less serious sites themselves. He sees continuing demand for hazardous waste management professionals in all areas.

PROFILES

Starr Dehn
Division Manager
Hazardous Waste and Industrial
Processes Division
CH2M Hill
Sacramento, California

Consultants play a vital role in implementing hazardous waste cleanup efforts, working extensively with the federal government and with private industry as well.

At one Air Force base in the western United States, there are no fewer than 40 different hazardous waste projects in progress or recently completed. Some are Superfund cleanups; others are RCRA or hazardous waste minimization efforts. Workers are improving the safeguards in a metal-plating shop, decontaminating a building soiled with mercury, cleaning up abandoned wells that are contaminating the water table, and assessing risks of airborne toxic emissions. The workers are all under the management of Starr Dehn, division manager of CH2M Hill's Hazardous Waste and Industrial Processes Division in Sacramento, California.

Dehn assembles teams of engineers, scientists, and managers from CH2M Hill's consulting resources around the country to meet the hazardous waste management needs of clients in northern California. He paints a picture of a field that is changing from the consultant's point of view. He feels that the majority of serious hazardous waste sites are now known. "The eighties were a decade of identification and characterization, but in the nineties we will see a lot more cleanup," he says. "That is going to mean a shift to more design than investigation, which probably translates into a greater need for people with engineering degrees and experience in construction, as opposed to people with paper study experience. The industry needs people familiar with the equipment used to clean up these sites."

Hazardous waste management professionals at CH2M Hill fit into a "matrix management structure" with four different career paths for employees. Technical experts concentrate on a particular area of knowledge and may work anywhere in the country where that knowledge is needed.

Discipline managers uphold the technical quality of the company within a particular area of knowledge, such as hazardous waste management, structural engineering, or solid waste management. Project managers focus on specific projects with a combination of skills in client management and business to pull together the resources needed to get a job done. Line managers like Dehn oversee all of the projects in a geographic region.

The company emphasizes teamwork and good organizational and communication skills to help clients move through a problem-solving process. The firm particularly values team leadership—leadership by people who do not necessarily have all the technical knowledge but are able to coordinate the efforts of others who do.

Dehn's own pathway to environmental engineering was a natural one. He studied at the University of Washington for his B.S. and M.S. degrees in civil engineering. "Most of the courses were very quantitative, like physics and engineering. Then I took a course that dealt with water quality and its impact on lake systems. It was very different from other courses and got me interested in the environmental field." After Dehn had spent some time working with a small consulting firm, an older brother suggested he apply to CH2M Hill.

Dehn suggests that for those who wish to join a consulting firm in the hazardous waste management industry, schooling in technical areas may outweigh experience. "Each consulting firm uses the credentials of its people on the project to help get the work, particularly the project engineers," says Dehn. "Nonrelated technical fields won't work."

At the same time, he adds, appropriate experience in the field is a plus. He recommends internship programs with the EPA and other state and federal regulatory agencies. "Get some familiarity with how the regulations work and you will be a much more valuable commodity to us."

Consulting in the hazardous waste management field, says Dehn, "is not a mundane type of job where you are doing the same thing every day. It is extremely challenging and rewarding for people who enjoy solving problems. That is what drives a lot of people in the consulting business. You work with a lot of different people and get involved with a lot of different things you've never dreamed of."

Manik (Nikki) Roy
Pollution Prevention Specialist
Environmental Defense Fund
Washington, DC

There is no inexpensive or easy way to eradicate hazardous wastes. The only workable long-term method is to avoid producing them in the first

place. Nonprofit firms provide guidance and exert pressure to ensure that
we eliminate hazardous waste production wherever possible.

Manik (Nikki) Roy, pollution prevention specialist with the Environmental
Defense Fund, defines success in hazardous waste management as avoiding its existence in the first place. He is trying to create a new breed of
specialist with "a whole facility approach to environmental protection,
including facility planning and trying to get existing programs such as the
Clean Air Act, Clean Water Act, and RCRA to collectively treat companies as whole things."

Some people call this cross-media pollution coordination, but Roy points
out that this label assumes that pollution already exists. He wants the
people responsible for enforcement and those who know technical systems
constantly thinking about how any changes affect not just one waste
stream but the entire company and its wastes. He talks about pulling the
right people into decision processes and encouraging companies to invest
in the right places to avoid pollutants of all types. He maintains close
contacts with both regulatory agencies and the companies their regulations affect.

Roy's appreciation of the problem on both the regulatory and producer
sides of the hazardous waste stream is no accident. In the summer of 1984,
Roy deliberately went to work at an electroplating shop struggling to come
into compliance with Massachusetts "right-to-know" regulations. "The
regulations were written to address a problem, not to be implemented by a
firm," he recalls. "There was little information about how to best comply
with the law. We had to hack our way through a wilderness of ignorance. I
reread the regulations about once per month, and each time, I found new
things."

The role of regulatory agencies needs to be reexamined, says Roy. "We
tend to think of [regulators] as the people who provide *the* answers.
Instead, we should think of them as devices for a social learning process.
Environmental protection issues have huge social components." He calls
for direct negotiating processes between the regulators and the regulated
in the form of advisory groups. He has experience with such efforts, but he
acknowledges that this approach is difficult.

A background that would produce the kind of balanced viewpoint Roy
demonstrates would have to be unusual. Roy's training is amazingly diverse and is driven by his own powerful recollection of the importance of
environmental protection. From his childhood in Arizona, Roy recalls
watching the tract of desert land across the street from his home developed
and, as he puts it, "trashed."

Roy's bachelor's and master's degrees in civil and environmental engineering from Stanford University included work for the city of San Francisco on sewage overflow problems. "It was a terrific case study on the intersection of environmental and political issues," he says. "And for the first time, I met people who were in love with their jobs."

The next several years took Roy to Washington, DC, and work as a clean water canvasser; efforts on the sewer and water issues of metropolitan Washington, DC; lobbying with legislatures and city councils; and campaigning for candidates in New Jersey, Maryland, and Florida. After gaining a Ph.D. in public policy from the Kennedy School of Government at Harvard University, he moved to the Massachusetts Department of Environmental Engineering as a source reduction policy coordinator, then went back to Washington as a toxic waste expert for the EPA, and, finally, landed at the Environmental Defense Fund. Now, says Roy, he is trying "to make history work."

Roy's advice to those entering the field is consistent with his example: "Be compulsively multidisciplinary."

Dave Galvin
Supervisor of Hazardous Waste
Management
Municipality of Metropolitan Seattle
Seattle, Washington

Tens of thousands of small businesses in every major city produce hazardous wastes that at present are excluded from regulation but that add up to significant amounts of pollution. Environmental education programs are emerging to enlist help from businesses in controlling the damage done by these wastes.

Dave Galvin, supervisor of hazardous waste management for the Municipality of Metropolitan Seattle (METRO), saves newspaper clippings to illustrate the problems of household hazardous wastes. "There was a person in Nevada who had fleas in her home, so she felt if one flea bomb was good, more was really good. She set off 15 of them and was smart enough to leave the house with her two kids. Her stove's pilot light ignited the fumes and blew the roof off and all the windows out. The last line of the clipping says, 'And not all the fleas were dead.'"

At times, the public clearly does not know what it is doing with hazardous materials, and often people seem not to comprehend how dangerous even common household chemicals can be. This situation is gradually changing as the public becomes more aware that some of what it uses, misuses, and discards are not just products that become trash but hazardous materials that become hazardous waste.

The Waste Watch Center in Andover, Massachusetts, reports progress. The United States has advanced from holding just two household hazardous waste collection events nationwide in 1980 to 855 in 1990. Permanent household hazardous waste collection sites, unheard of a few years ago, numbered 55 in 1990 and are rapidly growing. The Waste Watch Center estimates that household hazardous waste amounts to just 1 percent of the national waste stream. Because of its dispersed nature, however, it can inflict a great deal of damage by being tossed in with the week's trash to contaminate landfills. The most common offending items are used motor oil and paint.

The initial focus of hazardous waste programs has quite naturally been large, identifiable sources, says Galvin. "You can identify them, regulate them, issue permits, and take technology and apply it to the problem. But nonpoint, diffuse sources such as household hazardous wastes and conditionally exempt small business generators are a whole different challenge. Nonpoint sources are now more important than point sources in the amount of water pollution they create. It comes from everywhere and is much more difficult to address."

Enforcement does not work with diffuse sources. "We can't hire an army big enough to keep track of them all," says Galvin. "We have to approach them with education, by promoting stewardship. Now we encourage small firms to change the way they do business and reduce their generation of hazardous waste."

There are some significant success stories among nonregulated small businesses that have found ways to reduce or recycle their hazardous wastes. Dry cleaning firms are a classic case. "They used to produce horrendous amounts of soiled solvents, which they dumped on the ground or into sewers. Then they found that they could redistill them on-site, reuse the solvent, and produce a tiny fraction of the waste. The win-win is that by cutting their waste 90 percent, they avoid the cost of buying more solvent or paying to dispose of it."

Galvin cares a great deal about what is secretly dumped into the storm sewers of Seattle, for more than just professional reasons. He lives in a historic community of houseboats on Lake Union, nestled right in the city. His sensitivity to the condition of the environment is nothing new, however. While growing up in New England, on the opposite shore of the nation, Galvin recalls, he had a constant interest in clams, sea stars, and birds. By the time he finished grade school, Galvin was writing a weekly column on bird life for a local newspaper.

Galvin's studies in college included charting die-offs of lichens and comparing their distribution with patterns of sulfur dioxide pollution from paper mills in Maine and conducting other studies of wildlife as pollutant indicators. Pollution monitoring moved Galvin to water quality management and into hazardous waste management just as the field was developing in the late 1970s.

His job now is twofold. Galvin works to maintain water treatment in the Seattle area through METRO, particularly by monitoring sewers and storm drains to keep hazardous materials out of them. Second, he works directly with small hazardous waste generators not covered by federal RCRA regulations. In aggregate, this is no small task. Even if residents themselves did not present a problem, the 50,000 small businesses in Seattle do.

On a daily basis, Galvin jokes, although his work involves water, he sees much more of it at home from his houseboat. "My work is project administration and report writing, things that are more administrative and bureaucratic."

Most of the hands-on work is done by those who work with Galvin. He recommends that people headed for a career in fields such as his get out and work in the discipline while they are still in school. Galvin sees the professional focus of his part of the field as being different from some of the hard science orientation of the consulting field. "Your degree should not become an obstacle," he says. "When hiring, I look for experience rather than what the degree is. As a general rule, related work experience is more valuable." He uses interns in his department and has often worked with the Environmental Careers Organization.

Galvin's motivations for working with the environment go back to his earlier years. "Many in my generation wanted to change the world, and part of that [idealism] is still there. This work is something that has a lasting effect for the world and our society."

RESOURCES

Air and Waste Management Association. Trade association for personnel in the fields of air pollution and hazardous waste management. Publishes *Journal of the Air and Waste Management Association* and various special publications. April issue of *Journal of the Air and Waste Management Association* each year contains a useful directory of companies and government agencies in these fields. The association operates a job matching and referral service at its annual meeting. Send for a brochure on North American colleges and universities offering advanced degrees in environmental engineering, environmental sciences, and air pollution meteorology. P.O. Box 2861, Pittsburgh, PA 15230. (412) 232–3444.

American Chemical Society. World's largest organization devoted to a single scientific discipline. Publishes more than 20 periodicals, including *Chemical & Engineering News* (weekly), *Environmental Science and Technology* (monthly), and *Chemical Abstracts*. Also publishes materials on careers. Student memberships are available. 1155 16th St., NW, Washington, DC 20036. (202) 872–4600.

Chemecology. Covers health, safety, and the environment as they relate to the chemical industry. Subscriptions are free. Chemical Manufacturers Association, 2501 M St., NW, Washington, DC 20037. (202) 887–1100.

Citizen's Clearinghouse for Hazardous Wastes. A nonprofit, grass-roots organization that assists, through research and publications, community organizations that are working on hazardous waste issues. Maintains regional offices in Virginia, Pennsylvania, Georgia, and California. Publishes *Everyone's Backyard* (six times per year). P.O. Box 6806, Falls Church, VA 22040 (703) 237–2249.

Hazardous Materials Control Research Institute. Professional organization. Publishes *FOCUS* (monthly newsletter). 7237-A Hanover Pkwy., Greenbelt, MD 20770–3602. (301) 982–9500.

Pollution Engineering: The Magazine of Environmental Control (semi-monthly). Focuses on air and water pollution control and hazardous waste management. One issue each year includes a Yellow Pages–type listing of environmental instrumentation, equipment supplies, components, materials, and services. Cahner's Publishing, 1350 Touhy Ave., Des Plaines, IL 60017–5080. (708) 635–8800.

9 Air Quality Management

AT A GLANCE

Employment:
  60,000 air quality professionals nationwide

Demand:
  25 percent growth per year

Breakdown:
  Public sector, 13 percent
  Private sector, 83 percent
  Nonprofit sector, 4 percent

Key Job Titles:
  Air quality engineer
  Air quality planner
  Analytical chemist
  Environmental quality analyst
  Meteorologist
  Risk assessment specialist
  Safety and health manager
  Toxicologist

Influential Organizations:
  Air and Waste Management Association (AWMA)
  Association of Local Air Pollution Control Officials (ALAPCO)

California Air Resources Board
State and Territorial Air Pollution Program Administrators (STAPPA)

Salary:
Entry-level engineering salaries range from $23,000 to $35,000.

Air Pollution is uniquely egalitarian—it disperses rapidly to affect all living organisms, and it is a serious threat to the environment as a whole. In contrast, consider groundwater contamination, a dire threat in its own right. It at least is a slow process, often measured in years; at any point along the way, contaminants can be measured, analyzed, and cleaned up through remediation. Pollutants in the air, however, disperse within minutes, and retrieval is impossible.

WHAT IS AIR QUALITY MANAGEMENT?

Ensuring healthy air quality might appear to be a simple, straightforward proposition: Prevent pollutants, generated mainly in chemical reactions and combustion processes, from being released into the air. At one time, policymakers envisioned a relatively simple, albeit ambitious, regulatory agenda. Air pollution was seen mainly as a local problem that could be solved by regulating the primary pollutants being discharged in a region. Big industries and automobiles were the primary targets. This was the essence of early air pollution control efforts, including the landmark Clean Air Act amendments of 1970.

In some respects, the strategy worked quite well. According to the Environmental Protection Agency (EPA), the following reductions in air pollutant concentrations took place from 1981 to 1990:

- Airborne lead   79 percent
- Carbon monoxide   36 percent
- Total suspended particulates   24 percent
- Nitrogen dioxide   11 percent
- Sulfur dioxide   42 percent

However, as of 1990 virtually every major metropolitan area was out of regulatory compliance for ozone or carbon monoxide emissions or both. Furthermore, hundreds of toxic pollutants now recognized as health threats are just beginning to come under regulation.

Pollutants travel long distances, cross national boundaries, and combine in ways scientists do not fully understand to threaten human and environmental health. Even our homes can no longer be considered a safe refuge;

in fact, studies suggest our indoor air may be more toxic than that outdoors, even in industrial areas.

Michael Poe, technical manager for the Air and Waste Management Association (AWMA) in Pittsburgh, Pennsylvania, puts society's divergent viewpoints in clear relief: "If you are Joe Citizen, you are worrying: Will the air I am breathing harm me or my kid? If you are industry, you want to know: What will the next regulations look like, and how do I meet them and still stay in business? If you are government, you want to know how to assign the resources needed to enforce new regulations."

In short, solving air quality problems has proven to be much more complicated than originally envisioned. On top of these unsolved problems, other threats to air quality, such as acid rain and depletion of the ozone layer, are growing in severity and scope.

HISTORY AND BACKGROUND

The first Clean Air Act, passed in 1955, was replaced in 1967 by the Air Quality Act, which also is typically referred to as the Clean Air Act. Amendments in 1970, 1977, and 1990 strengthened the act considerably.

In 1971, the EPA established national ambient air quality standards (NAAQS) for any air pollutant that may "reasonably be anticipated to endanger public health or welfare." Under this regulation, the EPA developed standards for six priority pollutants: ozone, carbon monoxide, sulfur dioxide, lead, nitrogen dioxide, and particulates. Each state was required to submit a state implementation plan demonstrating how it would meet these standards within five years. State implementation plans included regulation of stationary sources (mainly industries) and automobile emissions testing. In the face of extensive noncompliance, however, Congress has extended the deadlines three times.

1977 CLEAN AIR ACT

It was not long before the limits of the original standards were realized. Congress attempted to correct the problem by producing national emission standards for hazardous air pollutants (NESHAPs). Only eight pollutants were controlled through the standards, however, leaving many unregulated.

1990 CLEAN AIR ACT AMENDMENTS

America's struggle for clean air entered a new era on November 15, 1990, with the signing of the 1990 Clean Air Act amendments. For people seeking careers in air quality management in the 1990s, nothing could be more important than a detailed understanding of this legislation and its impact. Although many environmentalists are dissatisfied with the new measures, the amendments will substantially improve air quality over the remainder of the decade and have already stimulated significant new employment in the industry.

Let us take a look at the crux of these new regulations, which will dominate employment in air quality management. Familiarity with the following few paragraphs may be essential to employment in this field. The amendments include seven titles.

Title I: Improving air quality standards. Title I is aimed at reducing the urban pollutants ozone (smog), carbon monoxide, and particulates. More than 100 million Americans live in cities in which ozone emissions exceed NAAQS limits. Cities are categorized in several groups, depending on the severity of pollution. Each group must meet specific milestones toward its attainment goals. Los Angeles, with the most severe urban pollution problem, is categorized as "extreme" and has 20 years to meet the standard.

Title II: Reducing motor vehicle emissions. Even though today's cars produce less pollution than earlier models, the growing number of cars, buses, and trucks in the United States accounts for a huge share of urban air pollution, including 90 percent of carbon monoxide emissions. The 1990 amendments put into place a rigorous schedule of restrictions on "mobile sources" of pollutants.

Titles I and II address the majority of conventional pollutants. Most states have met air quality standards for airborne lead, particulates, nitrogen oxides, and sulfur dioxide, but as mentioned earlier, virtually every U.S. metropolitan area is out of compliance with carbon monoxide or ozone standards or both. Carbon monoxide is primarily attributed to motor vehicle emissions. Ozone, often equated with smog, is a secondary pollutant formed in the atmosphere by a chemical reaction between nitrogen oxides, volatile organic compounds (VOCs), and sunlight. Nitrogen oxides and VOCs are discharged by fossil-fueled power plants, industrial operations, and motor vehicles. Both carbon monoxide and ozone present serious health problems and contribute to environmental degradation.

Title III: Controlling airborne toxic emissions. Airborne toxic emissions include dioxins, cadmium, polychlorinated biphenyls (PCBs), and hundreds of compounds linked to cancer, lung disease, birth defects, and other illnesses. Sources of these toxic emissions range from chemical plants, oil refineries, incinerators, and motor vehicles to dry cleaners and sewage treatment plants. The 1990 amendments name 198 airborne toxic emissions. Polluters have ten years to achieve reductions based on maximum achievable control technology (MACT).

Title IV: Preventing acid rain. The EPA estimates that electric utilities and other sources produce 20 million tons of sulfur dioxide emissions annually. Title IV of the amendments aims at cutting this roughly in half by the year 2000. More than 2,000 utilities will be affected.

Acid deposition, or acid rain, is an air quality issue attracting national and international attention. Scientists, utility officials, and policymakers have had great debates on the origin and effects of acid precipitation. Most agree, however, that sulfur and nitrogen emissions from power plants, smelters, and automobiles combine with atmospheric moisture to form an acidic rain that increases the acidity of lakes and streams, reduces forest growth, affects crops, and may contribute to coastal degradation.

Title V: Creating incentives. By 1994, to obtain an operating permit each polluter will be required to pay $25 per ton of pollutants emitted; this will provide an economic incentive to reduce pollution and will pay for state and local pollution control programs in the meantime. The provision is a key source of new funding for pollution abatement programs and a primary reason for optimism about employment growth in air quality management programs.

Title VI: Closing the ozone hole. Title VI phases out ozone-depleting chlorofluorocarbons (CFCs), halon, and carbon tetrachloride by the year 2000, as called for in an international accord known as the Montreal Protocol. Since the 1990 amendments, new regulations call for halting all CFC production in the United States by the end of 1995. (For a look at one person's work in this field, see the profile of Sharon Gidumal of DuPont at the end of this chapter.) Less harmful variants of CFCs, called HCFCs, will also be phased out.

Stratospheric ozone depletion and the greenhouse effect are global concerns. The culprits in depletion of the ozone layer are primarily CFCs found in aerosol propellants, refrigeration fluids, and plastic foams. CFCs, though stable in the lower atmosphere, slowly rise to the upper atmosphere, where they break down, releasing chlorine. Chlorine reacts with ozone in the upper atmosphere, depleting the ozone shield that blocks hazardous ultraviolet B radiation. The discovery that winter ozone levels in Antarctica have plummeted by 40 percent has shocked the world into action. As the damage worsens, a North American ozone hole remains a distinct possibility.

The greenhouse effect is caused by long-term buildup of carbon dioxide and pollutants such as carbon monoxide, which trap heat in the lower atmosphere. The result is global warming, which could have disastrous social and economic consequences worldwide.

Title VII: Increasing enforcement. Title VII provides more teeth for the EPA's regulations by increasing fines, which now range from $5,000 to $200,000. Willful violation now is a felony rather than a misdemeanor.

ISSUES AND TRENDS

In some disciplines, technology and policy are changing so quickly that the only way to keep your knowledge current is to maintain a careful watch on the newest issues and trends. This is definitely the case with air quality management.

NEED FOR FURTHER RESEARCH

Improved research methods and continued analysis of real-world data will be necessary to determine which toxic chemicals represent the greatest danger and what pathways they travel in doing their damage. Dr. Kathryn Kelly of Environmental Toxicology, Inc., in Seattle, Washington, cites an EPA evaluation of the pathways traveled by 13 toxic chemicals found in Lake Erie. From this study, the EPA concluded that atmospheric pathways contributed 8 to 66 percent of the pollution eventually found in the water. An understanding of these sophisticated relationships will require many additional researchers.

SHORTAGE OF TECHNICAL EXPERTISE

Established veterans in the air quality management field are closing in on retirement even as demand for air quality services increases, creating a shortage of qualified professionals.

INDOOR AIR POLLUTION

Indoor air quality is one of the biggest environmental issues of the 1990s. Dangerous chemicals found in indoor air include asbestos, formaldehyde, lead, combustion by-products, pesticides, and radon. These substances have produced what is now referred to as the sick building syndrome. One EPA study of seven cities found that indoor concentrations of toxic and carcinogenic compounds were 200 to 500 percent higher than outdoor concentrations. Ties between lung cancer and radon in the home make indoor air quality an area of considerable concern and growth.

REGULATION OF SMALL GENERATORS

The 1990 changes to the Clean Air Act do more than tighten standards for various pollutants. Charlie Pratt, senior environmental scientist with the EPA in Research Triangle Park, North Carolina, points out that until recently, the agency dealt only with the largest polluters. "EPA used to watch seven pollutants. Congress added 189 more, bringing hundreds of small businesses under regulation. How to regulate them all is the effort now."

NEW ROLES FOR COMPUTERS AND SOFTWARE

Computers will find increasingly useful roles in air quality control. Professionals foresee networks linking computers used by scientists in a laboratory with those used by inspectors in the field. Carrie Seringer, safety, health, and environmental manager for DuPont Fluorochemicals, says, "Permitting is getting much more complicated, and it requires sophisticated modeling."

CAREER OPPORTUNITIES

There will be tremendous employment opportunity in the air quality management field through the mid-1990s, according to William Becker, executive director of the State and Territorial Air Pollution Program Administrators (STAPPA) and the Association of Local Air Pollution Control Officials (ALAPCO) in Washington, DC. The 1990 Clean Air Act amendments and other activities are creating needs for the following:

- Environmentally oriented scientists and engineers, including chemists, public health professionals, and mathematicians.
- Managers who understand air pollution and how it relates to other environmental issues.
- People who can communicate, orally and in writing, with professionals and the public about issues of health risk, economics, and air quality programs.

- Lawyers who understand the web of federal, state, and local regulations.

PUBLIC SECTOR

Steady growth is expected for public sector air quality management organizations over the next several years. Federal positions will continue to serve a leadership role, although growth at the state and local levels will be more substantial.

Federal government. The EPA's air quality programs added 200 full-time positions during 1991 and will add another 100 by 1993, reports Keith Mason, a policy analyst with the EPA's Office of Air and Radiation. Gradual changes attributable to new air quality regulations will stimulate "steady growth over the next 15 years in the field," he says.

Stan Meiburg, director of the planning and management staff for the EPA Office of Air Quality Planning and Standards, explains a three-part role for the federal government. "First, we set national standards. Second, the federal government works to provide technical support to state and local air pollution control agencies. This role is very important as air pollution control regulations become increasingly technical, requiring expertise state and local agencies don't have and can't afford. Finally, we are responsible for oversight and administration of these programs and standards: Are we making progress? If not, why not?"

Federal air quality management jobs fall into several categories:

- Basic research and laboratory work carried out by both engineers and environmental scientists (chemists, biologists, physicists, mathematicians, microbiologists) will include engineering analysis and development and design of technologies to meet certain standards.
- Risk assessment, or determination of what pollutant levels constitute a risk to human health.
- Crop and environmental damage assessment.
- Mathematical modeling of air pollutant dispersion and the impact of various control strategies. Professionals with backgrounds in meteorology are examining how pollutants combine and disperse in the atmosphere. Computer science and data management specialists are needed to make sense of the reams of data collected in continuous monitoring across the country.

Professionals will also be needed to work with state and local air pollution control agencies. This work will include development, review, and oversight of state implementation plans; training of state and local air pollution control personnel; and establishment of inspection standards in each of the EPA regions. Increasingly, the EPA is using consultants for this work.

State government. State and local governments will be the rising stars in the public sector for air quality management, says ALAPCO's William Becker. "Not only will they expand their staffs, but the breadth of experience demanded will be increased dramatically. No longer will agencies rely only on engineers and technical people. They all need to hire a diverse group of professionals ranging from public policy people to scientists to risk assessment professionals and communicators, writers, attorneys, and accountants to track the regulatory reforms that are being developed on the state and local levels. That leads to a very exciting future in the air quality control business."

For instance, the EPA's Charlie Pratt notes that the state of Texas will expand its staff from 400 to nearly 1,200 people over four years to implement its permit program. Multiply this by 50 states and you will begin to understand the opportunities available in state government.

Local government. Local air pollution control agencies develop and enforce programs to ensure that their areas meet NAAQS. Personnel are needed in air quality engineering, modeling, inspections, and compliance monitoring. Chemical, mechanical, and environmental engineers evaluate sources of air pollution, design and set up networks to monitor ambient pollutants and emissions, conduct laboratory analyses, and analyze computer-generated data.

Environmental scientists, particularly chemists, analyze data and identify types and sources of pollutants. Some agencies use public health personnel for risk assessment. Inspections are generally conducted by teams of engineers, scientists, and technicians. Depending on the size of the agency, other personnel could include lawyers, metallurgists, microbiologists, meteorologists, toxicologists, and epidemiologists.

Much of the work of local air pollution control agencies, such as inspections, laboratory work, and maintenance of monitoring equipment, is done by graduates of two-year technical schools, and this will continue to be the case. However, as William Becker notes, "There is an increasing realization that [agencies] need managers, lawyers, public relations people, and writers, people who can communicate to the public, mediate, and negotiate."

PRIVATE SECTOR

Industry and consulting firms account for four of every five jobs in the air quality management field. Some people working in secondary supplier air quality control firms may not be fully aware that they are serving the environment, but this market segment is quite large. The EPA estimates that the private sector employs many more people in air quality management than are directly involved as professionals in air quality work.

Chrysler Corporation, Michigan. Paul Kantola checks the regulators on air cylinders used to calibrate Chrysler's emissions-testing equipment.

Private industry. Employment in private industry is expected nearly to double by 1995, representing 25 percent growth per year and 50,000 new jobs in the private sector alone. Positions range from entry-level field sampling and monitoring to engineering, project development, and management. Prospects are particularly bright for engineers with chemistry backgrounds and laboratory experience.

The AWMA's Michael Poe points out that industry's environmental affairs departments will need more help than ever. "Plastics, chemical, and refinery companies now have to control emissions they never had to worry about before. They can stop using those chemicals or modify the product, or they can install some sort of control equipment to treat and destroy the chemical. They are looking at all those options but are faced with trying to stay in business in the meantime."

Companies that manufacture air pollution control equipment can also expect their work to expand. According to the *Environmental Business Journal*, annual capital expenditures for air pollution control equipment in the United States are expected to double from $5 billion in 1991 to $10 billion in 1995, generating 31,000 new jobs.

Consulting firms. Consultants provide a growing number of air quality services to industry and government. The EPA contracts with outside firms for everything from training to monitoring to design and basic research. As hundreds of toxic emissions are regulated for the first time, state and local governments will need experts in many areas.

Consulting firms are hiring many of the same kinds of air quality management professionals as is the public sector. The focus again is on engineers, especially chemical engineers knowledgeable about airborne toxic emissions.

Dischargers are turning to consulting firms to bring them into compliance with new and tightening regulations. Consultants keep such companies informed about regulations; they design, build, install, and maintain systems and negotiate with regulatory agencies on behalf of their clients.

Acid rain provisions in the Clean Air Act amendments require utility companies to cut back dramatically on sulfur emissions. This requirement will create many in-house positions as well as more consulting work. Additional new markets include waste-to-energy and hazardous waste disposal facilities.

NONPROFIT SECTOR

Nonprofit organizations such as citizens' groups and environmental organizations constitute the smallest portion of the employment market for air quality workers, less than 5 percent. But because these organizations focus on improving the environment for all of us, the nonprofit sector has some unique appeal to its workers and unique value to our society.

Nonprofit organizations in air quality management range from industry associations closely tied to an industry, to environmental organizations lobbying for strict emissions regulations to organizations such as the American Lung Association, which is conducting research on the hazards of pollution to the lungs.

Workers in nonprofit organizations are generally paid less than their counterparts in other air quality management sectors. They provide a check on the more financially motivated activities of the private sector and on the more politically derived actions of the public sector. No great increase in employment is envisioned for nonprofits, but as the market expands it will generate increased demand for nonprofit efforts.

SALARY

Most of the salary information available for the air quality management field applies to engineers and chemists. Entry-level jobs for those with engineering degrees pay in the range of $23,000 to $35,000, depending on schooling and location. Local agencies pay at the low end of that range; state and federal agencies, a little higher; and private sector employers, in the low 30s and up to $70,000 or more.

An average federal salary for meteorologists and environmental engineers is $45,000. Michigan Department of Natural Resources salaries include the following ranges for air quality professionals:

Environmental engineer	$32,200 to $74,800
Environmental quality analyst	$24,500 to $57,700
Laboratory assistant	$18,600 to $35,600
Laboratory scientist	$24,500 to $57,700
Meteorologist	$24,000 to $52,000

Salaries are substantially higher in the private sector than for the majority of public sector positions. Even so, ALAPCO reports, top regulators' salaries in state and local positions can reach $50,000 to $70,000 or more.

GETTING STARTED

Entry-level jobs in air quality management are most plentiful in state and local government and in the consulting field. Engineering, chemistry, and laboratory experience will give you the quickest start. Have a specific skill to take to potential employers, along with some related experience, preferably more practical than academic. Plan ahead to apply for government positions, as the hiring process can be lengthy. If you are still in school, start networking now via independent projects and internships.

If you do not have an advanced degree, a marketable skill is particularly crucial in landing that first job. Many employees in air pollution control at state and local agencies are support personnel with two-year technical degrees. There is a good chance, however, that even with a B.A. or B.S. you will start as a technician: doing fieldwork, operating monitoring equipment, assisting in inspections, collecting data and entering the data into computers, and engaging in various laboratory activities.

EDUCATION

Because engineers and technicians account for a high proportion of new hires in the air quality field, the best route to getting a job in air quality management is to get at least one technical degree. The physical sciences, environmental science, and engineering make good basic starting points for a career.

Meteorology involves a great deal of computer modeling, which is an important tool in air quality management, so consider course work in this field as well. Toxicology, one of the fields highlighted by changes in air quality regulations, is another discipline in which not enough professionals are available.

Those with backgrounds in liberal arts, such as planning, law, economics, journalism, and political science, can find starting positions in technical writing, public relations, economic analysis, research, and state and local planning assistance related to air quality. To get an edge, take some technical courses, such as chemistry and computer science. Understand air quality regulations and how industries operate, and be able to make sense of technical data and studies.

ADVICE

Professionals in the air quality management field have offered the following advice to those entering the field.

Consider starting out in the public sector. Roger Westman of the Air Pollution Control Bureau in Pittsburgh's Allegheny County Health Department says: "State and local agencies are a good place to start an air quality career. They have the disadvantage of lower pay, but they offer unique experiences and opportunity for growth. Turnover is steady, as people tend to move on after two years to higher-paying jobs in the private sector."

Look for opportunities to broaden your experience. Stan Meiburg of the EPA offers a particularly useful bit of advice: "Yes, you're going to have to perform a specific task or tasks on your first job, but work to get as broad a preparation early on in your career as possible. Think about your career in a holistic way, always positioning yourself not just for the short term but for the long-term development."

Don't be discouraged by a lack of credentials. Although private sector companies often require more specific technical backgrounds than do those in the public sector, they also have more latitude in hiring. Brian Ketcham, founder of a consulting firm, says: "When I interview, I spend more time sizing up individuals, their attitudes, and their aptitudes than looking at their degrees. Are they enthusiastic? Do they appear dedicated? Do they demonstrate attention to detail?" There is plenty of entry-level work for consulting firms doing fieldwork and air sampling. One of the best ways to identify these firms is to look in the professional journals (see the resources section at the end of this chapter and the AWMA in the resources section of chapter 8).

SUMMARY

You could not ask for a better time to launch a career in air quality management than the mid- to late 1990s. The relative doldrums experienced in this field during the 1980s clearly came to a halt with the 1990 Clean Air Act amendments.

New regulations create a strong demand in every state for new professionals, particularly those with technical training. Many upper-level air quality professionals are reaching retirement age or are making parallel moves into other fields, ensuring that you need not remain on the bottom rung for long. As this nation and the world deal with global environmental problems that are clearly air quality issues, the air quality management field will remain a key source of environmental careers through at least the end of the 1990s.

CASE STUDY

South Coast Air Quality Management District

In one month's time, the 12 million inhabitants and 8 million motor vehicles of the Los Angeles basin propel into the air pollutants equivalent to those contained in the Exxon Valdez *oil spill.*

California's South Coast Air Quality Management District (AQMD) describes the extent of air pollution the agency must deal with: "Within 24 hours, snow-white filters placed in our air monitors turn black . . . from the suspended particulate haze which shrouds visibility. In 1988, one or more federal health standards for ambient air were violated on 232 days. Ozone alone exceeded the federal standard on 176 days. . . . Our air quality is nine times as bad as anywhere else in the nation outside California."

Yet the same organization also states: "We have just enjoyed the cleanest three consecutive years in the 40-year history of air quality monitoring here in the South Coast Air Basin. Levels of ozone—the worst ingredient in smog—are half the levels monitored in 1955."

The problem faced by southern Californians is that both statements are true. Much progress has been made in air quality, but much more remains to be done.

"This is a single-purpose agency with a very tough and controversial job," says Claudia Keith, AQMD spokeswoman. "Our mission is to achieve clean air. We set a target date of 2010 for meeting federal health standards. Everything [we do] is geared to that."

Cleaning up southern California's air is no small task. As of the early 1990s, the region exceeded federal health standards for all four primary pollutants, including nitrogen dioxide, particulates, carbon monoxide, and ozone, with ozone levels standing at 275 percent of the health standard.

"California's problem is population growth," says California Air Resources Board spokesman Jerry Martin from his office in Sacramento. The board sets motor vehicle emissions policy in the state. "We drive the cleanest cars and have the cleanest industry. But we have a huge influx of new population every year. About one quarter of Californians drive cars not designed for driving in this state.

"California routinely leads the nation in air pollution control," he adds. "We're moving now into controlling other forms of pollution in addition to cars, including lawn mowers, construction equipment, and household consumer products such as antiperspirants, hair sprays, windshield wiper fluids, and others, all of which combine to produce 10 percent of the hydrocarbon emissions in this state."

The cooperative efforts of both the California Air Resources Board and the AQMD are directed at a number of different targets. The agencies have little choice but to control a broad number of pollutants if the region is to meet federal health standards by 2010. Their efforts include the following:

• Two thousand major air polluters will take part in a smog reduction program that requires them to reduce emissions by 5 percent each year. The AQMD's Reclaim Program allows companies that reduce their emissions by more than 5 percent to sell excess "smog trading credits" to other companies unable to meet their annual goals. "Each company can decrease emissions in whatever way is best for it," says the AQMD's Claudia Keith. "This goes away from the command and control concept of the past to an economic, market-based approach." Program implementation begins in 1994.

- The AQMD and the Air Resources Board work together to reduce motor vehicle pollution. One of the most innovative programs is the AQMD's Commuter Program. Unlike ride-sharing programs elsewhere, this one is not voluntary. Companies employing 100 or more workers at a single work site must submit a plan to increase ridership to a target level within 12 months. Program enforcement is tough, carrying penalties of as much as $25,000 in fines and one year in jail for each day of violation.
- Emission limits are on the way for essentially all fast-evaporating chemicals. Producers of these volatiles will be encouraged to find less hazardous alternatives.
- Other measures aimed specifically at motor vehicles include prohibition of diesel vehicle sales in California by 2010. California's concern with motor vehicles is not an unthinking obsession. Fully 88 percent of the carbon monoxide measured in the Los Angeles basin comes from motor vehicles; only 1 percent comes from industry. Los Angeles's motor vehicles also produce 50 percent of the region's volatile organics, the precursors to ozone smog, while the next largest source, industry, produces half that amount.

By law, 50 percent of California's passenger cars in 2010 will be powered by electricity and 25 percent each will be powered by alternative fuels and gasoline. "Detroit is seeing that if they want to have any presence in California, they will have to make cleaner cars," says Keith. "There is pressure from the automotive industry saying that this is too expensive and they cannot meet our deadlines. But they can, in fact, do it."

In the meantime, the AQMD continues to grow at 30 to 40 percent per year as its newest collection of programs becomes operational and the task of reducing California's air pollution looms large in the near future. This will increase the need for air quality analysts, planners, air quality engineers, chemists, meteorologists, toxicologists, and public health specialists.

Other states are well aware of the progress of their western neighbor and are beginning to emulate its processes. Several northeastern and mid-Atlantic states have adopted or will soon adopt motor vehicle emissions standards like those of California, including requirements for cleaner, reformulated gasoline by 1995 and substantial sales of electric cars by

2003. Adoption of the standards is expected by the end of 1992 in Delaware, the District of Columbia, Maine, Massachusetts, New Hampshire, New Jersey, New York, Pennsylvania, Rhode Island, Vermont, and Virginia.

More than any other state, California demonstrates what can be accomplished through a strong commitment to environmental progress. Even in the face of airborne toxic emissions, global warming, ozone depletion, and smog, southern Californians may be relied on to persist and prevail.

PROFILES

Laura DeGuire
Environmental Quality Analyst
Michigan Department of Natural
*   Resources*
Lansing, Michigan

A gulf extends between air quality regulations and clean air, and that gulf is bridged by the efforts of those who climb on roofs in midwinter to make measurements day after day.

Laura DeGuire, environmental quality analyst with the Michigan Department of Natural Resources, began her professional life with a teaching degree in the midst of an oversupply of teachers in the late 1970s. In desperation, she went to work as a secretary until a telephone call out of the blue pulled her into a career she loves.

That call was from the city of Grand Rapids, where DeGuire had worked one summer as a noise pollution analyst. Her job had involved routine tasks such as conducting noise surveys and investigating noise complaints. A supervisor recalled DeGuire's work and wondered whether she would like a job in air pollution control. DeGuire laughs, recalling the conversation. "I was very interested in getting out of secretarial work and into air quality."

DeGuire's new job included tasks such as "climbing out on top of buildings in subzero weather." After a year in the position, she attended Michigan State University and earned a master's degree in environmental resources, which included studies in environmental law. The following summer, she took a temporary position as an assistant with the Michigan Department of Natural Resources (DNR).

"I realized there was no way I could be hired permanently without additional experience. And DNR wanted to hire an intern for a new program. I heard about the Environmental Intern Program through The CEIP Fund (now called the Environmental Careers Organization). I quickly called and asked how to sign up. It was exactly what I needed to get that experience."

During her six-month internship, DeGuire worked on the Great Lakes Atmospheric Deposition Program, which gathered important data on acid rain. DNR then hired her as a resource specialist, and she has since been promoted to environmental quality analyst.

DeGuire spends about half of her time ensuring the safety of the office's 130-member inspection staff. This includes making certain that their safety equipment is in good condition and that their health is checked periodically. She also monitors air quality for compliance with the Clean Air Act, paying particular attention to emissions that contribute to high ozone levels. When ozone levels exceed health standards, she notifies the appropriate authorities. DeGuire also writes the state's annual air quality report.

For those looking forward to similar duties, DeGuire suggests doing more than the typical technical studying—she advises giving psychology some consideration. "We have to work with the public to alter their daily activities and to change the way industry looks at producing goods and ensure that there is a strong environmental ethic. Everything in air pollution goes back to choices that we make in manufacturing and using products or conveniences. . . . It's not just cars. We have to change life-styles."

Her advice:

- Students working as summer help or interns have an excellent chance of getting full-time work if they perform with enthusiasm and professionalism.
- Growing concern about ozone depletion and airborne toxic emissions is creating increased demand for toxicologists. "Get toxicology experience and you cannot go wrong."

Sharon Gidumal
Environmental Specialist
Fluorochemicals Division
DuPont
Wilmington, Delaware

Private industry includes many thousands of professionals serving the environment from within industry, doing a job while also ensuring that "our days of simply polluting are over."

Sharon Gidumal, environmental specialist in DuPont's Fluorochemicals Division, Wilmington, Delaware, sees herself as a "passive environmentalist." As she describes it, her entry into environmental work was simple: "DuPont handed me these environmental opportunities, and I took them." Environmentalists working within the chemical industry have a crucial role to play, she adds. "Our days of simply polluting are over, but many environmentalists don't consider the business needs of industry."

Gidumal is a chemical and process engineer with a degree in chemical engineering from the University of Kansas and ten years of experience with DuPont. She now has a politically sensitive job helping to phase out chlorofluorocarbons (CFCs) in DuPont's product line. Gidumal keeps up with CFC regulations for DuPont and works with both the EPA and states passing their own regulations curtailing CFCs. She also represents Du-Pont's interests for substitute products that can replace CFCs without harmful effects.

Gidumal feels she is a good match for the job. "They need somebody who is diverse and who is willing to dig into things. I have to be able to write and speak and think on my feet—a lot of it is communication. It's also science, technical and process knowledge, and business priorities. It's not something you can do right out of school."

Still, she is aware that her task is essentially to work herself out of a job. When the CFCs are gone, so is the job, but Gidumal does not seem worried. "The expertise I'm developing in this job will not be wasted. Phasing out CFCs is sort of a template for many environmental concerns. The process will be repeated. Chemical products have emissions. We have to reduce them, report them, look for alternatives, and develop environmentally sound processes."

She advises people interested in air quality management to take environmental engineering electives. A solid base in some area of the sciences is important, she says. "There is a lot of math and modeling in this work, and that is really essential. You develop a thought process as part of that. An engineering curriculum is important, as it teaches you how to think logically."

Kathryn E. Kelly
President
Environmental Toxicology
International, Inc., and Alden
Analytical Laboratories
Seattle, Washington

Even in the service of planetary health there is room for the entrepreneurial spirit. A strong ethical code and good business do mix in the robust market for air quality management.

Dr. Kathryn E. Kelly, internationally known expert on airborne toxic emissions and founder of two Seattle-based environmental companies, says that even though industry releases large amounts of chemicals into our air, industrial chemicals are not our biggest air pollution problem.

"Of the quantifiable, controllable sources, the automobile is clearly the major contributor to air pollution in the U.S. and many other countries," she says. Kelly, a person of strong environmental convictions, is just as firmly grounded in the scientific method, which at times puts her in the position of having to debunk the misconceptions of citizens, industry, government, and environmental activists.

Kelly's firms help U.S. government agencies, private companies, and environmental groups understand and solve environmental contamination issues. Environmental Toxicology International, Inc. (ETI), formed in 1985, assesses health hazards posed by contaminated sites. Alden Analytical Laboratories, formed in 1988, analyzes samples of water, air, soil, and tissues for contamination.

What little we know of the extent of the airborne toxic emissions problem and how great a health threat it represents have largely been determined in the past ten years, says Kelly. Although numerous health problems have arisen from exposure to airborne toxins, most research has focused on cancer as the primary deleterious health effect. Study of other health problems has thus far been minimal, despite the fact that a 1987 EPA study ranking 31 results of pollution listed noncarcinogenic effects second after cancer.

The rise of public concern about these pollutants is far outpacing the rate of reduction. Kelly is convinced that "the real environmental problems are ozone depletion, radon, indoor air pollution in general, overall habitat destruction, and the attendant reduction in species diversity."

Kelly's road to owning two environmental companies at age 33 began when, as a premed major at Stanford University, she found herself less than enthralled with "the capital-intensive nature of curative medicine." She recalls: "I found myself on the way to Columbia University in New York and made a beeline to Love Canal. I got there just after the 700 families had been evacuated, and I decided this should not be happening. I want to prevent Love Canals."

After earning a graduate degree in environmental science from Columbia and studying environmental medicine at New York University, Kelly worked as an intern with a California chemical company through a program with the Environmental Careers Organization. "The internship was wonderful. I recommend it to anyone who wants to dip their toes in to see what it is like to work for industry or government or a consulting firm, even for just a short term."

Most of Kelly's time these days is spent on the move. She travels 60 percent of the time, flying around the United States and to Europe and the Pacific, negotiating the contracts that have built her businesses. Like other effective employers, she is careful about who she hires. She looks for qualities that are a bit unusual.

"Our available information is doubling every 12 to 18 months, and there is no conceivable way for the ability of the human brain to deal with this rate of growth in information. I want people who can look at fact and fiction and use critical thinking to know what to do with that information to solve problems.

"Ideally, I would like people with incredible depth in their field but who can also sit back and talk about how to bring in toxicology, meteorology, and computer studies to solve real-world problems, and who can do it on a scientifically sound basis."

RESOURCES

See also the Resources sections in other chapters for publications on environmental advocacy, education, and business; many of these publications cover air quality along with other environmental issues.

Air and Waste Management Association (AWMA). See the Resources section in chapter 8 for a description.

California Air Resources Board. Publishes *Employment Opportunities*, which does an excellent job of laying out employment opportunities at state and local air pollution control agencies, from the perspective of the state with the most significant air pollution challenge. State of California Air Resources Board, P.O. Box 2815, Sacramento, CA 95812. (916) 322–2990.

Environmental Protection Agency, Air Quality Management Division. Research Triangle Park, NC 27711. (919) 541–5551.

National Clean Air Coalition. 801 Pennsylvania Ave., SE, Washington, DC 20003. (202) 543–8200.

State and Territorial Air Pollution Program Administrators (STAPPA) and the Association of Local Air Pollution Control Officials (ALAPCO). 444 N. Capitol St., NW, Suite 307, Washington, DC 20001. (202) 624–7864.

10 Water Quality Management

AT A GLANCE

Employment:
143,000 professionals in all sectors nationwide

Demand:
9 percent growth per year for the first half of the 1990s, primarily in local government installations and private industry

Breakdown:
Public sector, 45 percent (5 percent federal, 40 percent state and local)
Private sector, 50 percent
Nonprofit sector, 5 percent

Key Job Titles:
Aquatic ecologist
Aquatic toxicologist
Attorney
Biologist
Civil engineer
Environmental chemist
Environmental engineer
Environmental specialist
Hydrogeologist
Hydrologist

Wastewater technician or engineer
Water quality technician

Influential Organizations:

American Water Resources Association
American Water Works Association
Association of State and Interstate Water Pollution Control Administrators
Environmental Protection Agency
National Society of Professional Engineers

Salary:

Entry-level salaries range from $16,000 to $24,000; the lower end of the range represents technicians, and the higher end represents chemists and inspectors. Average maximum salaries reach $40,000 for laboratory directors and superintendents, slightly less for chemists, $31,000 for inspectors, and $25,000 for technicians.

Water quality issues employ thousands of environmental workers in a broad range of disciplines and professions. Every city, town, and business in the nation uses water and produces wastewater, which requires treatment. In addition, fish and wildlife require healthy water for productive habitats. To meet this ubiquitous demand, a huge infrastructure of chemists, engineers, biologists, technicians, equipment makers and operators, lawyers, journalists, managers, and policymakers has grown into one of the environmental profession's largest fields.

WHAT IS WATER QUALITY MANAGEMENT?

Water quality management means different things to different people. The definition depends largely on who will be using the water and for what purpose. Is it being managed as drinking water? Do we want to draw healthy fish from it or go swimming without concern? Perhaps we need it for industrial purposes, irrigation, or hydroelectric power or to sustain habitat for fish and wildlife.

As we will see, the thrust of early water quality initiatives was to restore surface water spoiled by years of abuse. The problems were evident to eye and nose, and the sources were easy to identify. As our understanding of the multiple threats to our water resources has grown more sophisticated, we have added new layers of protection and found ways to meet our multiple, and sometimes conflicting, uses. Water quality management is both the means to and the result of this process.

Water quality management professionals generally divide the field into six categories.

DRINKING WATER SUPPLY AND TREATMENT

Management and treatment of drinking water includes identification of surface water and groundwater supplies, removal and transport of water, regulation of drinking water standards, operation of treatment facilities, promotion of water conservation efforts, and maintenance of the drinking water supply infrastructure.

WASTEWATER TREATMENT

Wastewater treatment is far and away the largest part of the water quality management field. Professionals in this area include the thousands of technicians working at industrial and municipal wastewater treatment plants; the people who design, build, and equip the plants; the chemists who collect and test water samples; and many others.

GROUNDWATER PROTECTION

Protection of groundwater resources is a field that is rapidly growing in importance. Groundwater protection professionals identify pollutants in groundwater; assess levels of risk to human, plant, and animal health; design computer models to predict the dispersal of pollutants; carry out remediation activities where resources are polluted; and design protection strategies to prevent groundwater contamination.

SURFACE WATER MANAGEMENT

Management of surface water resources goes beyond wastewater treatment to identify sources of pollution to lakes, ponds, streams, and rivers and find ways to reduce or eliminate them. Surface water managers often work with other environmental professionals in comprehensive watershed management efforts to protect water resources for fish and wildlife habitat as well as for human use.

ESTUARY MANAGEMENT

Coastal waters and estuaries (the meeting grounds between oceans and rivers) are crucial to breeding stocks of fish and wildlife. Estuarine managers help protect estuaries from the negative effects of development, industry, and agriculture.

WETLANDS PROTECTION

Inland and coastal wetlands moderate the effects of floods and droughts while serving as natural water treatment areas by removing silt and chemicals from the water. Wetlands are also important habitats for fish and wildlife. This part of the water quality management field includes a rapidly growing number of wetlands ecologists, surveyors, botanists, fish and wildlife scientists, planners, chemists, and water quality specialists.

HISTORY AND BACKGROUND

Water quality issues have been at the heart of the modern environmental movement since its beginning. Dead fish, oil slicks, and Ohio's famous burning river, for instance, provided much of the stimulus for the first Earth Day in 1970 and the subsequent growth of environmental legislation in the early 1970s. The issue of declining water quality seemed relatively simple and was highly visual and emotional—our waters were dying. Congress responded to the public outcry by passing legislation that set a broad goal to "restore and maintain the chemical, physical, and biological integrity of the nation's waters."

In some respects, progress has been remarkable. Our waterways certainly appear cleaner, and many are cleaner. Lake Erie, for example, pronounced biologically dead in 1972, now supports a thriving population of perch, walleye, and largemouth bass and enough fish to justify commercial fishing as well as sportfishing.

A survey of state environmental officials by the Association of State and Interstate Water Pollution Control Administrators found the overall water quality in the United States improved, in many cases dramatically, between 1972 and 1982. Linda Eichmiller, deputy director of the association, says that results of the 1992 survey should show continued improvement.

In our efforts to alleviate the most evident water quality offenses, however, we have discovered an entirely new collection of additional pollution problems, less visible but no less serious than the first. The fish are back in Lake Erie, but levels of pollutants make routine consumption of them a questionable practice. The *New York Times* reported in late 1991 that most game fish caught in the Great Lakes carry measurable amounts of dioxin, PCBs, and other toxic compounds. "Ten years ago, you couldn't even detect some of the toxics we can measure now," Eichmiller says. "It's like a teaspoon of something in a supertanker full of water. We're finding problems we didn't know we had because our measurements are getting better."

Discovery of these "new" problems created many of the major federal and state laws that drive water quality employment. The following are some of the major laws that will guide your water quality career.

CLEAN WATER ACT OF 1972

Federal involvement in water quality issues goes back to 1948, when Congress began to provide minimal funding for states to construct wastewater treatment facilities. It was not until the Water Pollution Control Act was passed in 1972, however, that the federal government took charge of regulating the quality of the nation's water supplies.

Two major strategies were embodied in the act. First, it mandated that the federal government provide financial assistance for the construction of local sewage treatment plants so that wastewater is treated before it is released into waterways. Second, it required that all industrial and municipal wastewater discharged directly into waterways receive a permit through the National Pollution Discharge Elimination System (NPDES). NPDES permitting has probably created more positions in water quality management than any other single action. The 1972 act also set up regulations governing dredging and filling, known as Section 404 regulations, which have since become the government's key tool for protection of wetlands.

CLEAN WATER ACT AMENDMENTS OF 1987

Responding to renewed public concern for water quality issues, Congress was unusually united in overriding a presidential veto and passing the Clean Water Act amendments in 1987. The new act focused on four main areas.

Water toxins. A key element was a shift of attention to toxic contaminants. These are substances such as heavy metals and organic chemicals that even in low concentrations may have a severe, possibly irreversible, effect on human health, the environment, or both.

Toxins enter water systems in many different ways. These include industrial discharge, urban and rural runoff, and airborne deposition. Acid rain also increases the tendency for certain toxic elements to leach out of the soil and into groundwater.

Nonpoint sources. Another significant change in regulatory emphasis was an increasing attention to nonpoint sources of water pollutants. A point source can be an outfall pipe that dumps factory pollutants from a manufacturing plant, whereas a common nonpoint source is fertilizer and pesticide residue from agricultural lands.

Other nonpoint sources include runoff from construction sites, mining areas, and city streets. In each case, the pollutants cannot be traced to any single identifiable (point) source. The Conservation Foundation estimates that more than half of the nation's water pollutants come from nonpoint sources.

Nonpoint source pollutants include heavy metals, damaging nutrients, sediments, and pesticides. Remedies for nonpoint source pollution are more complicated than those for point source pollution because of the huge number of nonpoint sources. As a result, nonpoint source pollution presents a formidable challenge to policymakers.

Increased state responsibility. The biggest change in the act is a shift of requirements and responsibilities to the states. The bill requires states to identify bodies of water that do not meet water quality standards, create programs to control nonpoint sources of pollution, and identify and regulate sources of toxic contaminants. This approach focuses on specific bodies of water and supplements existing industry-by-industry discharge regulations.

Reduced municipal aid. The amendments phased out federal assistance for construction of municipal wastewater treatment plants, a huge part of the nation's water quality cost. Instead, the federal government is required to provide seed money for loans.

Other job-generating responsibilities under the Clean Water Act amendments include a program for improving water quality in estuaries, aid for lakes damaged by acid rain, tightening of implementation procedures for industrial discharge regulations, and an increased commitment to comply with the Great Lakes Water Quality Agreement.

The community of water quality professionals expects new amendments to the act that will create additional employment. "All indications are that there will be a very interesting Clean Water Act reauthorization coming," says Linda Eichmiller. She estimates that the process will be completed in late 1993 or in 1994.

SAFE DRINKING WATER ACT

Whereas the Clean Water Act focuses on the quality of waterways, the Safe Drinking Water Act (SDWA) regulates the water we consume. The

1986 amendments to the SDWA provide for control of at least 83 trace substances, many of which were unknown when the act was first passed in 1974. Congress also inserted provisions to establish a groundwater protection program, particularly for areas surrounding drinking water wells.

In addition to the major federal water quality acts, there are others worth mentioning. For example, the Marine Protection, Research, and Sanctuaries Act (sometimes called the Ocean Dumping Act) regulates ocean disposal of sludge and industrial waste. Other laws governing airborne toxic emissions, toxic waste, and wildlife protection have broad implications for water quality protection.

ISSUES AND TRENDS

The following are some of the trends influencing the water quality management field in the 1990s.

IMPROVEMENTS IN MONITORING OF TOXINS

The Environmental Protection Agency's National Water Quality Inventory in 1984 included 37 states reporting elevated levels of toxins in some state waters. That number rose to 41 states reporting elevated toxins in the 1990 inventory. Although at first glance this appears clearly to indicate worsening pollution, it is also largely the result of more states investing in costly monitoring equipment and programs, according to Alice Mayio, an environmental protection specialist with the EPA's Office of Wetlands, Oceans, and Watersheds. People with abilities in water sampling and analysis will be needed in large numbers in this field.

INCREASED FOCUS ON CROSS-MEDIA ISSUES

Research suggests a strong link between airborne toxic emissions and water toxins, requiring programs that prevent the release of toxicants into either medium for the protection of both. Says Linda Eichmiller, "The more we know, the more we see that many water quality problems are visited upon us by air deposition of toxics and nutrients." A similar connection exists between land pollution (e.g., hazardous and solid waste disposal) and groundwater contamination.

POLLUTION PREVENTION

Federal, state, and local officials as well as many business leaders agree that cleaning up surface water and groundwater problems is difficult, expensive, and ineffective. In coming years, expect increasingly rigorous programs for pollution prevention and toxic use reduction aimed at keeping toxic and conventional pollutants out of our water in the first place.

CONTINUED WETLANDS LOSS

In spite of wetlands protection activities, the nation is losing these areas at a rate of 200,000 to 300,000 or more acres per year. Consensus is building that this cannot continue, and many areas are not waiting for further federal leadership. Expect a steady increase in local, state, and nonprofit innovations to purchase, protect, and reconstruct wetlands, including the construction of partially artificial wetlands for use as "natural" waste water treatment facilities.

INCREASED URGENCY ABOUT GROUNDWATER CONTAMINATION

More than half of the United States depends on groundwater resources for its drinking supply, and contamination rates are much higher than previously believed. Once contaminated, groundwater is more difficult and expensive to purify than surface water. As local, state, and federal agencies address the problem, expect the following trends to occur:

• The need for accurate information about groundwater contamination will grow. Computer-aided systems to monitor groundwater and project future patterns of contamination will be in high demand. A 1991 General Accounting Office report concludes that much of our groundwater data is unreliable.
• Hazardous waste cleanup projects around Superfund sites, landfills, military bases, and former dumps will focus on groundwater contamination.
• Pressure will grow for well-funded federal and state groundwater protection programs.

These and other groundwater issues will place hydrogeologists, computer modelers, environmental engineers, chemists, and bioremediation specialists in demand.

CONTINUED IMPROVEMENT AT LOCAL
WASTEWATER TREATMENT FACILITIES

"Overflows and bypasses from municipal wastewater treatment facilities are major sources of pollution," says Dave Peters, chief of the program section of the municipal facilities branch of the EPA in Dallas. Alice Mayio of the EPA's Office of Wetlands, Oceans, and Watersheds agrees, noting that in some areas, beach closings or shellfishing bans are caused by large increases in bacterial counts due to inadequately treated wastewater. Effluents from more than half of all U.S. wastewater treatment facilities fail to meet some water quality standards.

City of Hayward wastewater treatment plant, Hayward, California. Settling ponds are used in wastewater treatment.

INNOVATIONS IN NONPOINT SOURCE REDUCTION

As sewage treatment improves, the amount of pollutant-carrying surface runoff becomes an increasing percentage of the remaining pollution, says Jack Liebster of the California Coastal Commission in San Francisco. He reports that water quality in the Los Angeles area is seriously affected by oil, household pesticides, and wastes that accumulate in city streets and are washed into local waters through storm drains. Knowledge is limited about how best to reduce these pollutants, and water quality managers are experimenting with a wide range of planning, educational, regulatory, and enforcement programs.

IMPACT OF NEW TESTING METHODS

The standard tests for human disease hazards in the water supply and in recreational waters often fail to detect significant health threats, says Karen Taberski, an environmental specialist with the San Francisco Bay Regional Water Quality Control Board. "There is very little money spent on pathogen contamination methods," she says. Tests performed in the United States count coliform bacteria, but "viruses cause the most disease problems in more developed countries. Bacterial indicators don't represent or predict this very well." This may create increased demand for microbiologists.

CAREER OPPORTUNITIES

Water quality management is big business. In 1990, the Environmental Protection Agency calculated that the United States spent 2 percent of the gross national product, or $100 billion, to protect and clean up the environment. An article in the *Wall Street Journal* estimated combined expenditures for water infrastructure and utilities in 1991 at $27 billion; these areas thus account for more than 25 percent of all environmental work.

According to Grant Ferrier, editor in chief of the *Environmental Business Journal*, water industry employment for all sectors in 1991 totaled 143,000. He projects employment growth that will average 9 percent per year across the public, private, and nonprofit sectors, creating 55,000 new jobs by 1995 (well above the pace of the national economy in general).

How do these numbers and the trends described earlier translate into demand for people trained in specific disciplines?

- Water and wastewater laboratory technicians, equipment operators, managers, and engineers are still in demand.
- There will be a continued need for traditional water quality professionals: civil, environmental, and chemical engineers.
- Increasing concern about toxins is creating greater demand for people with chemistry backgrounds (chemical engineers and organic and analytical chemists) and also for toxicologists, environmental engineers, and public health and risk assessment specialists.
- There will be plenty of work for industrial engineers knowledgeable in process modification and chemistry to assist industry and government in implementing pollution prevention approaches.
- Groundwater scientists—chemists, hydrogeologists, and geological engineers—cannot be trained quickly enough to fill demand, which continues to grow quickly.

City of Hayward Waste Water Department, Hayward, California. Debora Anderson worked in both the laboratory and the field helping the city of Hayward's wastewater treatment plant conduct tests on wastewater content and treatment efficiency.

- People with strong skills in financial and program management will be needed to effectively manage initiatives that involve the expenditure of millions of dollars.
- Communicators and educators are in greater demand to educate the public in such areas as household hazardous waste disposal and water conservation.
- Watershed management approaches will require fishery and wildlife scientists, wetlands ecologists, and botanists to deal with the water needs of other species.
- Finally, all sectors need analysts, assessment specialists, and experienced managers who understand the relationships among environmental air, water, and waste problems.

PUBLIC SECTOR

Increasing numbers of jobs will appear at the state and local levels of government, while federal efforts will be redirected to emphasize the leadership and policy abilities of its staff rather than its technical expertise.

Federal government. "The EPA is moving toward a stewardship emphasis in Washington," says Rod Frederick, section chief for the EPA's Office of Water Quality Standards. Particularly at the agency's headquarters, he says, the agency is looking for "analysts and budget people in addition to technical folks." Technical strength in the EPA will gradually migrate out to regional offices, which will emphasize watershed approaches to problems rather than narrowly "water"-defined issues. This horizontal approach to managing EPA programs will increase the value of interdisciplinary training.

At the same time, however, the value of engineers will remain considerable. Maureen Delaney, chief of the EPA's National Recruitment Program, predicts that the demand for environmental engineers in all specialties will continue to outstrip supply. "We are [headed] for a work force crunch in the late 1990s and into the next century," she says.

Although the EPA is the major federal employer in water quality management, do not rule out other federal agencies. The U.S. Fish and Wildlife Service, the U.S. Geological Survey, the National Oceanic and Atmospheric Administration, the Soil Conservation Service, the Forest Service, the Bureau of Land Management, and the National Park Service all hire water quality professionals to assist them in protecting fresh and marine waters and in managing their extensive landholdings. The Army Corps of Engineers plays a key role as the agency that approves requests for the Section 404 permits required in order to dredge or fill wetlands.

Researching opportunities in water quality management at the federal level will require some digging but will be time well spent. The National Wildlife Federation's annual *Conservation Directory*, listed in the Resources section at the end of this chapter, and the *Directory of Environmental Information Sources*, listed in chapter 4, are good starting points. Federal agencies also provide career information and lists of job titles of professionals they employ.

State government. As we have seen, the 1987 Clean Water Act amendments significantly shifted responsibility to the states. Peter Piecuch, executive editor of the Water Environment Federation's *Research Journal*, says: "In environmental regulation, the federal government goes through cycles. Right now, there is an emphasis on state regulation, with the federal government setting the broad regulatory outline."

States are fulfilling their federal requirements by adding a variety of new programs that expand in-house personnel and expertise for program planning, development, and research and increase the number of inspection and laboratory personnel to implement and enforce new regulations.

States have also initiated water quality legislation and programs that go well beyond the federal scope, as is the case with so many other environmental issues. Groundwater management strategies now exist or are under development in nearly all states. The emphasis of these programs is on prevention and on developing information on land use and groundwater characteristics. These efforts include mapping of aquifers, development of state classification systems, and monitoring of groundwater quality. With the exception of consulting firms, states are the biggest public employer of groundwater scientists.

A more interdisciplinary professional is needed for nonpoint source pollution control programs, which states must develop with assistance from the EPA. Robbi Savage, executive director of the Association of State and Interstate Water Pollution Control Administrators says: "We need people with a management and scientific background who understand the regulatory and legislative process and also how surface water and groundwater move and interface. Environmental studies might be a useful degree for tackling this problem."

Finally, states are also responding to water quality problems unique to their regions and thus have staffs with corresponding specialties. Midwestern states are concerned with the water quality of the Great Lakes; the West and Southwest are working on issues of water supply; many East Coast and Gulf states are focusing on wetlands acquisition and protection; some of the mountainous states are working on river protection; and coastal states have developed or are developing legislation in response to the degradation of coastal waters and estuaries. If you are interested in employment in a particular region, look closely at the water quality programs and budgets of state governments in that area.

Local government. Ensuring adequate water quality is overwhelmingly a local and regional endeavor. Local units of government carry out two main functions in this field:

1. Treating most commercial, industrial, and residential wastewater that goes into the sewer system before being released into local bodies of water.
2. Purifying water for human use and consumption.

Efficient performance of these two functions at the local level is a goal that the federal government has both promoted and required by providing grants for construction of wastewater treatment facilities and by setting drinking water and wastewater standards. As a result, improvements by local governments have been dramatic. For example, in 1972, before the passage of the Clean Water Act, only 85 million Americans were served by secondary wastewater treatment. Ten years later, 142 million were served, and the number has continued to grow.

The cost, however, has been huge, and a greater and greater proportion of that cost has been borne by local governments. According to *Environment* magazine, expenditures on local wastewater treatment will increase from $37 billion in 1987 to more than $64 billion in the year 2000. This kind of money means an increase in local employment.

The reauthorization and expansion of the Clean Water Act and the Safe Drinking Water Act directly affect local staffing and expertise require-

East Bay Municipal Utility District, Jackson, California. Jonathon Strobel examines EBMUD maps of the Camanche Recreation Area to analyze use patterns of the watershed around the reservoir.

ments. The focus of these two acts on toxic trace chemicals will increase the need for technically oriented people to monitor and analyze water quality more thoroughly and for additional people to design, build, and sell equipment and supplies.

New systems to remove and detect toxic contaminants create additional needs for chemical engineers, industrial engineers, toxicologists, risk assessment specialists, analytical chemists, and organic chemists, as well as continued demand for civil and environmental engineers, the backbone of the wastewater treatment business. Finally, more complicated standards mean more enforcement and inspection personnel.

PRIVATE SECTOR

The same professionals needed by local government for dealing with toxic contaminants will also be in demand by private industries, which must implement pretreatment standards at their facilities.

Corporations. Since 1972, a significant number of large and medium-sized companies have installed their own wastewater treatment plants to comply with federal and state regulations, and these plants must maintain increasingly rigorous technical standards to meet the stricter guidelines. Private spending on wastewater treatment exceeded $4.7 billion in 1990 and continues to grow. Private water treatment facilities face the same issues as municipal plants in employing technicians and professionals.

Consulting firms. A major part of the water quality field, consulting firms handle everything from analysis of specific problems to design, construction, and installation of new systems to maintenance and regulatory paperwork for operating systems. Among all consulting and contract firms, private testing laboratories are a fast-growing part of the water quality management field.

The increased need for technical expertise cited earlier as a result of stricter regulations will also increase the demand for consultants. Chemical engineers, industrial engineers, laboratory specialists, analytical and organic chemists, groundwater scientists, and toxicologists are in demand at consulting companies to help government and industry comply with new requirements.

Consulting firms come in all shapes and sizes, from the one-person firm that handles only wastewater problems for electroplating firms in Chicago to the international firm that handles everything from engineering to economics to environmental remediation and has offices in New York,

London, Tokyo, Paris, and Washington, DC. Often, a large firm will get a federal contract and hire local firms or specialty firms as subcontractors. Entry-level positions are more common with the larger firms, as the smaller companies often do not have the resources to train people.

NONPROFIT SECTOR

Opportunities in water quality work are unusually abundant in the nonprofit sector, at least relative to the total number of environmentally related nonprofit positions. A national network of local, state, and regional groups has spent enormous amounts of time over the past two decades on legal, legislative, educational, and research activities aimed at bringing about effective water quality legislation and systems. And interest in water quality remains high.

According to the West Michigan Environmental Action Council, foundations are funding water quality work, especially for nonpoint source pollution and groundwater activities. Foundations have a lot to do with the issues and organizations that receive funding, so keeping attuned to the environmental priorities of foundations can be one way of measuring where jobs are going to be. Start by examining annual reports of foundations, and talk to veterans of the fund-raising scene.

In addition to carrying out advocacy and policy projects, organizations such as the National Audubon Society and various foundations fund water quality research and habitat restoration by nonprofit organizations and universities. These efforts include monitoring, laboratory analysis, pilot projects, and full-blown wetlands restoration and remediation initiatives. Generally, the work entails scientific research that deals with practical water quality problems and solutions, as opposed to academic research. Good preparation for this field includes field and laboratory skills, a diversified scientific background, and experience in designing and implementing projects.

Academia is also a major force in water quality research and education; jobs are found at universities that have substantial graduate programs in water quality, at community colleges that have technician's programs, and in biology and engineering departments at the undergraduate level.

SALARY

With the exception of particularly "hot" disciplines, such as hydrology and chemical engineering, salaries in water quality management vary less by speciality than by sector and region of the country. Entry-level positions at the local level pay in the mid-20s, and technicians start at around $16,000.

Pay scales in state and federal government are a little better, with entry-level salaries for those with bachelor's degrees close to $30,000 for most disciplines. Engineering degrees typically draw salaries in the $30,000 to $40,000 range. Hydrogeologists have been getting top pay straight out of school for several years, and similar performance will be possible for other specialties in which qualified candidates are in short supply.

Pay for private sector jobs in this field is roughly comparable to that in hazardous waste management, with starting salaries ranging upward from $30,000; groundwater scientists and engineers are at the top of the scale.

Managers in water quality management receive salaries that can be much higher, ranging to $60,000 or more.

GETTING STARTED

New opportunities in the water quality management field are being driven mostly by the new directions in major water quality legislation discussed earlier: reduction of toxic and nonpoint source pollutants, groundwater protection, increased attention to coastal issues and watershed management, efforts to stop wetlands destruction, and general improvements in water treatment standards.

These are some of the emerging issues, and training in these areas will place new entrants to the field in demand. To get your start, begin with a solid education.

EDUCATION

If your goal is to work at a private or public water or wastewater treatment plant, your best bet may be a two-year technician's degree at a community college. Community colleges are rapidly increasing the quality and quantity of their programs.

Concern over toxic materials in effluent, runoff, and groundwater is creating positions for people with the scientific and technical backgrounds to detect trace toxins, analyze the public health and environmental impacts of the toxins, and design methods of removing these contaminants from the water. Good backgrounds for this work include analytical and organic chemistry; toxicology; chemical, industrial, and environmental engineering; mathematics; and risk assessment. An advanced degree is sometimes needed.

As in many other fields, environmental engineers are required through-out the water quality management field. Further advances in pollution prevention approaches will require more process and industrial engineers as well.

Groundwater scientists are in extremely high demand. These profes-sionals monitor groundwater quantity and quality, develop computer mod-eling of groundwater flow, and engage in treatment of polluted groundwater. Hydrogeologists with advanced degrees and some experi-ence are among the most sought after and lucratively paid environmental workers. The most common undergraduate degrees in this field are geol-ogy, civil engineering, and chemistry. Most of those with undergraduate degrees find jobs doing on-site sampling and measurement. Undergradu-ate course work should include geology, groundwater engineering, water chemistry, inorganic chemistry, engineering hydrology, and calculus.

People with both undergraduate and advanced degrees in biology and chemistry are still needed in the water quality field, especially those who have taken strong laboratory and fieldwork classes in college.

Beyond technical requirements, another education is needed. Jack Lieb-ster of the California Coastal Commission sees an educational shift in the making. "There is a lot of engineering that needs to be done, but I think there is an emerging dimension of people who are essentially educators and communicators and who can create change in people's behavior," he says. "That is a new addition to the army of people necessary to solve our environmental problems." Steve Bagwell of the Water Environment Feder-ation in Alexandria, Virginia, agrees. New entrants to the field "need to understand how their work relates to the goals of our society, and they need to be able to communicate with communities about how and why things are happening."

ADVICE

Advice is a form of free education. However, you must sift through it to find what is useful to you. Here are some pre-sifted opinions of value to those seeking careers in water quality management.

Internships are essential. "Intern wherever you can, even if you don't get paid for it," says Liebster. "Get out there into the real world, not to supplant but to complement your education. Do it early and do it often. Hiring managers like experience, even in a new graduate."

Master technology. Become familiar with emerging high-technology tools. Learn to be comfortable with daily use of computers if you have not already done so, and explore some of the applications available in your field. Some of the most interesting computer work in water quality management involves new methods of determining groundwater movement that are greatly accelerating contaminant tracking. Knowledge of new areas such as this one will help you immensely.

Start specific. As in many environmental fields, if you have a B.A. or a B.S., entry-level jobs are easiest to find if you possess specific, technical field and laboratory skills. "Employers don't know what to do with an entry-level generalist," one professional offers. Those with master's degrees have broader options. Many consulting firms need research, laboratory and field technicians and hire entry-level workers, especially inspectors and laboratory technicians away from municipal wastewater treatment facilities, water purification plants, and health departments.

. . . But stay flexible. "Don't become too niche-minded and get into a narrow career path," warns Jon DeBoer of the American Water Resources Association. "The needs are very broad and the emphasis changes, so developing a broad background allows you to direct yourself in any number of pathways."

SUMMARY

Of all the environmental fields covered in this book, water quality management is among the most wide open as far as range and number of opportunities are concerned. Scientists and policymakers are still working to implement early water quality efforts, and a second generation of programs focused on toxins, groundwater, and nonpoint sources is now upon them. Whether you become a planner, a scientist, an engineer, a manager, or a lawyer or choose some other direction, the field of water quality management has a place for your skills.

CASE STUDY

International Cooperation Saving the Great Lakes

The roots of pollution in the Great Lakes are old. Dr. John Hartig, environmental scientist with the International Joint Commission in Windsor, Ontario, traces the issues back to waterborne diseases in the early years of this century and up through the large-scale visible pollution of the 1950s and 1960s, the phosphorus and eutrophication of the 1970s and 1980s, and the attention on toxic contamination of the 1990s. "The issues have changed as a result of pollution control and advances in science," he says. Pollution in the Great Lakes, as elsewhere, is a floating target. As each issue surfaces, is identified, and eradicated, another comes into view.

During the 1970s, water quality progress was already under way in the Great Lakes but at a pace too slow for many. Sewage discharge was still an issue, and industrial wastes of every type poured into the region's five vast lakes from rivers and streams and rained down from polluted skies. Lake Erie was pronounced dead, and the fish from some of the lakes were considered to be unsafe to eat due to accumulations of lead, mercury, PCBs, and other toxic chemicals.

Noah Eiger of The Center for the Great Lakes in Chicago says that the improvement began in 1972 with the Great Lakes Water Quality Agreement. This document states that national governments, states, and provinces of the region are responsible for setting and meeting pollutant guidelines to improve water quality. Progress took time, but the agreement marked a turning point in regional and international cooperation—a team began to form. Organizations that worked separately at first gradually began to work together. States, provinces, and environmental groups worked cooperatively, and binational organizations formed.

Eiger notes that the process has presented some difficulties: "The U.S. and Canadian governments make good efforts to work together, but different administrative systems and policies make joint efforts a challenge," he says. For example, "there are no Canadian counterparts to U.S. permits. The Canadians use consent decrees to control polluters."

By 1980, a number of environmental organizations had formed a coalition and begun to hold meetings to organize their activities. "We have meetings at least once or twice a year and share what each organization wants to propose and decide how we can work together," says Bill Brah, president of The Center for the Great Lakes. "Although [the coalition] comes across as a bunch of overlapping organizations, most of them consider one another allies. When we pull together, we can be formidable."

Teamwork has been essential, as U.S. federal funding for the program began dropping off just as the effort began to work. Brah says that this lack of priority turned around only in 1990, with the identification of the region as a focal point for water quality improvement. EPA administrator William Reilly, an Illinois native, decided that the Great Lakes could be a model for pollution programs—a national laboratory for an ecosystem approach to environmental quality.

That decision changed a proposed 1991 budget cut of $130 million for the lakes program into a 1992 budget increase of $19 million, with a further increase of $10 million projected for 1993, says Brah. "This indicates a shift in federal priorities, and it took an incredible effort by a number of groups to do it."

Action by the diverse coalition of governments and organizations has taken on the same themes as many other successful antipollution programs—stop pollutants at the source. "The new theme is recycle or reuse resources, remediate sediments and hazardous waste sites, and restore habitat," says Hartig.

Point and nonpoint source control of phosphorus pollution is credited with much of the improvement in Lake Erie and Saginaw Bay. Expenditures of $9 billion on phosphorus control slowed eutrophication of the upper Great Lakes and allowed considerable recovery in fish stocks.

But the process of bringing back the Great Lakes will be a long-term effort. Some have charged that at current spending levels, it will be 100 years before fish from the lakes are fit to eat. The International Joint Commission lists 43 toxic "hot spots" around the lakes. Even Lake Huron, the most remote of the five lakes, has four sites on the list, with two more on the waterways connecting it with other lakes.

Tracking toxic hot spots and polluted fish are examples of how environmental organizations intend to keep attention focused on the problem. The communication vehicles in use now include workshops, conferences, reports, newsletters, dedicated libraries, and media attention. Keeping the issues in the public eye has served well in this increasingly environmentally conscious time as citizens come to believe in the value of a healthy environment.

There is a growing awareness of the fragility of this huge shared system of lakes. Further, there is an appreciation for the fact that even the Great Lakes system, the world's largest body of fresh water, is not so large as to be immune from serious damage. This sense of the finite with regard to such a huge ecosystem is drawing the region together.

"We have looked at the various parts of this ecosystem as being separate compartments," says Judith Stockdale, executive director of the Great Lakes Protection Fund in Chicago. "But studying the Great Lakes teaches us that we are all connected. The effects of pollution on the Great Lakes show up more easily than elsewhere because this is a closed system. The problems are no different from [those in] other places, but you see the results sooner."

Public concern is generating increased funding to support the cleanup of the lakes, creating new career opportunities around the region. "The need for professionals will be phenomenal!" asserts Hartig. "We have to make sure we have the scientists and engineers to prevent pollution at the source and to use creative rehabilitation techniques at contaminated sites. We also need help to better understand integrated resource management. We need to have students come out who can work in interdisciplinary teams—there is a need for that now, and I only see it growing in the future."

PROFILES

David Powless
President
Ortek
Green Bay, Wisconsin

Environmental testing laboratories are a crucial part of the water quality management field, providing chemistry services for private and public wastewater treatment plants and assisting corporations and governments in a wide array of pollution assessment projects. Ortek, however, is not just any testing laboratory.

"There is nothing without water in it," says David A. Powless, head of Ortek, a Green Bay, Wisconsin, environmental testing company owned by the Oneida Indian Tribe. "Water is the blood of the Mother Earth. It is our duty to care for the waters as if it were our own blood—because it is."

Powless believes that Native Americans have a philosophical advantage in working to improve the environment. For him and for his tribe, "healing the earth" is no idle phrase. "Environmental problems exist because humans have not shown respect for the Mother Earth. If we do not learn respect, the Mother Earth will still be here, but we will not be here."

The Oneida Tribe purchased Ortek in 1988, when it had annual sales of $600,000 and 11 employees, none of them Native Americans. By February 1992, Ortek had increased sales to nearly $3 million and employed 64 people, of whom 38 were Native Americans. "Ortek is a nationally recognized environmental testing laboratory [that receives] water, soil, and other samples from every state in the country," says Powless. "We rank in the top 10 percent in sales and quality."

Heading up Ortek is the third successful career for Powless. The first followed close on the heels of his degrees in marketing and economics at the University of Illinois. The 1963 Rose Bowl propelled Powless into professional football with the New York Giants and Washington Redskins, until a back injury brought his career to an early end.

Career number two began with a National Science Foundation grant and work at the Colorado School of Mines on a process to recover hazardous wastes from steel mills. Two businesses resulted. And now he has Ortek, along with closer ties to his tribal origins.

"The whole program we are developing at Ortek is in alignment with our traditional culture," Powless says. That program includes employing Indians and non-Indians. It also provides Native Americans aged 18 to 50 who have high school and college educations with intensive training and environmental career development.

Ortek employees have previously worked in child care, construction, and printing and in raising children. They are trained to work in nondegreed positions running the latest in automated test equipment. "We have a woman who was a cook working for the tribe, and now she is an extraction chemist. She is taking chemistry, microbiology, computers, and laboratory math courses, and she loves her work."

Further expansion is planned. The Oneida Tribe is discussing a program called Shared Technology and Research (STAR) with other tribes. Powless and the Oneidas want to set up laboratories to be run by other tribes and have discussed their ideas with tribes in New York, New Mexico, Washington, and Florida.

"We intend to have five laboratories networked together on reservations, all doing environmental testing and employing Indian and non-Indian people. As Native Americans, this is what we can do. We take care of the Mother Earth and give her our thanksgiving for what she has provided for all of creation."

Richard McLean
Deputy Executive Director for
Resource Regulation
Southwest Florida Water Management
District
Tampa, Florida

Water management districts, like this one in Florida, create and implement comprehensive approaches to water use and water quality protection. For professionals who want to be "close to the action," local agencies like these are a good choice.

In a state that receives 52 inches of rain per year, Richard McLean is worried about running out of water. He is worried because Florida's environment evolved with that much rainfall. The porous limestone bedrock and sandy soil act as a vast sponge through which flows a network of subsurface rivers, or aquifers. He worries because human disruption of that aquifer network threatens the very qualities that draw people to his state in droves.

As deputy executive director for resource regulation with the Southwest

Florida Water Management District, McLean and others in his agency protect water quality for one-quarter of Florida's population. His responsibilities stretch from near the Florida panhandle in the north and down the Gulf Coast as far south as Charlotte Harbor. Across this prized portion of the state, people, industry, mining, construction, and agriculture place a huge burden on delicately balanced water resources. His goal: "We want to ensure that water use does not degrade the aquifer."

In Florida, one of the fastest-growing regions of the United States, so much water is taken from the underground rivers that in the central "highlands," some lake water levels have dropped 14 feet, says McLean. "There are docks 300 to 400 yards away from the water now. Some say it's a lack of rain, but I think it is large draws from wells all over the area taking the water table down. And if you happen to live on one of those lakes, you are not too fond of the problem."

High-quality fresh water in Florida moves in shallow aquifers running southward through the state. Below the best aquifers are others that carry fresh water of poor quality, and near the shoreline are lateral intrusions of subsurface salt water held in check by the freshwater flow. Drawing down freshwater aquifers too far pulls high-sulfate water up from below or pulls salt water over from the shore.

Managing water use involves controlling the drawdowns to minimize intrusion of poor-quality water and avoid permanent loss of wells to sea water when excessive water use moves the freshwater-saltwater interface inland permanently. "It may take years for the salt water to get to a well, but once it does, the well is shot," says McLean. The battle is one he believes in.

It is a battle of selectively controlling or even denying what some people want in order to protect what they have all come here to enjoy. The district controls water use activities through permits. Permitting in the district covers almost any new water use of any disturbance that might affect the water, such as construction of wells, roads, or storm sewers or other activities that create flooding or impact wetlands.

McLean spends half of every day working on the emergency issues that arise in each day's schedule. Planning and policy work take up a little more than one-third of his typical workday, and he spends the remainder of his time working with his 200-person staff.

"The district is the only place I've ever worked," he says. "I started as a water resource planner and worked my way up through the ranks." McLean studied marine biology at the University of West Florida and mixed environmental engineering, water chemistry, solid waste, biology, and microbiology in his master's degree work at the University of Florida in Gainesville.

"This is definitely a growing field," he says. "And just about any of the science or engineering specialties can lead you to it."

Pat Mulholland
Aquatic Ecologist
Environmental Sciences Division
Oak Ridge National Laboratory
Oak Ridge, Tennessee

Research scientists help increase our understanding of water's role in the environment, its fragility, and how human activities can be altered to maintain its quality. Such scientists work in a wide array of private and public organizations.

Picture yourself hiking along a stream in the Great Smoky Mountains. There is snow on the ground and the quiet beauty of an expectant early spring in the crisp air—the scene is hauntingly beautiful.

On the other hand, you are carrying 60 pounds of batteries, pumps, and testing chambers in your pack. You have slipped into the stream and are wet and getting chilled. You are trying to select just the right place to study stream ecology, to set up the chambers and pumps, to collect algae. You are hoping that the equipment will all work and this will not be a frustrating excursion, as are some of these trips. You are Pat Mulholland, aquatic ecologist and research staff member in the Environmental Sciences Division at Oak Ridge National Laboratory in Oak Ridge, Tennessee.

He drags equipment through snow and icy streams in search of knowledge in areas where our understanding of natural systems is scanty at best. "I'm particularly interested in nutrient cycling in streams and rivers," Pat says. "What regulates the entry of nutrients into streams? What regulates groundwater transport and how groundwater interacts with surface water? There is some information in this area, but it is not as well understood as it needs to be to address environmental problems."

The issues that concern Mulholland include the following:

- Defining the routes water takes through groundwater pathways to surface water. How do hydrological processes influence what gets through?
- Nutrient transport, including the mobility and movement of nitrates and phosphate.
- Biological and geochemical processes that regulate transport in soil, groundwater, and surface water. How do biological and geochemical processes influence the movement of problem substances?

The disciplines Mulholland brings to bear in his research include chemistry, environmental chemistry, hydrology and hydrogeology, microbial and algae ecology, and biogeochemistry.

As an undergraduate civil engineering student at Cornell University, Mulholland found himself fascinated with natural systems. He stayed on and earned a master's degree in environmental engineering, then moved to the University of North Carolina at Chapel Hill for his Ph.D. in aquatic biology.

Mulholland divides his average day equally among paperwork, thinking and writing, discussing ideas with colleagues and designing experiments, and conducting field or laboratory research. "I enjoy experimentation," he says. "It is an opportunity to think creatively about problems and design experiments to answer a question. I enjoy the whole analytical approach to trying to extrapolate information you gain on one scale to bigger and broader issues. I have the freedom to explore and design the kind of work I want to do."

Mulholland feels that many of the most important areas of environmental work cut across traditional disciplines. But that work needs to be done against a background of basic studies in chemistry, physics, biology, and mathematics. First, he advises, get basics in hand; then go after the interdisciplinary work.

"Issues of waste mobility and transport, and transport of agricultural chemicals and fertilizer to surface waters, will be very big issues. Those trained in these areas will be in demand with both government agencies and consulting firms."

RESOURCES

American Water Resources Association. A multidisciplinary organization dedicated to the advancement of research, planning, management, development, and education in water resources. Publishes *Water Resources Bulletin* (bimonthly), an annual association directory, and many special publications. 5410 Grosvenor Ln., Suite 220, Bethesda, MD 20814.

American Water Works Association. Organization for water works professionals. Publishes *American Water Works Association Journal* (monthly), which includes regulatory summaries, conference information, and job listings. Has state chapters, annual meetings, and special publications. 6666 W. Quincy Ave., Denver, CO 80235. (303) 794–7711.

Association of State and Interstate Water Pollution Control Administrators. The national professional organization of state water quality program administrators. Has many special publications on water quality issues in the United States. Holds membership meetings twice annually and seminars. 750 1st St., NE, Suite 910, Washington, DC 20002. (202) 898–0905.

Association of State Drinking Water Administrators, 1911 North Fort Meyer Dr., Suite 400, Arlington, VA 22209, (703) 524–2428.

Clean Water Action. A national citizens' organization working for clean and safe water. Needs volunteers to assist with computer data entry and donor research. 1320 18th St., NW, Washington, DC 20036–1811. (202) 457–1286.

Clean Water Report. CIE Associates, 237 Gretna Green Ct., Alexandria, VA 22304.

Freshwater Foundation. Publishes *U.S. Water News* (monthly), *Health & Environmental Digest* (monthly), and *Facets of Freshwater* (monthly). 725 County Rd. 6, Wayvata, MN 55391.

Journal of Soil and Water Conservation. Soil and Water Conservation Society, 7515 N.E. Ankeny Rd., Ankeny, IA 50021. (515) 289–2331.

National Ground Water Association. Professional association for those involved in groundwater protection. Publishes *The Well Log* (monthly newsletter) and *Water Well Journal* (monthly). Runs Job Mart, a job placement service. 6375 Riverside Dr., Dublin, OH 43017. (614) 761–1711.

National Wildlife Federation Conservation Directory. Has a section on the EPA. Published yearly; $18 plus $3.50 shipping per order. 1400 16th St., NW, Washington, DC 20036–2266. (800) 432–6564.

The Center for the Great Lakes. Publishes *The Great Lakes Directory of Natural Resource Agencies and Organizations*, produced for the center in 1984 by the Freshwater Foundation. Profiles hundreds of organizations working on natural resource management around the Great Lakes. 35 E. Wacker Dr., Suite 1870, Chicago, IL 60601.

Water Environment Federation. An international nonprofit educational and technical organization of 36,000 water quality professionals. Produces a products and services catalog that describes various educational training materials and industry-oriented publications offered by the WEF. A pamphlet titled "Test the Waters! Careers in Water Quality" is available on request. 601 Wythe St., Alexandria, VA 22314.

Water Quality Association. An international trade association representing more than 2,500 dealers and manufacturers of point-of-use water quality improvement technologies. 4151 Naperville Rd., Lisle, IL 60532.

Water Resources Review. U.S. Geological Survey, MS 20, 12201 Sunrise Valley Dr., Reston, VA 22092. (703) 860–6127.

Part IV

NATURAL RESOURCE MANAGEMENT

11 Land and Water Conservation

AT A GLANCE

Employment:
35,000 professionals in all sectors nationwide (includes some overlap with fields discussed in other chapters)

Demand:
1 to 5 percent growth through the 1990s

Breakdown:
Public sector, 75 percent
Private sector, 6 percent
Nonprofit sector, 19 percent

Key Job Titles:
Biologist
Ecologist
Environmental planner
Geographic information systems specialist
Land acquisition professional
Land trust or preserve manager
Lawyer
Natural resource manager
Soil conservation specialist

Influential Organizations:
Ecological Society of America
National Audubon Society

National Wildlife Federation
Natural Resources Council of America
Soil and Water Conservation Society
The Nature Conservancy
The Wilderness Society
Trust for Public Land

Salary:
   Entry-level salaries start as low as $12,000 to $18,000 but range up to
   $50,000 to $60,000 for those with experience and advanced degrees.
   Average salaries are around $27,000 to $34,000.

Just 300 years ago, the United States was a great wilderness. Huge stands
of ancient forest, a vast, uncharted prairie, millions of acres of wetlands,
and miles of pristine rivers and streams defined the American landscape.
Today, most of that original environment is permanently altered. Through
the work of today's land and water conservation professionals, however,
damaged land and water are being restored and remaining wild areas are
being preserved for the future.

WHAT IS LAND AND WATER CONSERVATION?

For many people, land and water conservation is the protection of wildlands, pure and simple. By this definition, conservationists have done their
work when land and water are preserved as much as possible in a pristine
state and protected from both use and abuse by human beings.

   Sharon Newsome, vice president of resources and conservation for the
National Wildlife Federation, defines the field more broadly as "making
sure that in our use of land and water, we do not hamper its ability to
support a diversity of wildlife, both now and in the future."

   To ensure the realization of this goal, a wide range of professionals,
government agencies, and organizations are involved in the conservation
and preservation of land and water resources. These people include natural resource managers, environmental planners, environmental advocates,
lawyers, ecologists, and land acquisition professionals, to name a few. They
work for a variety of employers, including local park systems, conservation districts, state agencies, private land trusts, consulting firms, the
federal government, and nonprofit organizations. The field of land and
water conservation draws on environmental protection, resource management, habitat restoration, pollution prevention, planning and education,
and many other areas.

A systematic listing of all professions involved in land and water conservation would include nearly every occupation described in this book. The following are some of the major types of work being done in the field.

PLANNING

A spectrum of planners are involved in local, regional, and national conservation efforts. These include environmental, land-use, water quality, and natural resource planners (see chapter 5 for a thorough discussion of the planning profession).

NATURAL RESOURCE ASSESSMENT AND MANAGEMENT

Natural resource assessment means inventorying flora, fauna, ecosystems, and watershed systems and other natural resources to produce databases and geographic information systems for informed decision making. Management of natural resources involves balancing human pressures with the conservation of land and water resources.

HABITAT PROTECTION AND RESTORATION

Protecting habitats in a watershed or an ecosystem involves limiting environmental contaminants, including acid rain, agricultural pesticide runoff into rivers, and hazardous waste dumping. Restoring damaged habitats can mean reforestation, decontamination, imposition of strict limitations on human uses, reintroduction of native species, and other active interventions.

PRESERVING OPEN SPACES AND NATURAL HABITATS

Some professionals work to ensure that land, water, or whole ecosystems are saved from development or extensive recreational use by outright purchase. Nonprofit land trusts generally work on a small scale, whereas professionals at state and federal land agencies designate and manage millions of acres for long-term conservation.

HISTORY AND BACKGROUND

An organized conservation effort began in the United States around the start of this century with concern for preservation of scenic western lands and issues such as the decimation of bird populations for fashionable clothing. Ladies' hats of the period often featured an entire stuffed bird or copious amounts of plumage from large southeastern waterfowl.

A growing sense that America was in danger of losing irreplaceable wilderness areas and the values they represented for both people and wildlife triggered formation of groups such as the Audubon Society and the Sierra Club, both formed in the 1890s.

Since then, land and water conservation has been among the most visible of all environmental fields, in part because the general public remains concerned about development pressures on open lands, recreational access, and loss of natural places. In the past three decades, nearly every metropolitan area has seen intense debate over protection of remaining agricultural lands, scenic areas, and wildlands.

As Ed Becker of the Essex County (Massachusetts) Greenbelt Association points out: "The public is taking a more holistic view of environment and resource protection and demanding appropriate action. It's as if the education and work of the past twenty years is coming to fruition. This is quite encouraging for professionals who want to get involved in this field."

LEGISLATION

Land and water conservation laws range from wildlife protection laws to regulations governing mining on government lands to legislation establishing wilderness areas, where activities disruptive of wildlife are prohibited. Compliance with laws such as the following is a major generator of employment in land and water conservation.

Forest Management Act. This act regulates use of national forest lands, including recreation as well as development of timber, mining, oil, and gas resources.

Federal Land Policy Management Act. The purpose of this act is to regulate management of federal land outside the National Forest System for recreational activities and resource development.

1872 Mining Law. This legislation regulates recovery of mineral resources from federal lands.

Wilderness Act. This act sets aside federal lands where mining, oil and gas exploitation and motorized vehicles are strictly prohibited.

Alaska National Interests Lands Conservation Act. This 1980 act increased Alaska's national lands system from one national park, two national monuments, and a few refuges to eight national parks, ten national preserves, four national monuments, nine national wildlife refuges, and 25 wild and scenic rivers.

Local and state land-use plans. The land- and water-use plans of local governments are among the most influential conservation laws in the nation. Outside of federally owned and state-owned lands, most protection in the United States must come from local laws.

These are just a few of the laws guiding conservation activities. Nearly all of the major laws mentioned elsewhere in this book have an influence on the land and water conservation field's successes and challenges.

ISSUES AND TRENDS

As in many of the other specialties within the environmental field, issues and trends point the way toward the areas where jobs will be in demand during the years ahead. Anticipating and following these changes will increase your value within the field.

INFLUENCE OF ECONOMIC CONDITIONS

Efforts to control land use are cyclical. The early 1970s saw a lot of concern in this field, but conservation efforts died out as the economy slumped. Since that time, there has been a multiyear boom of development that stimulated more conservation, followed by the recession of 1989–1992. During periods of booming development, people do not like to see change happen quickly and are driven to action because the open land next to them is being developed. Therefore, look for employment growth in areas with fast-growing economies.

INCREASED EFFECTIVENESS

Conservation efforts have become more sophisticated and productive. Land trusts dedicated to acquiring land for preservation have grown in number. State legislatures have passed comprehensive growth management legislation that mandates planning and inventorying, land acquisition, and often stringent curbs on development seen as detrimental to an area's character or a particular natural resource. As gains are institutionalized, the need for organized management grows.

DEBATE OVER PRIORITIES

At the federal level, the Land and Water Conservation Fund, started in 1965, has spent billions of dollars in matching grant programs, but it has been criticized because funds are often used for capital projects rather than for land acquisition. Some in Congress are working to establish a new fund, structured as an endowment, to acquire land and make grants to state and local governments for land acquisition efforts.

GROWING COOPERATION

There is an increasing number of cooperative ventures in land acquisition and preservation efforts. The Nature Conservancy, for example, often buys the development rights on a piece of land and holds the property until a government agency can work through the red tape to acquire it.

INCREASED SOPHISTICATION

The process of managing natural areas is becoming more technical, holistic, and complicated as part of a slow but fundamental change in the manner in which resources are managed. As a botanist with the Ohio Department of Natural Resources says: "It used to be you would acquire a piece of land and say, 'All right, we have a natural area.' Now we are realizing you can't just let that area sit and expect it to be the same 20 years from now—that area needs to be planned for and managed." Steve Starland, manager of the state of Washington's Scenic Rivers Program, comments: "It used to be we managed separately the trees, the fish, and the wildlife. Now, we need people to figure out how to put it all together. There are whole new fields developing."

ECOSYSTEM RESTORATION

Land and water conservation professionals are going beyond preserving and managing natural areas. Today's field might entail recreating a destroyed ecosystem, significantly altering a natural area, or creating an "artificial" ecosystem. One example of the latter is using wetland areas as "natural" wastewater purification systems. Other projects involve restoring prairies, planting local flora along highways, reintroducing wildlife to an area, or getting rid of non-native wildlife and vegetation. Engineers, biologists, botanists, ecologists, and landscape architects are involved in such projects. There are few areas not altered by humans, so biologists increasingly are setting out to recreate ecosystems.

USE OF COMPUTERS

Large-scale geographic information systems (GIS) and computer-assisted mapping are computerized database applications that allow users to locate many different types of information about parcels of land. In addition to natural features, GIS specialists track the location of underground storage tanks, aquifers, and wells; hazardous waste sites; and current uses of particular land parcels. These systems are likely to change dramatically the professions of environmental planning and natural resource management. A variety of professionals, including field biologists, cartographers, geologists, geographers, natural resource specialists, and computer personnel, are working to develop, maintain, and use these systems.

CAREER OPPORTUNITIES

With few exceptions, it would be misleading to describe any positions in this field as "hot jobs," meaning that available positions are far in excess of talented applicants. For one thing, those in land and water conservation tend to stay in their jobs longer than workers in many other environmental fields. For another, there has been a limited number of new land and water conservation initiatives from the federal government since 1980. Nonetheless, there are many challenging opportunities in every sector.

PUBLIC SECTOR

The public sector heavily dominates land and water conservation by accounting for some 75 percent of employment in the discipline. The federal government is a major employer in the conservation field.

Federal government. Federal landholding agencies own 700 million acres of land, roughly one-third of all land in the United States. The federal government is far and away the largest single employer of land and water conservation professionals. Conservation on these lands is managed primarily by six agencies within the U.S. Department of the Interior:

- Bureau of Land Management
- U.S. Fish and Wildlife Service
- National Park Service
- Bureau of Indian Affairs

- Bureau of Reclamation
- U.S. Geological Survey

Taken together, the Interior Department employs more than 74,000 professionals. Major holdings are also managed by the U.S. Department of Agriculture's Forest Service, which employs 36,000 full-time and 8,000 temporary workers. The Soil Conservation Service, the Tennessee Valley Authority, the Department of Energy, and, of course, the various components of the Department of Defense round out the federal picture.

The military will be needing more conservation professionals in the next few years. In addition to the day-to-day management of the thousands of acres in military bases owned by the Department of Defense, Congress has mandated an aggressive program of inventorying the natural resources of the military's landholdings. The Legacy Program will grow in importance because inventories will be required before the government can close and sell unneeded installations. Millions of dollars will be spent in this effort.

With minor exceptions such as this, none of the major federal land and water conservation agencies is expected to experience significant growth through the mid- to late 1990s. Positions, however, will still be available due to normal attrition and newly funded programs created by Congress.

What kind of land and water conservation professionals work for federal agencies? Robert Chandler, superintendent of Grand Canyon National Park, points out that each national park has a resource management division that does planning, environmental compliance activities, project design, and monitoring of resource management activities. At one park, there are four resource management specialists making sure that projects are completed as designed. The park also has a natural sciences studies group that includes wildlife biologists, fishery biologists, botanists, and biologists, all of whom conduct research activities. Says Chandler: "Over the last several years the National Park Service, at the administration as well as congressional levels, has realized the importance of resource management activities and has put more money into addressing these problems. Unfortunately, competition is tough for resource management jobs."

According to a wilderness coordinator with the Forest Service, recreational demands could boost federal hiring in the near future. "There is an ever-growing need for recreation in this country. Since we aren't acquiring new acreage to expand into, we intensify our efforts in managing what we have. This is eventually going to create new federal natural resource opportunities."

The Soil Conservation Service of the U.S. Department of Agriculture has a presence in virtually every county in the United States and is a quietly effective force in the conservation field. The 14,000 employees of the service work in partnership with local soil conservation districts to reduce soil erosion and pollution from soil runoff and to manage storm water. Other responsibilities include administering federal programs such as the Small Watershed Protection Program, the Rural Abandoned Mine Program, the Resource Conservation and Development Program, and the erosion requirements of the Food Security Act of 1985, or the Farm Bill. The service primarily hires soil scientists, agricultural and civil engineers, and biologists.

State government. "We try to balance different interests on the river, with varying degrees of success," says Steve Starland of Washington's Scenic Rivers Program. "Some want to dam up the river for hydropower; others want powerboating. Then there are the canoeists and hikers, commercial fishermen, and those who want the river kept in as natural a state as possible. We must decide the priorities, since you can't satisfy everyone."

State professionals involved in this process include planners (natural

State Coastal Conservancy, Oakland, California. Richard Retecki analyzes California coastal development with Mark Wheetley.

resource, urban, land-use, and recreational); general resource managers; resource specialists (water quality and hazardous waste management professionals and fishery and wildlife biologists) who offer data and help clarify specific problems; educators; and public involvement specialists. Another type of professional is a facilitator. This person, not necessarily trained in formal mediation skills, must have independent knowledge and background on the subject in question and must be able to bring together different groups and agencies at the table.

These professionals work in a variety of state agencies, from traditional departments of natural resources to state environmental protection agencies and departments of parks and recreation and agriculture, or in special bodies such as coastal commissions or watershed districts.

A key service of state governments is the administration of natural heritage programs. These programs are designed to identify and preserve biological diversity within a state by tracking the status and distribution of rare and natural elements and making this information available to policymakers and the public. The impetus and staffing for natural heritage programs originally came from The Nature Conservancy. This nonprofit organization works with state natural resource departments nationwide in its efforts to preserve biological diversity.

Forty-eight states now have such programs. Susan Crispin, now director of The Nature Conservancy of Canada, coordinated five full-time staff members and two to six seasonal interns when she worked for the Michigan Natural Features Inventory. "We conducted county-by-county surveys to find rare natural plants and maintained a database that is used by local, state, and federal agencies as well as developers and environmental activists. A typical information request might be something like 'What is the most important wetland community in the state?'" Michigan's program employs field biologists and ecologists who understand the ecology of communities and ecosystems and work in a new field called conservation biology.

States vary greatly in their involvement in natural heritage programs, and some people wonder whether states will maintain this level of commitment to conservation in less healthy economic times. If you are considering entering the public sector in this field, follow these issues closely.

Local government. Agencies and citizens are becoming more involved in the conservation and management of natural resources at a local level. However, expect significant variation in the level of activity from region to region and even among neighboring municipalities.

Local government activity takes place on a number of fronts. Towns and regions are expending resources to plan where they want to be in the

LAND AND WATER CONSERVATION   257

future—developing master plans and working to implement them through zoning and development regulation as well as land acquisition and conservation strategies. The work of some of these planners is outlined in chapter 5.

Assisting these local efforts are lawyers with experience in real estate and conservation issues, real estate professionals, planners, and natural resource staff members, who manage land owned by land trusts and local units of government. Positions are also being created by local units of government and conservation districts to enforce environmental and natural resource regulations.

Another local presence is soil and water conservation districts. There are 3,000 of these districts nationwide, and they are staffed by a combination of local and state personnel as well as federal employees of the Soil Conservation Service. They work with individual landowners and units of government to reduce soil erosion, preserve long-term viability of the land, and limit nonpoint source water pollution. Urban conservation districts work on such issues as storm water management and nonpoint source erosion and toxic pollution from development and redevelopment activities.

Small but valuable natural areas are managed by local agencies. Tom Stanley of the Cleveland Metroparks System says: "Organizations and agencies with relatively smaller parcels of land under their jurisdiction are hiring people to plan and implement natural resource management; places like arboretums and nature centers are no longer viewed as collections of plants but as ecosystems. This may be just one person, and [his or her] responsibilities might include fixing the chain saw, but it is a position where one previously did not exist."

Indian nations. Indian nations own and manage significant parcels of land in the West and hire the gamut of land and water conservation professionals, especially natural resource managers and specialists. Contact these tribes separately, as each has its own hiring procedures.

PRIVATE SECTOR

Utilities, timber companies, and consulting firms make up the private sector in conservation. They employ a small number of conservation professionals.

Utilities and timber companies. Timber companies and utilities manage large tracts of land across the United States. Utility companies often leave significant portions of the land they use relatively undisturbed, making it available for plants and wildlife. Timber companies have very large pieces of land that for years at a time lie relatively undisturbed. Wetlands within timber tracts, for instance, must be preserved.

Consulting firms. Consulting work in the land and water conservation field is less common than in the environmental protection fields. Nevertheless, corporations and government agencies look to consultants for expertise not found on staff. Consulting firms work primarily with government agencies but also with corporations and utilities that have large parcels of land to manage. Much of the work done by consulting firms in land and water conservation will revolve around specialties covered in other chapters: water quality management, hazardous waste management, forestry, and planning.

Other areas in which consultants are getting involved include habitat and ecosystem restoration and provision of expert testimony in legal action. One factor limiting consulting work in this field is that government agencies often contract work to universities that might otherwise go to consultants. Entry-level consulting jobs are difficult to find in this area. It is far more common for experienced professionals to leave a public sector career to join a consulting business.

NONPROFIT SECTOR

During the 1980s, an increasing number of natural resource management jobs became available with private nonprofit organizations such as nature centers, arboretums, community land trusts, and national organizations such as the Trust for Public Land (TPL), The Nature Conservancy, the National Audubon Society, and the National Wildlife Federation. However, the recession of the early 1990s has reversed this trend, at least temporarily.

"There is downsizing at all the environmental groups when the economy is bad," says Sharon Newsome of the National Wildlife Federation (NWF). NWF and other organizations were not hiring at all in early 1992, and in some nonprofit organizations the layoffs were large. This is in stark contrast to the mid- to late 1980s, when NWF grew at 10 percent per year, says Newsome. These boom and bust cycles are nothing new, so expect employment in the nonprofit sector to rebound with the economy.

Nonprofit land trusts are a major force behind land acquisition efforts, working to acquire land outright or purchase easement or development rights on properties. Of these, the largest and best known is probably The Nature Conservancy (TNC). TNC manages more than 1,100 preserves in 50 states as well as in Canada, the Caribbean, and Latin America. The organization employs more than 1,000 full-time staff people and a seasonal staff as well.

Beyond national groups like TNC, however, is a growing land trust movement. According to Susan Witt of the Community Land Trust in the southern Berkshires of Massachusetts, the function and strategy of land trusts vary considerably: "In the Northeast, land trusts are being used to keep the scale of development in proportion to a community; in a midwestern community they might work to save family farms; in the Ozarks, to better manage the forestland, economically and environmentally." Excluding TNC and TPL, there are some 900 local land trusts in the United States, employing nearly 1,700 full-time and 1,100 part-time workers.

Another significant development is the flourishing of statewide and grass-roots organizations. This is a trend that R. Montgomery Fischer, director of the Northeast Natural Resource Center of the National Wildlife Federation in Vermont, believes will not be short-lived. "There is quite a future in local nonprofits. One reason nonprofits are so important at the local level is their work to ensure implementation of a tremendous flood of state legislation related to growth management, planning, and land preservation. In Vermont, we have had 35 to 40 major pieces of state environmental legislation enacted in the past several years."

Eric Partee, executive director of Little Miami, Inc., which is working to preserve the Little Miami River near Cincinnati, comments: "Besides riding herd on government agencies to live up to their legally mandated responsibilities, it is a responsibility of nonprofits to be creative, to come up with new initiatives. We must also educate, communicate, and sell our ideas. I try to think of what we do as a product. I try to market this product so that people are so enthralled by it that they can't do without it and will pay for the work of Little Miami, Inc."

Land and water conservation jobs in the nonprofit sector require a wide range of skills. Real estate backgrounds are in high demand where land acquisition is the key function. Speaking and writing, policy analysis, management, fund-raising, resource inventorying, and legislative work are all needed.

SALARY

Federal salaries in land and water conservation start at about $18,000 for professional positions, and technical degrees may bring more than $20,000. Federal conservation salaries average $35,000, and high salaries can reach $60,000. Law degrees bring a higher salary.

Salaries in state and local conservation districts and agencies are generally lower than federal salaries, although there may be local exceptions in urban areas. Starting salaries are $16,000 to $20,000, with average salaries reaching $30,000.

Private industry salaries run higher than public sector salaries, starting closer to $25,000 and averaging more than $35,000.

Nonprofit organizations are working to compete with public sector agencies in their range of salaries. The National Wildlife Federation provides starting salaries for new hires with a master's degree in forestry of $25,000 to $35,000. Attorneys at the National Wildlife Federation may make $40,000 to start, and advanced degrees and experience can raise salaries up to $60,000.

GETTING STARTED

There are many ways to get involved in land and water conservation. A variety of backgrounds not specifically related to natural resource management—planning, environmental education, recreation, and the environmental protection fields—can provide a start. Whatever your starting point is, consider the following ideas.

EDUCATION

Employers like applicants with a broad-based education—it might be a double major in politics and biology or in business and natural resource management. If natural resource management is your major focus, there are many specialties within this discipline. Although technician-type jobs exist for those with two-year degrees or those with bachelor's degrees, because of competition most professional jobs go to those with master's degrees. There are exceptions, such as opportunities for people who have unique experience and skills.

If you pursue only one undergraduate major, the basic sciences are recommended: biology, botany, zoology, chemistry, physics, and geology.

Although graduate school is a time for specialized training, professionals repeatedly stress that they are looking for applicants who are not overly narrow. Steve Starland of the Washington State Scenic Rivers Program advises, "We are not looking for someone who just understands the trees or the fish or the streams or the timber industry but for people who can put it all together."

Good preparation for a career in land and water conservation would include course work in biology, the ecology of ecosystems and communities, and, possibly, population biology. Course work on public policy as it relates to resource management is also useful, but it should not be pursued at the expense of a hard scientific grounding. Master's degrees that encompass this type of work include natural resource management, ecology, botany, conservation biology, and forestry.

While completing your degrees, do not neglect opportunities to gain volunteer or internship experience. Professionals have pointed out that it is best to try out the sector you are most interested in. "We like to see someone who has experience working with nonprofit organizations," says Eric Partee of Little Miami, Inc. "Become an officer in a local nonprofit; learn what it takes to get things done, to coordinate volunteers, run meetings, and deal with the Army Corps of Engineers and local members of Congress. If you want to work for a local organization or land trust, understand the local politics and issues."

ADVICE

Some of the sources for this chapter gave us the following advice for those entering land and water conservation careers. These are the points that they feel are essential to keep in mind as you approach this area of work.

Contract work may be your first step. Jim Burns of the Ohio Department of Natural Resources counsels: "Very rarely will you get out of school, even with a master's, and land a permanent position right away. I was doing contract work for two years and had to relocate a lot. Some people give up and go back to school and become a teacher. I'm glad I stuck it out."

Use cooperative education. In addition to universally advising the use of internships to get experience, federal and state agency staff members strongly encourage participation in cooperative education, noting that "co-op ed" workers often receive preferential treatment in civil service hiring.

Get legal, real estate, and financial skills. Before an area can be managed, it must be protected. Before it can be protected, it must be purchased or at least have limitations placed on its use. The business aspect of conservation is growing, and these skills are in demand.

Use the Student Conservation Association. For anyone interested in a career with federal land management agencies, a volunteer position through the Student Conservation Association (SCA) is a great way to start. SCA has placed thousands of people in conservation positions over the past three decades and also provides other career services.

Know the "hot" issues. Because job growth in the field often depends on a new funding source, it pays to know what these sources are and gain appropriate academic or practical experience. From this chapter, for instance, you know that the inventorying of natural resources at military bases and recreational growth on public forestland are two current boomlets.

SUMMARY

Land and water conservation is a very popular field, and the number of applicants seeking jobs far exceeds the supply. If this is the field for you, getting established will take imagination, persistence, and patience. Go beyond the departments and agencies traditionally associated with land and water conservation—there are conservation jobs tucked away in the most unlikely places.

Employment in land and water conservation will probably always be relatively tight because funds for agencies involved in this field are usually scarce and many applicants want to fill the jobs that do exist. The good news is that the work is strongly supported by the public, and that support is growing. Those who succeed in this field as we enter the twenty-first century will possess strong, integrated scientific backgrounds, relevant experience, and, above all, commitment.

CASE STUDY

Finding a Water Balance in
Southern Colorado

Water conservation professionals quickly discover that water issues are political, social, and economic as much as they are ecological and technical. The case study that follows is just one example.

In the isolated, arid San Luis Valley of south central Colorado, plant ecologist Dr. David Cooper spent weeks digging holes into wetland preserves in an effort to ensure the survival of those wetlands. The valley is home to 40,000 people, primarily farmers and ranchers, including many Hispanics and some Lakota Sioux. The valley also is home to more than 50,000 acres of wetlands in four state and national wildlife refuges and a pulsating spring in the Great Sand Dunes National Monument—all of it at risk.

Risk in the West can have no more frightening form than the loss of water, and the crucial natural resource of the San Luis Valley is the underground aquifers that keep its crops and wetlands watered in spite of a desert climate. Since the mid-1980s, American Water Development, Inc. (AWDI) of Denver has worked hard to gain approval for its plan to remove huge amounts of water from those aquifers for sale to Denver and other thirsty western places.

"Their theory was that much of the water in an area known as the closed basin was evaporating anyway and they could use it," says Patty Mercer, administrative officer and litigation coordinator for Colorado's Division of Wildlife. Another part of AWDI's argument was that some of the underground water was trapped and not connected to any surface tributaries. The Division of Wildlife became involved when it realized that wetlands under its jurisdiction would be damaged by proposed wells.

Meanwhile, the federal government became alarmed that its federal wetlands might be damaged and that downstream water required for the Rio Grande watershed might not flow from the San Luis Valley.

AWDI had studies and computer models for evidence, as well as experts and some big-name personalities who have argued that the company's plans will cause no harm to the state's wetlands. The firm's board of directors includes William Ruckelshaus, former director of the Environmental Protection Agency, and Richard Lamm, former Colorado governor.

Fearful that large-scale pumping would decimate the valley and its resources, San Luis residents decided to tax themselves to pay for an effort to block AWDI. They were joined by the U.S. government, the state of Colorado, and many others, each with individual reasons for fighting the proposal. The case illustrates the kinds of conflicting claims to resources that typify such lawsuits.

Water rights law has developed such complexity and monetary importance that judges and attorneys now specialize in the field. The case concerning the water rights of AWDI spanned many months of procedures before Robert W. Ogburn, water judge for Water Division 3, State of Colorado. AWDI traces its claims to water rights back at least 130 years through previous owners of the land it now holds in the valley.

Sprinkled through Judge Ogburn's background and ruling in the case are quotations, including the following quote from Stanley Crawford: "Next to blood relationships, which rule the valley, come water relationships. The arteries of ditches and bloodlines cut across each other in patterns of astounding complexity."

Complexities lie below the ground as well, in geologies and hydrogeologies of silts and blue clays, confined and unconfined aquifers, alluvial fans, volcanoclastic formations, horsts, and grabens. These are subterranean complexities that pitted a computer modeling program against itself as the same program was used in two different ways by opposing sides in the case.

Samuel Langhorne Clemens (Mark Twain) neither figured in nor testified during the case, but Judge Ogburn's opinion quotes him just the same: "There is something fascinating about science. One gets such wholesale returns of conjecture out of such a trifling investment in fact."

But although science versus science comprised much of the case, the investments were far from trifling. As AWDI geologists and hydrogeologists sought to prove that pumping water from the underground aquifers would neither affect existing water rights of farmers and ranchers nor reduce the water supply to refuges, the objectors labored to prove otherwise.

Experts for the objectors showed evidence of a serious drop in the water table after prolonged pumping by AWDI, damaging or ruining agricultural and ranching wells. "There are only seven to eight inches of rain per year here, so they have to rely on wells for their water," says the Division of Wildlife's Patty Mercer.

Plant ecologist David Cooper received a telephone call from AWDI one day asking him to serve as their expert on the case for drilling the wells. "I said no, but [the offer] was very hard to turn down," admits Cooper, who teaches at the University of Colorado and Colorado State University and consults as well. AWDI was willing to pay handsomely for his testimony. They hired another ecologist.

A telephone call from the objectors in the case came the next day, and Cooper accepted on the condition that he be funded to do original research for the case. "I've got to tell you that the other guy made a lot more money than I did," he laughs. "They worked five or six weeks and made a lot of money, while I worked for six months."

But good science can lead to good law, it seems. "You need a good enough data set so you can present a full perspective," Cooper says. "You need to do some original research because on almost any project in the West, there is not enough data. We did a great study, and the original research did the trick in court."

Cooper quantified the relationship between water supply to the wetlands and the health of the plants in those wetlands. His uncontested testimony, states the judge's opinion, showed evidence that based on the hydrogeology determined by other experts, the proposed well drawdowns would "cause the total eradication of at least 26,000 acres of wetlands . . . [and] . . . at least an additional 24,000 acres would be substantially injured."

The application for San Luis Valley water rights by AWDI was denied and dismissed by Judge Ogburn on February 10, 1992. AWDI has appealed the decision to the Colorado Supreme Court.

PROFILES

Dr. Robert Halley
Geologist
Coastal Center
U.S. Geological Survey
Saint Petersburg, Florida

Research scientists are key members of the land and water conservation community, providing increased understanding of how the earth works so that we can devise better conservation strategies. The work of Dr. Halley and his colleagues is one example.

Walking through the U.S. Geological Survey's Coastal Center with geologist Dr. Robert Halley is the scientist's equivalent of being a kid in a candy store. All around him, members of a select team of researchers do exactly what they have prepared themselves for. It seems that behind each doorway, another fascinating coastal study is going on.

Land and water conservation professionals focus on coastal lands not only because of their biological importance but also because the vast majority of the nation's population lives within 100 miles of an ocean or one of the Great Lakes.

At the Coastal Center, geologists and other scientists research the following issues:

- Coastal erosion throughout the United States. Time-lapse studies of mid-Atlantic shores show patterns of sand removal and deposition during storms. Maps show the relative changes in shore topography over decades. There are places along the Gulf Coast of Louisiana, says Halley, "where you can just about watch the shore erode." Detailed data on the nation's entire coastline accumulate here for the center's studies.
- Coastal pollution and its effects on ocean geology. A classic study in Hawaii two decades ago detailed the effect of pollutants that raised nutrient levels on a coral reef, encouraging algae growth, which in turn killed the reef. Coastal Center divers and scientists study reef die-offs around southern Florida and the Caribbean.

It was the outdoor activity of classic geology that wooed Halley away from his premed studies at Oberlin College and into that institution's program in geology. He continued his study of geology by earning a master's degree at Brown University and a Ph.D. from the State University of New York at Stony Brook.

U.S. Geological Survey Coastal Center, Saint Petersburg, Florida. Geologist Robert Halley (right) and divemaster Keith Ludwig of the USGS take a core sample from a Bahamian coral head as part of the agency's coastal studies. The hole is sealed with cement and heals in about four years.

Ironically, he says, "We spend a large portion of our time now in front of a computer, and less and less time is involved with those activities that brought us into our profession." Automated electronic equipment makes it possible to collect far more data than ever before. "And the only way to process that much data is with computers," Halley says.

At the Coastal Center, computers analyze data on weather patterns, winds, waves, and sediment movement collected through satellite imagery and chemical analyses. "The sheer volume of information that can now be collected and analyzed allows us to look at far more than we used to." Even data more than 100 years old are subject to sophisticated computer analysis. Workers at the center are gradually entering data from old coastal maps, including water depths and topography, to provide more data points for analysis of modern data.

One of Halley's greatest concerns is the lack of high-caliber people entering the field since the end of the period of scientific optimism in the 1970s.

"What we really need is analytical folks," he says. "You have to have an incredible background to sort your way through what has already been done and isolate a problem from a host of other factors over which you have no control." He cites the help of organizations such as ECO as "a real gold mine in helping to filter through a lot of people and find the sort of folks we need, including talented scientists of color."

With the right people and the right research, says Halley, "on occasion I am able to discover some basic truths about how the world works, and I find that absolutely fascinating and exciting. It is easy to get caught up in everyday life and forget that. This job allows me to stay in touch with those truths."

> ### *Jennie Gerard*
> ### *Senior Vice President*
> ### *Land Trusts and Development*
> ### *Trust for Public Land*
> ### *San Francisco, California*

When rapid development along the California coast during the 1970s was converting acres of open land at any price, a few people decided to do something before all the open lands were gone. They formed a "land trust": a citizens' organization to acquire and manage open lands for the public benefit. The trust's first battle produced two famous results: first, the preservation of miles of California coastline around San Francisco, since taken over for management by the National Park Service; second, the formation of the Trust for Public Land, one of America's most successful and best-known land trusts.

For Jennie Gerard, senior vice president for land trusts and development with the Trust for Public Land (TPL), land trusts provide "an opportunity to work on a daily basis in a field in which I have a tremendous personal stake. I care very much about what the earth looks like and what it will look like for future generations. TPL allows me to fit that concern together with my need for a paycheck."

Gerard joined TPL in 1977 at the start of TPL's land trust program and has worked with the organization ever since. "There are now 900 land trusts in the United States, and TPL worked on 300 of those," she says. The results of the program include the protection of properties as varied as the first winter encampment site of the de Soto expedition in Tallahassee, Florida; community gardens in the middle of Boston; and part of the Columbia River Gorge National Scenic Area on the Washington-Oregon border.

The Trust for Public Land, San Francisco, California. Jennifer Dere, benefits administrator for TPL, plants a tree in San Francisco's Golden Gate Park during a California ReLeaf event. Photograph by Susan Ives.

"I have an abiding interest in working with community groups on open space issues. We respond to community groups that feel passionately about something—a watercourse, an endangered historic building. We are working from the agendas of these groups." When Gerard began her work with land trusts, California had "fewer than five—now there are more than 80."

Before being bitten by the land trust bug, Gerard gained an undergraduate degree from Wellesley College and a master's degree in city and regional planning from the Illinois Institute of Technology and worked as a private land-use consultant with firms in Boston and, later, Berkeley, California.

"I knew I wanted to work with citizens' groups on their land-use issues," she recalls. "When I heard about TPL, I asked what kinds of people they worked with. I found out they were turning the agendas of citizens' groups into protected open space, and I joined the organization."

Land trusts may be one of the few exceptions to the slump in land and water conservation growth. Gerard says that there has been "exponential growth" in land trusts since the early 1980s. A new land trust forms every week, she says. However, this is a small field in terms of total jobs. TPL employs a total of 165 people nationwide. The most numerous positions in TPL are field positions, called project managers.

TPL's project managers "figure out how to arrange for permanent protection of privately held public space," says Gerard. "A community group or public parks agency comes to us and asks for help to protect a particular piece of land. Sometimes it's a group that tried their local government or others and got no help. These groups are candidates to form land trusts."

The project manager determines whether the landowner is willing to sell and whether there are public agencies willing to buy it. Is there a community group willing to help raise money for the purchase?

"The job of the project manager is to look at the interests of local groups and identify how to put together a deal, use staff attorneys and financial analysts to figure out the transaction, and use development staff to do fund-raising, if that is needed. There are about 50 project manager positions in 11 TPL offices around the country."

Gerard envisions further growth in land trust positions in TPL, with "great career opportunities and new challenges in the 1990s and beyond."

Mike Soukup
Research Director
Everglades National Park
National Park Service
Homestead, Florida

Although a great deal of land and water conservation work is done on a small, local scale, some environmental professionals are preserving whole ecosystems of value to people all over the world. Members of the research staff at Everglades National Park are among this lucky group.

Mike Soukup cannot decide where in the Everglades he would most like to be. It might be "in the middle of a vast expanse of that open and remarkably subtle, shallow marshland," or it might be "in the mangroves—I haven't spent enough time there," or it might be far out in Florida Bay amid thousands of small islands, where "I saw four species of endangered sea turtles surface by the boat in 15 minutes."

As research director for Everglades National Park, Soukup presides over the largest research facility in the National Park Service. He is also a field general in a protracted battle to preserve and protect what he describes as an internationally significant "biosphere preserve." Much like the tropical rain forests Americans are asking South American governments to preserve, the Everglades includes unique habitats and rare species, all of them threatened.

By the time Everglades National Park was formed in 1947, says Soukup, "the ecosystem was already headed downhill." At the time, a nearby municipality called Miami boasted some 500,000 residents. By 1980, the population of Miami alone was 4 million, and other cities to the west and north were growing as well. Florida is still in its "expand and explode mode," says Soukup, and has not yet come to grips with the limits that will be necessary to preserve the state's fragile environment.

Even as Soukup's research teams study the Everglades and work to preserve the ecosystem, other groups battle on behalf of their own interests. Man-made canals connecting various bodies of water allow boats to move quickly to fishing spots but also alter the flow of water through the park. Soukup wants the canals filled—but fishermen, including Native Americans, say that removing them would take away their fishing rights.

Sugar cane and vegetable farmers divert water for their own use and then create nutrient-rich runoff waters that damage the Everglades ecosystem. Continued development in south central Florida would take more of the water that eventually flows into the park, damaging it further.

Exasperated, the Park Service took the state of Florida to court, charging the state with failure to enforce its own environmental regulations that would protect the park. Soukup's team of a half dozen scientists won an out-of-court settlement in favor of the park; some parts of the settlement were written by Soukup.

Research chief Soukup is no stranger to difficult scientific and managerial dilemmas. Before taking over the research center, Soukup had been a regional chief scientist for the Park Service, providing scientific answers to management questions from New Jersey to Maine. In school, he earned a degree in biology at the University of Richmond, then worked on a local water control board, followed by a year at the Woods Hole Marine Biological Laboratory. A master's degree in population ecology from the University of Massachusetts and a doctorate in limnology, the study of freshwater ecology, followed.

Soukup took a one-year contract with the Park Service working on Cape Cod limnology issues and joined the service as a result. He traces his personal motivations for doing environmental work to the experience of watching the gradual loss to development of the Virginia lowlands near Richmond during his youth.

Preventing a similar fate for the Everglades will be a difficult, long-term effort, says Soukup. He and his team are developing a restoration plan to reverse the park's decline by putting Everglades water back in the right places, at the right times, with the right quality to restore the ecosystem. For the plan to work, however, a number of groups must cooperate. These will include local governing bodies that control water use and runoff, urban and agricultural interests, and the sovereign Miccosukkee Indian Tribe.

Soukup's team has brought a reluctant state government into efforts to preserve a fragile ecosystem, while helping both farmers and urbanites understand the benefits of a restored Everglades. This progress is possible because dedicated conservation workers exemplify the qualities Soukup recommends to those entering the field. "Master the fundamentals of science," he says. Then "be flexible and willing to take risks."

RESOURCES

Listed here are only some of the trade and professional organizations active in the land and water conservation field. The National Wildlife Federation's annual Conservation Directory *is an excellent source of information on additional organizations as well as state and federal agencies and departments active in the conservation field.*

Conservation International. 1015 18th St., NW, Suite 1000, Washington, DC 20036. (202) 429–5660.

Ecological Society of America. Publishes *Ecology* (bimonthly). Center for Environmental Studies, Arizona State University, Tempe, AZ 85287–3211. Write for "Careers in Ecology" pamphlet.

National Association of Conservation Districts. Publishes *Tuesday Letter* (monthly) and "Guide to Natural Resources Careers" (1990), a pamphlet with a bibliography of publications on careers in conservation. 509 Capitol Ct., NE, Washington, DC 20002. (202) 547–6223.

Natural Resources Council of America. Federation of national and regional conservation organizations and scientific societies interested in conservation of natural resources. Publishes *NRCA News* (bimonthly). 801 Pennsylvania Ave., SE, Suite 410, Washington, DC 20003.

Society for Ecological Restoration and Management, University of Wisconsin Arboretum, 1207 Seminole Hwy., Madison, WI 53711. (608) 262–2746.

Society for Range Management, 1839 York St., Denver, CO 80206. (303) 355–7070.

Soil and Water Conservation Society. Advances the science and art of good land and water use worldwide. Publishes *Journal of Soil and Water Conservation* (bimonthly). Career brochure available, "Want to Be a Conservationist?" 7515 Ankeny Rd., Ankeny, IA 50021–9765.

The Center for Marine Conservation. A nonprofit membership organization dedicated to conserving coastal and ocean resources and to protecting marine wildlife and habitats. 1725 DeSales St., NW, Washington, DC 20036. Regional offices in Austin; San Francisco; Hampton, VA; and Saint Petersburg, FL.

The Conservation Foundation. 1250 24th St., NW, Washington, DC 20037. (202) 293–4800.

The Job Seekers Guide to Opportunities in Natural Resource Management for the Developing World. See the Resources section in chapter 4 for a description.

The Nature Conservancy. Preserves habitat for rare and endangered plants and animals. Publishes bimonthly magazine. Has land and water conservation programs operated by professionally staffed field offices in 50 states. Job hunt line ([703] 247–3721) is a weekly update of all jobs available with The Nature Conservancy. 1815 N. Lynn St., Arlington, VA 22209.

The Wilderness Society. Publishes *Wilderness* (quarterly). 900 17th St., NW, Washington, DC 20006.

Trust for Public Land. Works to acquire land for public use as parks, community gardens, recreational areas, and open space. Provides technical assistance in land acquisition. Publishes *Land and People*, which highlights current projects around the country. 116 New Montgomery St., Fourth Floor, San Francisco, CA 94105. (415) 495–4014.

U.S. Department of Agriculture, Soil Conservation Service. P.O. Box 2890, Washington, DC 20013. (202) 447–4543.

12 Fishery and Wildlife Management

AT A GLANCE

Employment:
33,000 fish and wildlife management professionals in all sectors nationwide; 18,000 in wildlife and 15,000 in fisheries

Demand:
3 to 5 percent growth per year in wildlife management; 5 to 8 percent growth per year in fishery management

Breakdown:
Wildlife management:
Public sector, 70 percent (20 percent federal, 50 percent state and local)
Private sector, 15 percent
Nonprofit sector, 7 percent
Education, 8 percent (includes both public and private sectors)
Fisheries management:
Public sector, 50 percent (25 percent federal, 25 percent state and local)
Private sector, 16 percent
Nonprofit sector, 3 percent
Education, 31 percent (includes both public and private sectors)

Key Job Titles:
Aquaculturist
Botanist
Data management specialist

Endangered species biologist
Environmental specialist
Fishery or wildlife biologist
Fishery or wildlife manager
Hatchery manager
Marine biologist or ecologist
Naturalist
Professor (education)
Refuge manager
Senior research scientist
Wetlands ecologist

Influential Organizations:
American Fisheries Society
National Audubon Society
National Wildlife Federation
U.S. Fish and Wildlife Service
Wildlife Society

Salary:
Entry-level salaries range from $15,000 to $20,000 but can go as low as
$12,000. Salaries for more experienced positions are in the $30,000 to
$40,000 range, with some higher.

Something about the field of fishery and wildlife management attracts a lot
of people, people who envision a life of tracking elk across mountain
meadows or tagging wild salmon on remote rivers. Their passion for the
outdoor life and their love of animals are what draws them to the environmental professions. That dedication and love for the environment are just
as important now as they have ever been, but today's fish and wildlife
manager must bring more than just desire. The field now is as reliant on
"people" skills and computer modeling as it is on rugged fieldwork.

WHAT IS FISHERY AND WILDLIFE MANAGEMENT?

Management of fisheries and wildlife used to mean maintenance of adequate populations of game fish and animals to satisfy sportfishermen and
hunters. Although this is still part of the profession, the field is now
considerably broader. Management now often means regulation or manipulation of natural resources and human activities in the best interests of
fish, wildlife, and plants. The field might be called ecosystem management

to point out that the concerns of fishery and wildlife managers now extend far beyond the welfare of a few individual species useful to human beings.

With its broader and more sophisticated responsibilities, the field has grown from one dominated by outdoor biologists with undergraduate degrees to one in which advanced degrees are all but essential. These changes have produced professions with a wide variety of management specialties, as we shall see. Nonetheless, the outdoor mystique remains. Biologists and their activities are still at the heart of fishery and wildlife management.

A look at the tasks of fishery and wildlife management professionals serves as a good definition of the field. The U.S. Fish and Wildlife Service defines these positions as follows:

- *Wildlife biologists* study the distribution, abundance, habits, life histories, ecology, mortality factors, and economic values of birds, mammals, and other wildlife. They plan and carry out wildlife management programs, determine conditions affecting wildlife, apply research findings to the management of wildlife, restore or develop wildlife habitats, regulate wildlife populations, and control wildlife diseases.
- *Fishery biologists* study the life history, habits, classification, and economic relations of aquatic organisms. They manage fish hatcheries and fishery resources and gather data on interrelationships between various species of fish and the growth of fish. These professionals determine rearing and stocking methods best adapted for maximum success in fish hatchery operations and devise methods to regulate fishing to secure an optimum sustained yield.

These are accurate but bureaucratic definitions. The reality behind them is an exciting and world-preserving career.

HISTORY AND BACKGROUND

"Wildlife management is both very old and very new," says Craig Rieben, an information officer with the U.S. Fish and Wildlife Service. "Native Americans burned clearings to maintain them for wildlife long before Europeans knew about it, for instance."

The modern wildlife management profession in this country, however, can probably be traced to the beginning of the National Wildlife Refuge System. The protection of Pelican Island in Florida around 1903 helped stop mass killings of waterfowl for their large feathers, which were prized by northern dressmakers and milliners. Since then, more and more threats to wildlife have been identified and more species have come under the protection of refuges and human managers.

Modern fishery management began shortly after the Civil War, as New England's rivers, gradually polluted and impounded by industrial development, produced fewer and fewer fish. "Most New England rivers were dammed to produce power for mills to make shoes or textiles," says Paul Brouha, executive director of the American Fisheries Society. "Dams blocked passage for spawning fish such as the Atlantic salmon, striped bass, and shad." In 1870, concern over these declines led to the formation of the American Fish Cultural Association, and members started to apply scientific practices to fishery management.

It was not until establishment of reliable funding mechanisms in the 1950s, however, that the field became a serious and widespread profession. The Dingell-Johnson Act of 1951 led the way by providing continuing allocation of funds to state fishery programs.

LEGISLATION

As is the case with many environmental fields, careers in fishery and wildlife management are driven by laws intended to eradicate mistakes of the past, design programs for effective management, and ensure funding. Some of these influential laws are as follows.

Federal Aid in Fish and Wildlife Restoration Act (1950). This act established an excise tax on fishing tackle sales and apportions resulting funds to state fishery programs based on a formula of land area versus licenses sold.

Magnusen Fishery Conservation and Management Act (1976). The 200-mile exclusive economic zone around the U.S. coastline to protect U.S. fishing stocks from depletion by foreign fishermen was established by this legislation.

Fish and Wildlife Coordination Act. This law requires government agencies to coordinate and advise one another about activities and their effects on fish and wildlife populations.

Endangered Species Act. This is potentially the most significant and far reaching of all fishery and wildlife protection legislation and a true landmark in environmental management. The act directs the U.S. Fish and Wildlife Service to determine when a species is threatened with extinction and requires government agencies to take actions aimed at recovery.

Migratory Bird Treaty Act. This act regulates waterfowl conservation activities and was one of the first wildlife protection laws. This act prohibits many forms of exploitation, including hunting, killing, selling, purchasing, shipping, or delivering migratory birds, except under specific regulations.

National Wildlife Refuge System Act. More than 470 refuges encompassing 90 million acres are protected today by the National Wildlife Refuge System established by this act. Many of the largest tracts are in Alaska, but the refuges include land throughout the nation. Most of the refuges have employees on site.

Migratory Bird Hunting and Conservation Stamp (Duck Stamp) Act. Duck stamps are required for all adult waterfowl hunters, generating funds for purchase of new wetland refuges.

This legislative base provides the framework within which fishery and wildlife professionals carry out their work, receive their funding, and measure their success.

ISSUES AND TRENDS

The following are some of the broad concerns affecting fishery and wildlife managers in the 1990s.

WETLANDS PROTECTION

"Wetlands are probably the most biologically productive habitat type for fish and wildlife," says the U.S. Fish and Wildlife Service's Craig Rieben. Yet they are being destroyed at a rapid rate. Some areas of the United States have lost as much as 90 percent of their wetlands. Wetlands that border our oceans, including salt marshes that account for large percentages of commercial fishery "nurseries," are also under attack. Identifying, protecting, and restoring valuable wetlands is a major employment area for this field, and not all of the work involves advanced science. "In many cases," says Paul Brouha of the American Fisheries Society, "action as simple as adding a culvert where a road has blocked off a marshland may restore an area as a productive part of the fisheries ecosystem."

ENDANGERED SPECIES PROGRAMS

Public support for efforts to protect such endangered species as the California condor, the bald eagle, and the alligator is strong. The U.S. Fish and Wildlife Service notes that at least 600 plant and animal species are in danger of extinction in the United States. Continuing additions to the list generate further research needs and require teams of managers to design protection strategies. Will such support continue as more species qualify for legal protection? Some experts expect confrontations to become more intense as the needs of wildlife conflict with economic realities (see the Case Study in chapter 14 for an example of such a controversy).

HABITAT PROTECTION

Fishery and wildlife professionals are agreed: Saving any living thing means protecting its habitat. As this philosophy is incorporated into long-range plans and government regulations, expect an increase in new "conservation" careers requiring legal, financial, real estate, business, and similar skills to purchase land or control its use.

TOXINS AND WILDLIFE

Contaminants from old oil spills, pollutant outflows, and other sources may continue to have effects on fish and wildlife many years, or decades, after the incidents that created the contaminants. Research is needed to determine which contaminants are present in ecosystems, what effects they have on the health of fish and wildlife, and how to remediate or reduce those negative impacts.

URBAN WILDLIFE

Urban wildlife areas are a likely area for significant employment growth during the next several years, reports Harry E. Hodgdon, executive director of the Wildlife Society. This work will include restoration of urban wetlands, he says. Look for job opportunities in previously unexpected places, such as utility companies, local government agencies, and development companies.

MIGRATORY BIRD ISSUES

Habitat needs of migratory birds will grow as a concern not only in the United States but also throughout the Americas as habitat modification and fragmentation in the United States and habitat destruction in South and Central America continue. Knowledge of these issues is still spotty, as is knowledge of the significance and extent of destruction of bird habitat. Whether or not funding will be available is an open question.

PUBLIC ACCESS

"We are getting increased support for and interest in wildlife from the public, which translates into increased demand for public access to refuges," says Hodgdon. "Future wildlife managers must be managers of people to a much greater extent than ever before. This places strains on the educational system. Wildlife management is no longer just animals and habitat training. Now there are psychology, sociology, recreation management, and other human studies thrown into the process."

INTEGRATED NATURAL RESOURCE PLANNING

Fishery and wildlife professionals increasingly work with other environmental professionals and agencies to plan, develop, and implement fishery and wildlife programs in conjunction with overall natural resource management plans. For example, when preparing its ten-year plans, the Forest Service is required to make provisions for maintaining viable populations of wildlife. This integrated planning requirement brings new people from a variety of local, state, and federal agencies into the service's planning and has increased its role as an employer in the field. Watershed planning efforts are another example. As more agencies and companies require fishery and wildlife considerations in their work, job opportunities should expand.

COMPENSATION

"Regulatory agencies used to let development happen as long as losses of habitat were minimized," says Ron Klein, a wildlife biologist for Portland General Electric in Oregon. "Now, if your development leads to destruction of habitat, you may be required to compensate by finding a chunk of land in poor condition and restoring it to increase its habitat-carrying capacity." Requirements for compensation and restoration will necessitate not only biological skills but also legal, financial, and real estate abilities.

CAREER OPPORTUNITIES

On the fisheries side, Paul Brouha of the American Fisheries Society reports that there are currently fewer qualified fishery management graduates than has been the case generally. "There are a lot of fisheries jobs now, and there is not tremendous competition for them," he says. "There may be several reasons. One is the perception that it is a small field. A lot of people are not going into fisheries studies in colleges and universities. We do not have a lot of high-quality candidates from diverse cultural backgrounds available."

This comparative abundance of jobs in fishery management should continue for some time, considering the following trends:

- Aquaculture is expanding and will create new hiring both in the private sector and in federal agencies.
- Marine sport fisheries will need expert help in the coming years. The population of coastal areas now exceeds half of the nation's total. There are increasing pressures on marine sport fisheries among a segment of voters, who will insist on more access to this resource.
- "We've done a poor job of managing commercial fisheries since passage of the Magnusen Act in 1976," says Brouha. "Of 180 commercial marine fish stocks, 140 are overfished. Fishery management institutions are based on a model that doesn't recognize present technological abilities of commercial fishermen." He expects emerging pressure for management of international waters to create demand for sophisticated managers.

Today's trends, however, could change quickly. Will Sandoval, a harvest management biologist with the Muckleshoot Indian Tribe, says: "The job market in fisheries has been quite cyclical, with the highest proportion of openings dependent on what is trendy. For example, when the United States and Canada were working on fishing treaties in the early to mid-1980s, this meant a lot of modeling, tagging, computer work, and basic research. The focus has now shifted toward habitat and water quality issues."

On the wildlife side, the picture is not as bright. The Wildlife Society concluded in a study of 1986 graduates that overall, only 44 percent of the graduates obtained employment one year after graduating (34 percent of those with B.A.s, 66 percent of those with master's degrees, and 87 percent of Ph.D.s). Little has changed since then.

Destry Jarvis, executive vice president of the Student Conservation Association, points out that these data may be misleading, however. "Wildlife people tend to have a broader education. They feel they can go into more things than specifically wildlife. The vast majority work in some area of conservation."

Although the job market in wildlife management is tough, you would be doing yourself—and the field—a disservice if you made your career decision based solely on how many jobs are available. A wildlife management professional says: "Yes, the field is tight, and if you have only a casual interest there is not a high probability you will get a job. However, the country needs as many people trained in fisheries and wildlife as we can get. I am also of the opinion that 90 percent of the jobs that will exist five years from now haven't been invented yet."

PUBLIC SECTOR

The federal government has the highest number of fishery and wildlife managers, but state and local programs undertake some of the most interesting work, such as carrying out endangered species recovery programs and managing local fisheries.

Federal government. The federal government is by far the largest single employer of fishery and wildlife managers. The two largest employers are the Department of the Interior's U.S. Fish and Wildlife Service and the Department of Agriculture's Forest Service. Surprisingly, the Forest Service is the larger employer of wildlife managers. Other federal agencies employing fish and wildlife professionals include the Bureau of Land Management, the National Marine Fisheries Service, the Army Corps of Engineers, the Environmental Protection Agency, the National Park Service, the military services, and the Peace Corps.

Federal agency employment in wildlife programs remains relatively unchanged since the reductions of the 1980s when the U.S. Fish and Wildlife Service, the Forest Service, the National Oceanic and Atmospheric Administration, and others cut back. However, federal employment of fishery personnel is headed upward again. The following are some examples of this trend:

- The Forest Service's expansion to 300 fishery biologists from 100.
- The National Park Service's expansion to 130 fishery experts from 7.
- Bureau of Land Management requirements for about 100 new fishery experts.

State and local government. Much of the most innovative and important fishery and wildlife work is done at the state level. Important state agencies for fishery and wildlife management include departments of fish and wildlife, forestry, conservation, environmental protection, and parks and recreation. One survey found that state agencies hire more applicants with master's degrees in these fields than do other organizations.

Rupert Cutler of The River Foundation in Virginia adds: "It is encouraging to see more comprehensive fish and wildlife management at the state level. Part of this is made possible by enlarged databases such as the information collected by natural heritage programs and geographic information systems. We are also paying attention to nongame species and their habitat, not just the white-tailed deer and largemouth bass. This is aided by the nongame income tax checkoffs available in many states. In addition, some states have passed their own Endangered Species Act. Finally, a direct result of this activity is that states are getting more involved in fish and wildlife education and are also taking these educational efforts to major urban areas."

This interest in urban areas generates more involvement on the part of local governments. Harry Hodgdon of the Wildlife Society observes: "The demographics of the United States are rapidly changing, with the population becoming more urbanized. We are looking for open space and wildlife enjoyment closer to home. This is creating positions in and around urban areas ranging from habitat enhancement to wildlife education to professionals controlling wildlife damage and also human damage to wildlife."

A little-known employment sector for fishery and wildlife professionals is Native American tribal government. According to Dewey Schwalenberg, executive director of the Native American Fish and Wildlife Society, there are at least 167 tribes with resource management functions, employing more than 1,300 personnel.

PRIVATE SECTOR

Private sector employment in fishery and wildlife management includes a diverse range of occupations, such as work for forest-products firms and utility companies with large landholdings, environmental departments of large companies, consultants, and commercial game farms and aquaculture ventures.

Private industry. "Mitigation projects are popping up around the country, carried out by utility companies, developers, timber companies, and other businesses with large landholdings," says Portland General Electric's Ron Klein. "Some are doing these projects with in-house staff, and others are using consultants. In effect, these companies are becoming natural resource management agencies [and] owners and managers of wildlife preserves." Of these, forest product companies are probably the largest single employer, with utilities second.

Fishery and wildlife professionals outside of the natural resource companies will usually be found as part of a general "environmental" department with their air, water, and toxic wastes counterparts. Even more than with other types of employers, projects are likely to require a variety of skills beyond those of traditional biologists.

There are many employers with one-of-a-kind jobs to offer, such as wildlife ranges, scientific foundations, zoological parks, and hunting and fishing clubs.

Consulting firms. Nearly all of the major full-service environmental consulting firms in the United States employ a cadre of fishery and wildlife professionals, usually with significant experience and advanced degrees, to work on contracts with the public and private sectors as well as with universities. In addition, there are a large number of small or one-person consulting firms with extremely specialized skills in a specific discipline or type of client.

Commercial aquaculture. Finally, the dramatic increase in aquaculture, or fish farming, has produced fish stocks requiring staff and controlled by corporations, states, and individuals. Catfish farming is a prime example. In 1976, the annual harvest of wild catfish exceeded cultured production by more than 10 million live-weight pounds. Twelve years later, however, more than 90 percent of catfish marketed in the United States came from aquaculture. This trend has created and will continue to create fishery positions, predominantly in the private sector but also technicians and regulatory jobs in the public sector.

NONPROFIT SECTOR

As is true through much of the environmental field, nonprofit organizations in fishery and wildlife management are but a small portion of the industry when measured in terms of employment. But, as elsewhere, this sector has more impact than its size would indicate.

Among the important nonprofit organizations working in fishery and wildlife management, the best known are Greenpeace, the National Wildlife Federation, the National Audubon Society, the World Wildlife Fund, the Izaak Walton League of America, and the Sierra Club. As of this writing, these nonprofit organizations are not expanding. This does not mean that no jobs are available, but it does mean that jobs are difficult to get. And, as noted in other chapters, salaries are typically at the lower end of the scale.

If the nonprofit sector is of interest to you, keep in mind that there are large numbers of small, grass-roots organizations spread throughout the country, many of them low-profile organizations that are not widely known.

Use networking techniques to inquire about organizations in parts of the country that interest you, and be persistent.

Colleges and universities hire a significant percentage of fishery and wildlife management graduates with advanced degrees, not only to teach but also for various research projects. Many of these are temporary positions.

SALARY

Not much has changed since a National Wildlife Federation salary survey of state fishery and wildlife workers showed the following entry-level salaries (adjusted to 1989 dollars):

Game or fishery technician	$16,200 to $23,000
Junior fishery biologist	$19,700 to $27,800

Once a job is obtained, however, salaries for more experienced personnel are not bad. The most recent data available from the U.S. Office of Personnel Management show the following average federal salaries:

Wildlife biology	$33,400
Wildlife refuge management	$33,600
Fishery biology	$35,800
Biological science	$36,500
Fish and wildlife administration	$58,000

Technicians' and entry-level salaries in the private sector are roughly the same as those shown here. Scientists working in consulting firms, however, earn significantly more with advanced degrees and skills in well-funded areas.

GETTING STARTED

So where do you go from here? As in any career, your formal education is the first step.

EDUCATION

Graduates with the best chances of having successful careers in fishery and wildlife management are those who have stressed a broad, ecologically based approach in both their formal education and their work experience. Increasingly, wildlife professionals work on issues of habitat destruction, contamination, and restoration; comprehensive natural resource management planning involving numerous types of professionals and agencies; and multispecies wildlife issues. This requires not only a broad scientific education but also skills in such areas as planning, administration, communications, and negotiation.

Most professionals recommend an integrated course of study stressing ecosystems as well as fish or wildlife biology. Besides the fact that it prepares you to be a better professional, there is a practical reason for this: You broaden your job options. Some schools now offer a combined undergraduate degree in fishery and wildlife management for that very reason.

A state wildlife supervisor illustrates this call for a broad-based education: "Rather than a straight wildlife degree, consider getting a solid biology degree with a lot of field experience. Take courses in everything from limnology and forest ecology to ornithology and organism biology. Go to a school with a biological station and stay there one summer."

In addition to this focus on interdisciplinary study, advanced degrees are now often essential as a passport to careers above the technician or field biologist level.

Rupert Cutler of The River Foundation says: "I recommend taking some courses in business administration, office management, planning, programming, budgeting, finance, and public relations. This will make you a better professional and will give you an edge in the job search. The bottom line in your education is that you should be attempting not to take the cookie cutter approach and be like everyone else but, through a diversity of study, to make yourself uniquely qualified for a niche."

For those who want to work on a daily basis with fish and wildlife in the field, the foregoing advice may be counterproductive. An associate's degree from a two-year college may be a better idea. One state supervisor says: "I think students should step back and look again at technicians' jobs. Technicians do the work most students seem to want to do when they originally go into fishery and wildlife programs. They are the ones who get to wrestle with the animals and catch the fish while we biologists are looking at aerial maps and arguing with foresters."

At any level, formal education alone is unlikely to get you a job in the fishery and wildlife management field. Seasonal and part-time work, internships, and special projects are almost essential for obtaining full-time employment. Not only must you acquire numerous field skills, but, given the competition and scarcity of openings, it is also useful to be a known commodity. Many state, local, and federal departments operate under protracted hiring freezes and can rarely create new staff positions. But there may be latitude to move money around when there is an individual they know and want.

ADVICE

Here is the best of the advice given to us by established professionals in the field, who have faced most of the trials and tribulations you will encounter on the way to your profession.

Get computer skills. Experience and skills in computers, statistics, and computer modeling are useful as habitat management tools. Such areas as harvest management, population dynamics, and other statistics-related areas are growing in importance.

Get some experience. Look for opportunities to do traditional entry-level and seasonal work, such as conducting surveys, measurements, and other research; assisting a biologist; overseeing the work of seasonal or part-time employees; or interacting with the public regarding fishing and hunting regulations. Other entry-level work includes computer data entry, report drafting, paperwork, statistical analysis, and equipment construction and repair. Use unpaid internships and volunteer experiences if paid opportunities are not available.

Join the Peace Corps. Another way to get started in the fishery management field is with the Peace Corps. Helping to increase food production in developing countries through growing and harvesting fish is one objective of the Peace Corps. Volunteers work in aquaculture, inland fisheries, and marine fisheries. Besides the hands-on experience, volunteers also receive one-year noncompetitive eligibility for positions with the federal government. Many have used this edge to gain positions in fishery and natural resource management.

Use the back door. Use a back door or side door approach to get a job in the field. This strategy entails starting at an agency in an unrelated position that is easier to get, then transferring to a fishery or wildlife management job. Such positions include natural resource specialists and managers, employees of natural heritage programs, and water quality personnel. Take this route with some caution, since there is no guarantee of later transfer and you may become a specialist in another area, limiting your ability to move back to fishery and wildlife management. Obviously, you must also be qualified for your interim position—another argument for a broad-based education.

Get on registers. Look at the federal, state, and even local employment procedures and get on these agencies' job registers as soon as possible, either for job openings or just to be informed of the next test for the position you desire (some tests are held several years apart).

Join professional associations. It is advisable to join and become involved in the professional associations: the Wildlife Society and the American Fisheries Society. Both have student chapters at universities. Go beyond these chapters to meet active professionals. Both associations offer accreditation for fishery and wildlife professionals and have combined to establish JOBSource, an up-to-date, detailed bank of national and international job vacancies, summer jobs, and internships (see the Resources section at the end of this chapter).

Know yourself. Resist the temptation to take whatever position is available just because it is available. Initially, of course, you cannot be too picky in this field, but keep in mind your longer-term career goals. Is the position something you will enjoy? Will Sandoval of the Muckleshoot Indian Tribe offers some insight on this subject: "My job is unpredictable, requiring me to juggle a number of projects at a time. I like that. Some prefer more structure, finishing one project before they move on to another. If, for example, I worked for the U.S. Fish and Wildlife Service, I would likely have a particular specialty, say chinook salmon or coho, or maybe harvest statistics. Think about these types of issues when you consider your career."

SUMMARY

The popularity of the fishery and wildlife management profession is both a blessing and a curse for the field and those who enter it. In many cases, there are more highly qualified applicants than there are jobs. Many applicants are overqualified for the jobs they seek, and the frustration of some who struggle to find permanent employment is legendary. Professionals who work for years to gain field experience and knowledge end up behind a desk, while those who are doing the fieldwork complain of low salaries and a limited career path.

Opportunities in fishery management will be more plentiful for the next several years than they have been in the past, but the wildlife management field will still feature tough competition. Advanced degrees are all but assumed in many cases. But the lure of fishery and wildlife management remains strong, and for those with persistence, talent, and creativity, a satisfying career will be the reward.

CASE STUDY

Exxon Valdez *Oil Spill Triggers* *Extensive Wildlife Surveys*

Today the name Exxon Valdez *is synonymous with "oil spill." This environmental disaster in a prized wildlife region ironically triggered what may have been the largest wildlife surveys ever undertaken in a single ecosystem.*

The *Exxon Valdez* strayed into shallow waters in Prince William Sound, Alaska, early on the morning of March 24, 1989. Bligh Reef tore away part of the underside of the massive oil tanker, releasing some 11 million gallons of North Slope crude oil, the largest U.S. oil spill ever, into the pristine waters of the sound. Prince William Sound is near the top of the arc formed by the Gulf of Alaska, with remote and stunning scenery that teems with fish and wildlife, including herring, salmon, whales, seals, bears, bald eagles, puffins, murres, sea lions, sea otters, and many other species. The sound has 2,000 miles of shoreline and water surface area, roughly equal to that of Chesapeake Bay.

Oil from the spill reached some 1,200 miles of coastline as the slick moved westward through the gulf. Shoreline was damaged in Prince William Sound and elsewhere, including seven different national forests, parks, and refuges. *Valdez* oil traveled as far as 600 miles from the site of the wreck. Skimmer ships recovered some oil but had too little equipment and too little time to contain such a vast amount of oil.

The U.S. Coast Guard coordinated the program, but Exxon assumed responsibility for the spill, thus termed a "nonfederalized spill," and organized its own large team of contractors and employees to work on saving wildlife and cleaning up the oil. Other organizations involved included the U.S. Fish and Wildlife Service, the National Oceanic and Atmospheric Administration, the Environmental Protection Agency, several Alaska state agencies, the Prince William Sound Alliance, and many local fishermen.

A small army of workers, boats, helicopters, and land-based staff recovered dead animals and birds, brought live oiled animals into recovery stations for cleaning and care, surveyed the extent of the spill, and made estimates of wildlife populations. Some of these population estimates took place before the spill reached wildlife, making comparative population estimates possible for more accurate estimates of wildlife damage.

Once the early wildlife cleanup and rescue work were under control, cleanup of oiled shorelines began. Cleanup methods used in 1989 ranged from simply pushing oiled masses of debris down into the surf, to hand-cleaning rocks using high-pressure water, to spreading fertilizers to encourage oil-consuming bacteria. The U.S. Fish and Wildlife Service's "Summary of Effects" concerning the spill notes: "When deteriorating weather brought an end to cleanup work in the fall of 1989, a great amount of oil remained on the shorelines." Winter storms removed or buried a substantial portion of this oil. Crews continued to clean shorelines during 1990, using primarily manual cleanup methods. Exxon reported that it spent more than $2 billion on cleanup actions during 1989 and 1990.

Much of the data about wildlife damage collected during the cleanup effort are only partially available for use because much of this information is being used in ongoing legal discussions about damages between Exxon and the U.S. government, along with specific agencies. Many in government agencies appear somewhat critical of Exxon's efforts but are constrained in their ability to speak freely while the matter remains in legal limbo. Some, however, are proud of the cleanup effort and happy to talk about it, including Ed Owens, senior consultant in the Coastal Science and Engineering Center of Woodward-Clyde Consultants in Seattle.

"We conducted the largest single coastal survey that has ever been done," says Owens. "We surveyed 8,000 kilometers of shoreline in 1989, and we did it in about four months." Owens, who managed the survey project his firm carried out for Exxon, explains that the effort included managing a team of as many as 50 professionals who collected data on shoreline oil conditions and the ecology of the shoreline. The team comprised coastal geologists, ecologists, oil spill experts, chemists, and wildlife and cultural experts.

Owens recalls the early days of the effort, with all of the oil still on the shore: "I can remember standing on one beach and seeing 50 vessels with 800 to 1,000 people in the operation. I remember standing there and saying, "I'm not quite sure that this one is going to go away." The fact that Owens had worked with oil spills for many years places this comment in perspective.

The spill took a toll on human workers as well as wildlife. Except for brief visits, Owens scarcely saw his family from March 1989 through September 1990. From March to July 1989 in particular, the schedule was "18 to 20 hours a day, seven days a week. You got up and went to your desk and stayed there—you ate at your desk." The only breaks workers had were to go out and work on the shorelines at the twice-daily low tides. To deal with the high stress and fatigue, workers shifted to a work style that

Owens compares to that of a military operation. "Sometimes you just had to decide what was the right thing to do and go do it."

By the second week of January 1990, Owens says, the visible evidence of the spill had changed dramatically. "We were going around in a rubber boat to some of the sites we sampled and photographed repeatedly over time, and we just kept saying, 'It's all gone.' To have seen it in the spring of 1989 and to go back in January and see the difference was stunning.

"One of my real problems today is that people still think of Prince William Sound as completely covered with oil, and that is a very erroneous picture." Indeed, there have been large catches of salmon, and Owens reports seeing otters "all over the place."

But the damage to wildlife was and is very real. The numbers of animals killed by the spreading oil are only estimates because there is no way to assess the losses accurately. Wildlife loss estimates from the *Exxon Valdez* Oil Spill Trustees' report of April 1992 include the following:

- 3,500 to 5,500 sea otters, with continuing abnormal mortality.
- 200 harbor seals.
- 25 killer whales, three times the normal mortality rate.
- No identifiable terrestrial mammal deaths, although deer in the area had elevated levels of petroleum hydrocarbons in their tissues.
- 300,000 to 645,000 birds, including 300,000 murres, 580 bald eagles, and many others.
- 25 percent lower pink salmon catch in 1990, with analysis of the 1991 catch continuing—abnormally low yields of wild salmon fry, including gross physical abnormalities, have been observed.

The 1992 report proposes few actions to restore wildlife populations directly, instead leaning heavily toward management of human uses to allow natural populations to recover and expanded habitat protection and acquisition measures with essentially the same intent. The report rejects proposals to intervene directly with specific species restoration projects. This is in line with current thinking that except in extraordinary cases, habitat protection achieves species protection more effectively than any direct action.

Chief among the obstacles in determining accurately the losses of wildlife and the best measures to speed its recovery is the need for increased knowledge about the region's wildlife ecology and species. Many of the options detailed in the report, including benchmark monitoring sites, a comprehensive monitoring program, an endowment fund for restoration, and a marine environmental institute, will require fishery and wildlife management professionals as the effort fully to restore Prince William Sound unfolds.

PROFILES

Tom French
Assistant Director
Natural Heritage and Endangered
* Species Program*
Massachusetts Division of Fisheries
* and Wildlife*
Boston, Massachusetts

State natural heritage programs protect species that are not hunted,
fished, trapped, or commercially harvested. The Nature Conservancy
started its Natural Heritage Programs in the 1970s to keep inventories of
wildlife in each state. In Massachusetts, this program protects 175 species
of vertebrate and invertebrate animals as well as 250 species of plants, all
considered at risk.

Wildlife management professionals caution new entrants into the field not
to expect glamour and drama in their careers, but there are some professionals who make even the desk jobs look exciting. Tom French is one of
those. In his capacity as assistant director of the Natural Heritage and
Endangered Species Program for the Massachusetts Division of Fisheries
and Wildlife, he has the kind of busy management position that you would
expect, complete with long hours.

What you might not expect, however, is to see French on television,
rappelling down the side of an office building to rescue a baby peregrine
falcon in need of medical attention or far above the ground on an old iron
catwalk, netting young barn owls from the interior of a building sealed off
for reconstruction.

"I enjoy being outside and getting dirty and being involved in projects,"
says French. "That is what I was trained for. But the better I got at it, the
more administrative responsibilities I took on as I moved up. Now my
position is essentially an administrative job. But that doesn't mean I don't
have pet projects that allow me to keep my hand in and have fun."

French's program is responsible for the protection of 175 species of
vertebrate and invertebrate animals and 250 species of plants that are
considered rare, threatened, or endangered in Massachusetts. This includes species as diverse as bog turtles, the small whorled pogonia (a
plant), the bald eagle, the piping plover, and the American burying beetle.

The peregrine falcon has been reintroduced to downtown Boston by
French's department, and as this chapter was being completed, young
hawks hatched in a peregrine nest on the historic Custom House clock

Natural Heritage and Endangered Species Program, Massachusetts Division of Fisheries and Wildlife, Boston, Massachusetts. Tom French, assistant director of the program, prepares to release a rehabilitated peregrine falcon. The falcon later became part of a breeding pair in central Boston. Photograph by Bill Byrne.

tower. French often stops by to check on the nestlings on the way to or from his Boston office or on a lunch break.

French says he traces his consuming interest in animals "back as far as I can remember." His youthful interest in catching frogs and turtles and playing in the creek gradually evolved into a career—but he started early. French went from earning a sixth-grade science project award for a display of animal skull brain capacities to pouncing on the museum vertebrate collection during his first week as an undergraduate student in biology at Georgia State University in Atlanta.

French worked in the museums at each of the three universities he attended, including Georgia State University, where he earned his degree in biology; Auburn University, where he earned his master's degree in zoology; and Indiana State University, where he obtained his Ph.D. in ecology and systematics.

His broad-ranging interests have resulted in published papers on focused areas of mammalogy, herpetology, ornithology, and entomology. His level of comfort in an array of different fields makes French an ideal administrator. It does not, however, protect him from the work load. "I usually have four or five large projects, like work plans or contracts, that make up my work expectations for the day when I get to the office, but the reality is that most of my time is taken up by brush fires and emergencies, usually on the phone." Other activities during the day may include "a frighteningly small amount of creative time, a law enforcement issue or two, tons of meetings, and lots of networking." There may also be calls about oil spill hazards to wildlife, rabies, or special wildlife collection permits, all of which fall into French's domain.

To ensure that all of these responsibilities are met, French has assembled a varied team of ten professionals. He points out, however, that "not a single one of them has a wildlife management degree." The heritage program employs a botanist, a computer and data management expert, and a botanical ecologist, among others. Four of the ten have Ph.D.s, and virtually all the rest have master's degrees.

These varied talents are put to the test on most days by the range of issues the department must address. Today's emergency involves a female red-tailed hawk well known to French. Once again, she is nesting in an area frequented by lots of people—and dive-bombing golfers who come too close to her tree.

The last time this happened, French personally removed the chick to another hawk's nest and released the mother bird after taking down the nest, thus stopping the protective behavior pattern without losing the chick. This time, he is unsure whether to fence the area, remove the chick, or take the unusually aggressive mother into captivity for good. Another day at the office for Tom French.

Dr. Mamie Parker
Chief, Division of Federal Activity
U.S. Fish and Wildlife Service
Region Three
Fort Snelling, Minnesota

The U.S. Fish and Wildlife Service conserves, protects, and enhances fish, wildlife, and their habitats. The agency's 7,000 employees care for migratory birds, endangered species, fish, and some marine mammals.

First and foremost, Mamie Parker sees herself as an ambassador. Others know her as Dr. Parker, chief of the Division of Federal Activity for the U.S. Fish and Wildlife Service, Region Three, Fort Snelling, Minnesota. But as an African American from the Louisiana bayou country of the Mississippi Delta, she knows it is also her job to lay stereotypes to rest using her wit, charm, and intellect—the job of ambassador is one she knows well.

"I consider myself a child of the integration generation," she says. "I was born in 1957, during the civil rights movement. Six years later, I was one of the first black children to attend the all-white school in Wilmot, Arkansas." The school principal asked Parker's mother to send one of her 11 children to the school. Pointing out little Mamie, Parker's mother said, "Take that one; she'll talk her way out of anything." An ambassador was born.

As a young girl, Parker converted her excursions along the bayous with her mother and grandmother into a source of biological information. "I kept collecting things and learning about their habitats and the order and balance of their ecosystems." She earned a degree in biology from the University of Arkansas at Pine Bluff, followed by both a master's degree and a Ph.D. in aquatic biology and limnology from the University of Wisconsin–Madison.

During college, Parker accepted summer internships with the International Fish Hatchery and Fish Health Laboratory in La Crosse, Wisconsin, and a U.S. Fish and Wildlife Service National Hatchery in New London, Minnesota. "In New London, I was the only black in a town of about 1200. I was a novelty, a black woman working in a Minnesota fish hatchery." She learned to say "uffda," and New Londoners had their first taste of fish fried in cornmeal batter and served with collard greens.

During her 15 years with the U.S. Fish and Wildlife Service, Parker has continued her ambassadorial efforts. She once explained to an irritated group of 20 Missouri farmers that they could not mow down trees along waterways or divert streams because these activities threatened the Indiana bat. By the time she left, Parker recalls, "they were slapping me on the back and laughing."

Her positions since joining the U.S. Fish and Wildlife Service have involved ecological service work in the Green Bay, Wisconsin, field office; lake and rainbow trout raising with the national hatchery at Lake Mills, Wisconsin; and endangered species work in Columbia, Missouri. "In order to move up, you have to move around," she says.

Today, Parker is responsible for guiding policy on federal activities for a region of eight midwestern states. She reviews hydroelectric power projects, provides policy and guidelines for U.S. Fish and Wildlife Service field biologists, and reviews the biologists' work. And in her spare time, Parker helps students with their personal problems during her summer course at Tennessee Technological University, works as a Girl Scout troop leader, and provides encouragement for women in an outpatient program for recovering substance abusers in Minneapolis. True to her calling, Parker remains an ambassador.

Joseph Pavel
Manager of Quantitative Services
Northwest Indian Fisheries
Commission
Olympia, Washington

The Snake River sockeye is now an endangered species, and the salmon stocks of several Northwest fisheries are depressed. Effective fishery management programs executed by dedicated biologists are essential to help preserve both the fish stocks and the fisheries.

Joseph Pavel of the Skokomish Tribe on the southern end of Hood Canal, part of Puget Sound, faced a difficult choice ten years ago. He could keep on making good money, working as a logger in the Pacific Northwest's timber country, or he could make use of his new degree in fisheries biology and work with the Northwest Indian Fisheries Commission to help regulate the salmon fisheries—and earn a lot less.

Logging provides a good income and instant gratification: trees fall down. But for Pavel the logger, the work failed to provide any real goal. It was not a career.

Fishery work, on the other hand, requires patience, imagination, and a great deal of faith. "It will take another 10 or 20 years to evaluate our progress," he says. "In that time frame, we will see that it is working." But the very fact that fishery work requires a long view also means that the field provides a strong sense of direction. Pavel's work, though at times frustrating, has the goal of preserving Northwest salmon species and simultaneously maintaining a viable Native American fishery.

In his first position with the commission, Pavel helped maintain a database for the salmon catches of 20 Northwest tribes that belong to the commission. By monitoring the amount of fish caught, their species, and where they were caught, the commission built a database of information to use in determining the health of existing salmon stocks and to predict future safe harvests.

The data were relayed to a large mainframe computer housed at the University of Washington in Seattle. As the program developed and personal computers became more affordable, the tribes began to use them in the program. Now each tribe has several computers linked to the commission via telephone modem links. Pavel worked with the computers from the start, increasing his knowledge of the systems as he worked with them.

Today, Pavel is manager of quantitative services for the commission. The Quantitative Services Unit manages database applications, sets up and maintains new computer applications, maintains the local area network linking the computers, and manages data processing and computer simulation modeling for the commission's fishery data. Pavel manages a staff of several workers, spending 50 percent of his time working with the staff on specific projects, 30 percent on maintaining and coordinating information, and the remaining 20 percent on carrying out administrative and managerial work. Pavel's department labors to produce the information crucial to making informed decisions about which fish are safe to catch and when and where to catch them so that the fishing will be good and the fish stocks will also be protected from overfishing.

The Snake River sockeye is now an endangered species, and other valuable stocks are in danger as well. "We will never have the amount of fisheries resources that will make everybody happy," says Pavel. "We need to reach levels of compromise and realistic expectations for the catch. Some stocks are quite strong, and others are depressed. It takes intense scrutiny and hard work to direct the catch. We are trying to halt the downward spiral of fish populations and bring the stocks back."

Three of the data sources Pavel uses to track fish stocks are as follows:

- Fish receipts, which record the general species caught on the tribal fishing boats and the location where they were caught.
- Genetic stock identification uses protein electrophoresis analysis to determine the genetic stock source of a particular fish. Based on database records, Pavel uses the analysis to determine the geographic origin of the fish.
- Tiny coded wire tags implanted in fish at hatcheries or at wild fish traps. After implantation of the tags, the fish is marked with a clipped fin so that when the fish is caught, the wire can be recovered and the resultant data on the fish, as well as where and when it was caught, can be entered in the database.

This kind of fishery work requires skills in three crucial areas. Pavel says: "I'd rate biology number three. It is by far the easiest of the three skill areas you need. Go with a core curriculum of math and English. You have to be able to communicate and understand the numbers. Computer skills are also very important."

Used well, those skills will help fishery management professionals rebuild salmon fish stocks over the years ahead while still allowing careful harvesting by the Northwest tribes around Puget Sound.

RESOURCES

American Fisheries Society. Holds an annual meeting as well as symposia and workshops. Has regional chapters. Publishes an annual membership directory, *Fisheries* (bimonthly), and the *Journal of North American Fisheries Management* (quarterly). 5410 Grosvenor Ln., Suite 110, Bethesda, MD 20814–2199. (301) 897–8616.

American Institute of Biological Sciences, 730 11th St., NW, Washington, DC 20001–4521. (202) 628–1500.

American Society for Biochemistry and Molecular Biology, 9650 Rockville Pike, Bethesda, MD 20814. (301) 530–7145.

Botanical Society of America, Dr. Christopher Haufler, University of Kansas, Botany Department, Hayworth Hall, Lawrence, KS 66045–2106.

Center for Marine Conservation. A nonprofit membership organization dedicated to protecting marine wildlife and its habitats and to conserving coastal and ocean resources. Regional offices in Austin; San Francisco; Hampton, VA; and Saint Petersburg, FL. 1725 DeSales St., NW, Washington, DC 20036.

Chronicle Guidance Publications. Publishes *Oceanographers* as well as *Zoologists*. Aurora St., P.O. Box 1190, Moravia, NY 13118–1190. (315) 497–0330.

Defenders of Wildlife. Promotes the preservation of wildlife, particularly endangered species, through education, litigation, research, and advocacy. Conducts public education and runs an activist network. Publishes *Defenders* (bimonthly). 1244 19th St., NW, Washington, DC 20036. (202) 659–9510.

Fisheries Scientist. Occupational Brief 190. Single copy $3 from Chronicle Guidance Publications, Moravia, NY 13118.

International Association of Fish and Wildlife Agencies. Publishes a bimonthly newsletter. 444 N. Capitol St., NW, Suite 544, Washington, DC 20001. (202) 624–7890.

JOBSource. See the listing in the Resources section in chapter 4 for a complete description. Has a special program for the American Fisheries Society and the Wildlife Society. Offers a computerized, up-to-date listing of positions.

National Audubon Society. Publishes *Audubon* magazine and *American Birds* (both bimonthly). 950 Third Ave., New York, NY 10022. (212) 546–9100.

National Wildlife Federation. Largest conservation organization in the world. Has state chapters and holds an annual meeting. Awards fellowships for graduate study in conservation and sponsors paid internships. Publishes annual *Conservation Directory, National Wildlife Magazine* (bimonthly), and numerous other publications. 1400 16th St., NW, Washington, DC 20036. (202) 797–6800.

Peace Corps. Recruitment Office, 1555 Wilson Blvd., Suite 701, Arlington, VA 22209. Or call (800) 424–8580 for the Peace Corps office nearest you.

Trout Unlimited. Publishes *Lines to Leaders* (monthly). 800 Follin Ln., Suite 250, Vienna, VA 22180. (703) 281–1100.

U.S. Fish and Wildlife Service. The service manages more than 450 national wildlife refuges. U.S. Department of the Interior, Washington, DC 20240. (202) 208–5634.

Wildlife and Fisheries: Career Opportunities (1986). West Wind Productions. (800) 228–8854.

The Wildlife Society. Conducts annual and various special meetings. Has regional chapters. Publications include the *Journal of Wildlife Management* (quarterly), the *Wildlife Society Bulletin* (quarterly), and the *Wildlifer* (bimonthly). 5410 Grosvenor Ln., Suite 200, Bethesda, MD 20814. (301) 897–9770.

World Wildlife Fund. Publishes *FOCUS* (bimonthly). 1250 24th St., NW, Washington, DC 20037. (202) 293–4800.

13 Parks and Outdoor Recreation

AT A GLANCE

Employment:
75,000 full-time parks and recreation professionals nationwide, with an additional 40,000 part-time and seasonal workers

Demand:
2 to 5 percent growth per year in the early 1990s, followed by 5 to 8 percent growth from 1994 to 2000

Breakdown:
Public sector, 80 percent (25 percent federal, 55 percent state and local)
Private sector, 10 percent
Nonprofit sector, 10 percent

Key Job Titles:
Administrator
Archaeologist
Biologist
Botanist
Concession manager
Ecosystem restoration expert
Geologist
Historian
Landscape architect

Maintenance manager
Natural resource manager
Planner
Ranger
Wildlife biologist

Influential Organizations:

Army Corps of Engineers
Forest Service
National Parks and Conservation Association
National Park Service
National Recreation and Park Association

Salary:

Base starting salaries for federal rangers vary from $15,000 to $18,000. Experienced individuals draw salaries of $30,000 to $40,000. State and local park salaries start as low as $10,560 per year for trainees, but with a degree they jump to $22,000 to $26,000. Top salaries fall in the $75,000 to $100,000 range.

Many people considering environmental careers trace their interest to a memorable outdoor experience they had as a child. Parks provide a large percentage of these experiences for children and adults in locations ranging from the centers of our largest cities to places so remote that the night sky has not a hint of city lights in it. Parks and recreation workers are the people who guide us within these special places of enjoyment, education, and contemplation.

Perhaps that is why many people first look to the parks when they think about environmental careers. You should be aware, however, that many career opportunities exist beyond the most visible jobs of ranger and forest fire fighter.

WHAT IS PARKS AND OUTDOOR RECREATION?

Parks and outdoor recreation is a surprisingly complex field, for which the Indiana Department of Natural Resources lists 90 distinct positions. The following is a breakdown of some of the major categories of professionals involved in parks and outdoor recreation. In addition, many positions held by park personnel are discussed further in other chapters: natural resource managers and specialists, chapter 11; environmental educators and interpreters, chapter 6; and planners, chapter 5.

ADMINISTRATION

Parks and other outdoor areas are physical and organizational entities that must be managed just as any other agency or company is. To do so requires skilled personnel in the areas of budgeting and finance, public affairs and procurement, and contracting, as well as people to perform personnel management, management analysis, and related support services. Informational resources management is one growing area in these agencies; records managers and computer and telecommunications specialists can find interesting and innovative work in outdoor recreation agencies.

INTERPRETATION

Interpreters are the park personnel whom the public is most likely to see. The most visible, perhaps, is the park ranger. (The title itself is a generic term for professionals who carry out a variety of tasks.) Rangers are involved in law enforcement—they provide for the safety of park visitors. They are also involved in education, maintenance, and natural resource management activities and in planning and executing recreational programs for visitors. In small park systems, a ranger might handle all of these functions; elsewhere, specialists handle the diverse functions. Thus, there are park police, interpreters, recreation planners and programmers, maintenance staff members, and natural resource managers (of which there are numerous specialties). The current trend is to separate the roles of interpretation and law enforcement into different jobs and career tracks.

NATURAL RESOURCE MANAGEMENT

The specialty of natural resource management tends to emphasize the component of parks and outdoor recreation that makes resources accessible to the public. Equally important, however, are those professionals who actually manage natural resources. These include foresters, range managers, fishery and wildlife biologists, ecologists, soil scientists, and various natural resource specialists and planners. These professionals are covered more extensively in chapters 11, 12, and 14.

RESEARCH

Closely related to natural resource managers are personnel involved in research on federal and state lands. Public lands are repositories of biological information, gene pools, and species diversity and are ideal natural research facilities. Researchers include those listed under Natural

Resource Management as well as virtually every type of scientist imaginable. An area that is receiving increased study is the impact of contaminants—airborne and waterborne toxins and pollutants—on ecosystems and on individual plants and animal species. The effect of acid rain on park ecosystems, for instance, is undergoing considerable scrutiny.

SITE OPERATIONS AND MAINTENANCE

Whether parks and outdoor recreation facilities are maintained in a roughly natural state or are intensively managed facilities, their maintenance and upkeep is a formidable and often chronically underfunded task. Besides providing maintenance and facilities for visitors and staff members, maintenance personnel must manage large amounts of land. This work is carried out by landscape architects, engineers, property managers, and administrative staff members as well as laborers, technicians, and seasonal workers.

HISTORY AND BACKGROUND

Although we tend to think of our park systems as long-standing entities, the idea of publicly supported parks is actually a fairly new concept.

- Yellowstone National Park, the oldest national park in America, was established as a federal reservation in 1872 and placed under control of the U.S. Army.
- The Lacey Act of 1894 gave the army authority forcibly to stop interstate shipment of wildlife, bringing damage to wildlife and other park resources under more control.
- The National Park Service was founded as a civilian agency in 1916, allowing the army to concentrate its resources on the war in Europe. The 1916 act charged the new agency with conserving scenery and natural and historic objects as well as wildlife in the national parks. The act also requires the Park Service to provide for the public's enjoyment of the parks while protecting them for future generations. Future acts added to the scope of the National Park Service.
- The Wilderness Act of 1964 established wild buffer zones around national parks to insulate them from nearby human activity.
- The Alaska National Interest Lands Conservation Act in 1980 set aside large tracts of land in Alaska for new national parks.
- Other laws, including the Endangered Species Act, greatly influence the operation of parks nationwide.

The National Park System now includes some 361 parks that encompass 80 million acres. But as large as this federal park system appears, it is dwarfed in numbers of parks by the size of U.S. state and local park systems. Barry Tindall, director of public policy for the National Recreation and Parks Association, estimates that there are now more than 108,500 state and local recreation sites around the United States. The total number of full-time workers in the parks probably approaches 75,000, with seasonal workers swelling the ranks beyond 100,000, says Tindall.

ISSUES AND TRENDS

Trends point the way toward the areas where the most is happening in your chosen field. These grow, fade, and change over time, so watch them closely throughout your career. They may provide the opportunity to focus your efforts and maximize your value in the employment marketplace.

IMPORTANCE OF URBAN PARKS

With park acreage so immense, it would be easy to assume that parks and recreation priorities are dominated by the needs of vast, comparatively remote domains of bear and beaver, elk and antelope. But Tindall and others argue that the parks of greatest importance to the majority of Americans are urban parks, whether they are run by federal, state, or local agencies.

"The urban setting is the last place to be reached by the environmental movement," says Mark Primack, executive director of the Boston Green-Space Alliance. "Urban parks are being taken seriously as a social issue and an environmental issue."

URBAN PARK DEMOGRAPHICS

Demographics present the most convincing reason for the growth of urban parks: In one generation, there has been a phenomenal increase in the proportion of people who live in or near major metropolitan areas. Moreover, the annual two-week vacation by the two-parent family, though not a thing of the past, is being overshadowed by life-style changes, including the rise of single-parent families, an aging population, an increase in dual wage-earner families, and more single people. All of these changes create a demand for more and better recreation closer to home.

"Recreation close to home is absolutely the top priority," says Tindall. "It must be within 15 minutes by foot or bicycle or ten miles by car or public transportation. Understanding the demographics is critical, yet very few natural resource managers even begin to look at demographics." Demographics say that urban parks will soon begin to dominate the recreational landscape.

OPEN SPACE NEAR HOME

Some urban groups are focusing on smaller and smaller pieces of open space. Kathy Dickhut of the Open Lands Project says: "We are working on establishing permanent community gardens and parks in neighborhoods because people want open space where they live. Again and again I hear, 'We want a place where we can watch our kids play while we are cooking dinner.' This is day-to-day open space."

URBAN WILD PLACES

At the other end of the urban recreation movement is an emphasis on creating nearby outdoor recreational opportunities that border on wilderness. Wetlands, rivers, seacoasts, meadowland, and old farmland are being used and often reclaimed for such purposes. The Boston Harbor Islands State Park and the White River State Park in Indianapolis are just two examples of the federal, state, and regional outdoor parks in and around urban areas. The rails-to-trails movement, which calls for converting abandoned railways to biking, skiing, and hiking paths, is another example of this trend. Finally, the President's Commission on Americans Outdoors in 1985 called for the creation of greenways. Greenways are corridors of private and public recreational lands and water that provide access to open spaces, and habitat for wildlife, close to where people live.

INCREASED PARK USE

People now use parks for a wider variety of activities and at all times of day, so year-round staffing and varied programming are much more important. Why has this shift occurred? As the population ages and as more workers take advantage of flexible work schedules, more people can use parks in off-hours. People come to parks for weekend picnics, but they also return during the week to exercise, play, and learn about their environment, culture, and history.

ACCESS VERSUS PRESERVATION

As parks move closer to people and the use of outdoor areas increases, multiple-use issues—the often conflicting goals of access and preservation—become an increasing challenge. This is true for urban parks as well as for national outdoor recreation areas. Professionals must face the divergent demands of large crowds, including hikers, hunters, and anglers as well as researchers and preservationists. They contend with increased demand for consumptive uses of public lands such as timber cutting, mining, and oil and gas extraction. At the local level, these conflicts often surface in issues such as paving for bicycle access, off-road vehicle use, marina construction, festival activity, and concessions. As one professional says, "With increased use and expanded constituencies, we don't have the slack we used to have; decisions must be better thought out and more professional and then [must be] implemented efficiently."

OUTSIDE THREATS

Outside threats to parkland health, such as development on park borders, acid rain, water pollution, and the introduction of foreign species, also command the attention of outdoor recreation professionals. Says Mark Primack of the Boston GreenSpace Alliance: "Park professionals are realizing that they cannot limit their activity to within park boundaries because actions and decisions made outside the park will directly affect them." Park personnel are becoming more active in working with local community organizations and political bodies and are engaging in public relations and media strategies. Interpretive staff members who previously were concerned only with helping people enjoy their visits to the park are now making visitors aware of the park's health.

PARK ACCESS FOR ALL PEOPLE

The democratization of outdoor recreation is an issue in many areas. Recreation coordinators spend a lot of time worrying about those who are left out, including the poor, the elderly, and the disabled. Legal requirements will force improvements, and park workers will be charged with ensuring some park access for the physically challenged.

PRIVATE PARKS

The question of access to outdoor recreation areas brings up another topic: the increasing incidence of private as opposed to public ownership of such areas. Professionals are quick to point out that all privatization should not be assumed to impair equal access. Privatization of concessions in the national parks, for example, can raise money for the National Park System and free staff members for other responsibilities.

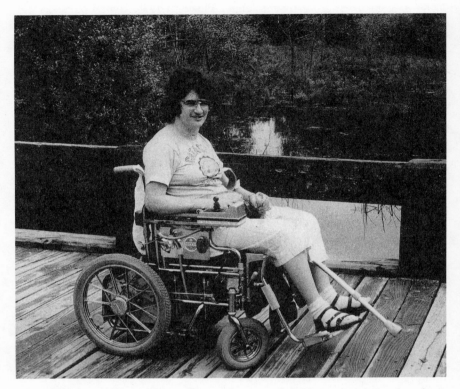

*Blue Hills Reservation, Milton, Massachusetts. Ceil Blumenstock developed rec-
ommendations for redesigning the facilities at Houghtons Pond, Massachusetts,
to make the public park fully accessible to handicapped visitors.*

There is, however, marked concern that a move toward privatization
could create a class-based system of recreational opportunities. Waterfront
access is a prime example. As private development takes over more and
more shoreline, concern is growing over exclusion of the public from waterways and beaches.

SCARCE FUNDING

The scarcity of funding for outdoor recreation at the federal, state, and
local levels is a persistent, significant problem for park professionals.
Bernard Conn of the New York State Office of Parks, Recreation, and
Historic Preservation says: "This ongoing scarcity of resources means
park professionals must be inventive and creative since the resources don't

exist to do everything you need to do. So, we spend a lot of time working with volunteers and writing grants. This requires flexibility."

INCREASING PROFESSIONALISM

The outdoor recreation field has become increasingly professional. There is less patronage hiring, and there are fewer old-boy networks and more national job listings. More people enter the field with specialized training. And as the field becomes more sophisticated, employees also need skills outside of natural resource management or recreation programming, including written and oral communication, management, and budgeting.

UNDERFUNDED RESEARCH

Research in our park systems has historically been funded with less than 2 percent of the National Park Service budget. Research left undone creates a host of problems all across the nation. For instance, in an article from *National Parks*, Dr. John C. Gordon, dean of Yale University's School of Forestry and Environmental Studies, notes that the saguaro cacti of Saguaro National Monument are failing to reproduce and no one knows why. The effect of runoff of agricultural fertilizers on the Everglades National Park is also poorly understood. "Almost 90 percent of the National Park System's 80 million acres has never been surveyed adequately for cultural resources," Gordon writes.

CAREER OPPORTUNITIES

Opportunities in parks and outdoor recreation in the United States vary greatly from one facility to another, even within the same sector. The Detroit park system, for instance, has a different mix of personnel from that of Yellowstone National Park. Still, all agencies hire rangers and law enforcement professionals, interpreters, maintenance and recreational program personnel, and administrative staff members.

Although a job with Yellowstone may at first glance appear more exciting than one with an urban park system, both rural and urban parks provide their own challenges and satisfactions. Be sure to examine carefully the full range of outdoor recreation careers.

PUBLIC SECTOR

Although a part of this sector, the National Park Service employs only a small fraction of the total park workers in the public sector. Other federal agencies, and state, county, or city parks are more likely employers.

Federal government. Working at a national park is often presented as the career path of choice for those entering the parks and outdoor recreation field. But the National Park Service, with 13,000 full-time employees, many of whom work in maintenance, employs a relatively small percentage of recreation professionals.

The National Park System includes 361 sites covering 80 million acres and encompasses two broad categories: historical parks, found primarily in the eastern United States, and large western parks, which exhibit the characteristics and hire the types of professionals (rangers) most commonly portrayed.

Although national parks come to mind first, the public uses many other federal lands as well, including national forests, wilderness areas, wildlife refuges, and scenic rivers. These lands are managed by numerous federal agencies that are often overlooked by job seekers. The Forest Service, for example, with more than 30,000 employees, manages 200 million acres of land in 44 states and hosts 100 million visitors each year. The Bureau of Land Management, with 9,000 employees, manages 300 million acres, to which public access is mandated. The U.S. Fish and Wildlife Service provides public access and recreation at its wildlife refuges and other landholdings.

Although federal park rangers are the image many have in mind when they consider an outdoor recreation career, breaking into the Park Service as a ranger is not easy. "We hire only about 50 rangers in an average year," says Leonard Emerson, personnel management specialist with the National Park Service. "We went through tremendous growth in the National Park System and pretty well loaded up on those people." The Park Service is unlikely to increase the number of rangers it hires until 2005 to 2008, when older employees will retire in large numbers.

The definition of "ranger" itself is so broad that many people consider it absurd. The National Park Service lists the functions of a federal ranger as list supervision, conservation management, natural resource management, interpretation, forest fire control, predator control, traffic control, accident investigation, and even folk art demonstration. "I don't even know if it's possible to hire that kind of a superperson anymore," says Emerson. Rangers already tend to specialize in one area or another, and this trend is likely to continue.

State and local government. All of the federal agencies combined, however, provide far fewer opportunities for parks and outdoor recreation professionals than do the 50 state parks and recreation agencies and numerous state forests, scenic rivers, and wildlife refuges. Although it is not as well publicized as federal employment, employment in state park systems is growing relative to federal positions—despite hiring freezes in many state governments. Even small towns have parks, and in large cities the park system is often run by a major department. Consider as well the numerous regional and county park systems.

Metropolitan District Commission, Boston, Massachusetts. Vicky Gobetz put her artistic talent to work by painting interpretive signs for the Boston regional park district.

More so than federal agencies, state and local park and recreation systems are faced with the need to provide for urban populations. Growth in urban park requirements, says the National Recreation and Park Association's Barry Tindall, calls for skills not found in the typical parks and recreation curriculum. "These people are service brokers as much as they are managers or initiators," he says. "It requires good people skills, organizational ability, and effective management of resources and resource users." Environmentalists in urban systems often need social intervention skills as substance abuse activities and gang intervention become increasingly common.

"How do you manage a park and recreation system to be in compliance with the Americans with Disabilities Act? These are the conditions that, in our opinion, define a new mission for professional recreation preparation." Tindall explains as well that these kinds of changes are accompanied by new concern about legal issues. "I get more calls on laws and regulatory issues than on anything else," he says.

PRIVATE SECTOR

The private sector is founding or taking over more and more recreation areas; thus, private sector employment is a growing proportion of the recreation field.

Privately owned facilities. A majority of privately managed facilities tend to be artificial, such as golf courses, marinas, health clubs, and resorts. However, significant numbers of private operations do manage outdoor activities in the proximity of large parklands, including hiking, skiing, climbing, fishing, white water rafting, whale watching, and other activities. In 1991, private businesses clustered in and around the nation's parks garnered revenues of $3 billion from the 260 million park visitors.

Still, it would be easy to discount the importance of opportunities in private recreation when contemplating an environmental career. But consider this, for example: the majority of the 5,000-plus U.S. golf courses include significant plant and animal wildlife and water resources. Additionally, private nature centers and other organizations not easily classified employ parks and recreation personnel.

Ecotourism and direct mail merchandising. Ecotourism, run by both private businesses and nonprofit agencies, is one of the fastest-growing portions of the recreational field. *Buzzworm* magazine's March/April 1992 issue listed 118 outfitters ready to transport vacationers to nearly any part of the globe for the environmentally correct time of their lives. The expansion of this glamorous field—the environmental equivalent of working on a cruise ship—means that jobs are available, but competition may be fierce.

Finally, opportunities exist for writers, marketers, merchandisers, and graphic production specialists in burgeoning environmental mail-order catalog operations.

NONPROFIT SECTOR

Nonprofit agencies—the smallest set of employers in the parks and recreation field—have made the same discoveries that private firms have, namely, that mail-order catalogs and ecotourism are big business.

The most dedicated of these organizations, such as the National Parks and Conservation Association and the National Recreation and Park Association, provide invaluable information tailored to suit the needs of this field. In addition to carrying out such information-intensive programs, they also lobby for improvements in parks organizations and espouse new techniques and programs that will benefit both their members and the environment.

SALARY

Traditional entry-level positions in parks and outdoor recreation are fairly uniform in salary—and no one goes into parks and recreation to get rich. The result of sometimes heavy job responsibilities coupled with mediocre pay is that "most rangers can't afford to stay with it," says Lazaro Garcia, chief operating officer for the National Parks and Conservation Association. Garcia says that in some areas with high costs of living, as in the case of urban national parks, "local housing is beyond their financial limits." Associations are lobbying hard to solve this problem.

Interpretive, ranger, and recreational positions offer starting pay in the range of $16,000 to $23,000, usually near the low end. (See chapters 11, 12 and 14 for additional salary information on related careers.) Entry-level federal park ranger positions are usually graded GS-4 or GS-5 and occasionally GS-7; check current federal pay ranges for these grades.

"Rangers are grossly underpaid," states Garcia. He notes that federal park police, with duties similar to those of rangers, receive 30 percent more pay. According to the National Park Service's Leonard Emerson, average pay for experienced rangers is $30,000. He notes that in 1994, all federal salaries will be augmented by "locality pay" for areas where federal pay is out of step with the cost of living.

Seasonal employment in entry-level positions is likely to pay $250 to $300 per week. Seasonal federal positions in interpretation are graded between GS-2 and GS-7, and those in law enforcement are graded between GS-3 and GS-7, depending on education, skills, and experience; this means that these positions may pay as little as $13,000 per year. Seasonal employees who have been working for some time can make as much as $300 per week, though with few if any benefits.

Entry-level salaries in state and local parks average $22,000 to $26,000, according to the National Recreation and Park Association. Many experienced people earn salaries in the $40,000 to $50,000 range, and the high end of the salary scale can reach $75,000 to $100,000.

Jobs in the nonprofit sector yield salaries roughly comparable to federal salaries, while private positions can be somewhat more lucrative. Emerson notes that salaries in the federal parks lag behind private pay "in all areas."

Many park employees function as specialists in their respective fields. See chapters 11, 12, and 14 for further information on salaries in land and water conservation, resource management, fishery and wildlife management, and forestry.

GETTING STARTED

Because parks positions are often in high demand, getting hired will require more effort and careful planning than will other segments of the environmental field. Careful consideration of your educational plans is essential.

EDUCATION

There are so many different careers in parks and outdoor recreation that it is impossible to note one particular way to prepare for such a career. Furthermore, professionals say that it is difficult to specialize until you get a job, and they recommend against attempting to specialize as part of undergraduate training.

Mark Primack, a former park employee and now executive director of the Boston GreenSpace Alliance, says: "People come out of school thinking park management is all about managing natural resources. Not so. Today's open space manager needs people skills to interact with subordinates, seasonal employees, the public, businesspeople, and the local community. Those who have the technical skills without the skills in communications and politics do a disservice to us all.

"We used to speculate that the perfect park employee worked at a five-and-dime retail job: high pressure, low budget. Something else we looked for was combined backgrounds: combinations that included such skills as public relations, planning, computers and graphics, education, and horticulture."

This advice drives home an important point: You need specific skills and a careful strategy to get your first job in parks and outdoor recreation. However, you also need a broad arsenal of skills and education to have a successful career in the field. The National Parks and Conservation Association's Lazaro Garcia recommends that in college you study one or more of the following topics: biodiversity, animal and habitat protection, agriculture, natural and cultural resources, and journalism (you need to be a good writer, he says).

The National Park Service's Leonard Emerson recommends studies in botany, fisheries biology, history, archaeology, biological sciences, biodiversity, and geology. "We need applicants with 24 to 30 hours [or more] of natural science," says Emerson.

One way to choose a field of study is to decide where you want to work and query that organization about its educational requirements.

If you are fairly certain of your long-term goals, there exist some distinct career paths that you can work toward as an undergraduate. If your major interest is in natural resource management or research, a hard science background with a strong ecological base is recommended, and a master's degree is probably needed (see chapters 11, 12, and 14). If state park management and administration is your ultimate goal, a degree in recreation and parks management, perhaps combined with some hard sciences, is a good path. These are not the only ways to get started in these subfields, but they are among the most common.

No matter what their educational background may be, most parks and outdoor recreation professionals start at the bottom and work their way up, specializing as they go along. To advance your career, it is important to have held some of the entry-level jobs, especially those that entail contact with park visitors; most administrators were once rangers, interpreters, or foresters. This speaks for a broad-based education designed to develop a variety of skills, both technical and interpersonal.

With the exception of some specialized positions, a master's degree is not absolutely necessary—and probably will not guarantee the raise in salary that it can in other fields. Parks and outdoor recreation professionals view a graduate degree as a way to specialize later in a career or as a way to broaden oneself, as a complement to an undergraduate degree. For example, if you have a B.A. in a hard science, you might consider a master's degree in management.

Whenever possible, gather expertise in additional areas such as communications, writing, fund-raising, negotiation, and computer applications. Knowledge of a foreign language, especially Spanish, is often valuable to your parks and recreation center. In addition, the application form for the position of seasonal park ranger, besides focusing on law enforcement and medical and safety experience, asks about outdoor skills (hiking, rock climbing, canoeing); leadership and ability as a tour guide; experience in dramatic arts; operation and repair of equipment (chain saws, fire-fighting equipment) and vehicles (farm equipment, boats); knowledge of archaeological and historical preservation; and ability to work with people of varying ages, abilities, and backgrounds.

ADVICE

The tougher the job market, the more useful it is to heed those who have been this way before you. It is important to actively gather and consider the advice of professionals in the field as you embark on and progress in your career.

Get some experience. Experience is often a prerequisite to getting a job in parks and outdoor recreation. One way to gain valuable experience is to attend a school that has a cooperative program with the agency for which you would ultimately like to work. If you do a good job, you might be hired full-time on completion of your degree.

In addition, the breadth of your work experience is important, as is the strength of your professional references. Work in part-time, seasonal, or volunteer positions (which can provide valuable references) with more than one agency if possible—broaden your experience. Consider starting your career at the state or local level, where competition is not as harsh and there are more openings.

Start with seasonal work. The entry-level job in the parks and outdoor recreation field is the seasonal position. Few people are hired for full-time jobs without previous seasonal experience. Seasonal positions are found in all areas of park operations, and include jobs as interpreters, law enforcement workers, park rangers, laborers, researchers, and recreation programmers.

Be aware of application requirements. You do not have to be a college graduate to be eligible for seasonal employment, but to qualify for a job at the federal level you must be 18 years old and have a driver's license. Application deadlines are mid-January for summer positions and mid-July for fall and winter jobs. The National Park Service allows you to apply for positions in only two parks at any one time. To increase your chances of acceptance, consider applying at lesser-known parks, which receive fewer applications. In addition, check with state and local park systems for their seasonal application requirements.

Once you have worked as a seasonal employee, you can complete the federal application (Standard Form 171) for full-time work. This form is part of the procedure allowing you to apply for openings in the federal government.

One thing working in favor of most people reading this book is a decline in patronage, which is the hiring of relatives and political friends. This is especially relevant to people considering careers in municipal or regional park systems. It still helps to know your city council member or local elected official, but such a connection probably does not carry the weight it once did.

Do some research on agencies you are interested in. One final piece of advice: Examine the philosophy of an agency before you devote significant time and energy to getting a position there. Are you comfortable with its priorities, both mandated and informal? With its traditional career paths? With its programs and special projects? Spend some time on these questions; your investment will pay off later.

SUMMARY

In 1991, on its 75th anniversary, the National Park Service organized several working groups to explore nontraditional ways of working within the agency. In addition, impetus for reorganization came from the outside as environmental associations poked and prodded the agency to consider change.

That change is coming for all parks and outdoor recreation organizations is a given. The multiple, simultaneous, and often conflicting pressures of reduced budgets, special needs, endangered species, demands for urban recreation, low salaries, and other issues present parks and recreation organizations with both demand for, and obstacles to, change.

Salaries will increase somewhat, and demand for well-trained professionals will expand this area more strongly beginning in the mid-1990s. The National Park Service's Leonard Emerson expects that rather than asking rangers to serve an inordinate number of functions at parks, the agency will turn some jobs over to specialists by reclassifying the jobs as professional positions.

CASE STUDY

Yellowstone National Park

Yellowstone National Park epitomizes the central quandary of the parks and outdoor recreation field: preserving nature while simultaneously ensuring its enjoyment by the humans who place it at risk.

More than 120 years after it was first set aside as a national park, Yellowstone is just a few years from being perhaps the only intact large-scale ecosystem in the United States. "The gray, or Rocky Mountain, wolf is the only native animal missing from Yellowstone," says Norm Bishop, research interpreter for the National Park Service at the park.

This statement reflects some of the pride that Park Service employees feel at managing a park that sustains a relative balance between conflicting responsibilities. The act that established Yellowstone National Park in 1872 required preservation of the park's wildlife as well as its abundant geothermal features—Yellowstone contains more active geothermal sites than the rest of the world combined, says Bishop. That same act also required that Yellowstone be available for the enjoyment of citizens, and that has been the crucial dilemma for the National Park Service since its formation in 1916, when it took over management of the park.

Today's Yellowstone functions with an assortment of different divisions to meet its assigned tasks. These divisions include the following:

- The superintendent's office, home of management, public affairs activities, and planning.
- The Administrative Division, which manages payments, supplies, and personnel.
- The Maintenance Division, which maintains physical facilities in the park.
- The Service Center, located in Denver, which designs larger park projects.
- The Ranger Division, which is responsible for police, fire, and rescue operations, wildlife preservation, visitor information, and other functions.
- The Interpretation Division, which helps educate and guide park visitors.
- The Concessions Division, which manages food distribution throughout the park.

Whatever the range and qualities of a park's professionals, however, the central challenge of all parks remains the same—how do you ensure the human enjoyment of a complex wild ecosystem without doing that ecosystem harm?

The relative isolation of Yellowstone in its mountain-range retreat in the northwestern corner of Wyoming is an important ally in the efforts of the Park Service. This remote location, coupled with a buffering layer of wilderness areas around the park, insulates the ecosystem from much of the outside world. But the lure of the park is such that roughly 3 million visitors each year make the journey. Although the Park Service officials feel that the impact of humans on the park is being contained, the effect of humans is nonetheless significant:

- Modification of wildlife habitat in nearby lands outside the park is a constant concern. Mining, oil and gas exploration and extraction, and housing development on these lands, much of it in private hands, make changes to wildlife habitat that tip the balance away from survival for some species. One extensive national forest now contains hundreds of miles of logging roads and extensive clear-cutting. "Such a huge amount of timber was removed that lands which once supported a 45-day elk-hunting season can now sustain only a 5-day season," reports Bishop.
- Each year, the National Park Service spends $200,000 hauling solid wastes out of the park to incinerators and landfills well away from Yellowstone. "We take the wastes that far away and spend that money to protect the bears from getting into it and becoming used to human foods," says Bishop. "Our experience is that when bears become accustomed to human food, they can become dangerous and have to be killed."

  But the Yellowstone bear story has changed substantially in recent decades. The grizzly has been moved from the backwoods habitat to its former central role in the park. Human fishing is almost entirely limited to catch-and-release sportfishing, allowing fish stocks to return to their former abundance. Grizzlies now fish the streams during spawning season in full view of visitors on the famous Fishing Bridge, and campgrounds close to the bears' favorite fishing spots have been removed. Yellowstone now supports roughly 200 grizzlies, with some populations reported outside the park. Through the grizzly, the Endangered Species Act has been both a contentious and a unifying force for the Park Service, says Bishop. "It forces resource managers in different agencies to work together."
- Large ungulates, those honored herbivores that include both bison and elk, present the park with their own set of resource issues. Yellowstone boasts the last continuously wild herd of bison, and parts of the herd roam where they please, including areas outside the park. Neighboring ranchers are terrified of brucellosis, a disease carried by the bison that can cause spontaneous abortion of calves, because of their belief that the bison can spread the disease among cattle. Recent findings indicate that bison cannot infect cattle, says Bishop, but the controversy rages on.
- Elk have their issues as well. Without the wolf as a predator, the elk population in the park has increased, raising concerns that the large animals might be destroying their crucial winter range in the northern end of the park. However, Bishop says that 30 years of studies make it clear that overgrazing by elk is no danger.
- Wolves may be on the way for Yellowstone. As this book was being completed, the National Park Service was writing its environmental impact statement to justify reintroduction of the predator to its former

range. Among the results of such a change would be a check on elk populations, but the move would have other effects that would be every bit as beneficial. "Many small animals depend on large predators to provide them with dead animals for winter forage," says Bishop. "Foxes, fishers, weasels, and others depend on these oases of meat to survive in winter." Restoring the wolf would also bring these other species back to their normal populations in the park.

Interestingly enough, Bishop says, for all the driving along park roads and tromping over boardwalks that people do in the geyser basins, the human impact on wild ecosystems at Yellowstone is comparatively slight. The average visitor's stay is 2.4 days, most of it spent on well-traveled roads and pathways. "Only about 30,000 people per year get out into the back country," says Bishop. That is a number he feels the park can tolerate with Park Service guidance.

Education, policing, and herding of humans is still the most demanding of tasks faced by the National Park Service in this the oldest of our parks. Bishop sees his own role in interpretation as providing the education necessary to enjoy the park without doing it harm.

Bishop believes that some of the criticism of parks has a beneficial side to it. "When our elk and bison populations increased in the 1980s, we got money to study the possibilities of overgrazing on the northern range." The criticism of national parks that was surfacing as this book went to press, he concluded, would likely provide resources badly needed to solve some of the National Park Service's problems.

PROFILES

Armando Quintero
Bay District Ranger
National Park Service
San Francisco, California

National parks include not only the great and remote giants of the system but also the smaller parks, often located in population centers, which are often more intensively used.

Growing up in the San Francisco Bay Area, Armando Quintero was unaware that he lived less than a mile from a small national park. While attending junior college, Quintero volunteered his time at the John Muir National Historic Site because he liked working outside and enjoyed studying biology in his spare time. Parks sounded like the place to be. "By the time I went to work on my four-year degree, I had learned a lot about the agency and knew I wanted to work for the National Park Service," he recalls.

Once he knew what he wanted, Quintero made park work the focus of all his studies. "I focused on national parks issues during my college work whenever I had a choice. I worked as a recruiter for the Park Service and contacted the Environmental Careers Organization, which is a source of good minority candidates." Quintero has a bachelor's degree in environmental studies and natural history from California State University, Hayward.

Quintero has been with the National Park Service for 15 years and is currently Bay District ranger for the service. His responsibilities include managing the Golden Gate National Recreation Area as well as Alcatraz Island, where park rangers conduct tours of the infamous old prison.

"I manage a district that includes Alcatraz and the coastline along the bay of San Francisco. I set policy, manage how events take place, and work with nonprofit tenants in Park Service buildings. A lot of what I do involves maintaining the infrastructure of the park facilities to make sure they are available to the public."

Quintero's 30-ranger staff manages a mix of historic, cultural, and natural sites that draw an average of 10,000 visitors each day. Events at the parks gather crowds of as many as 120,000. Demands on the professionals at such a diverse park are daunting, requiring the ability to coordinate children's events as well as linguistic expertise. "At Alcatraz, we provide information in six different languages," says Quintero. "A third of our usage is by non–English speakers, and we need to provide information to all of them."

Quintero's typical day defies description. As an experiment, for a year he kept his watch set to sound an alarm at 10 A.M. each day and noted what he was doing when the alarm went off. "It was never the same twice," he recalls with a laugh. Activities ranged from attending congressional hearings on Park Service needs to diving to an underwater shipwreck with an archaeologist, participating in long-term planning meetings, followed by a small boat trip to a natural or cultural site out on the bay that needed study, and working with an internationally known environmentalist at a public event or hosting a European dignitary's tour of Alcatraz.

Quintero's career seems to flow naturally from his lifelong concern for the environment and the people around him. His advice for people who want similar careers is to think carefully about what they want to accomplish and keep it in mind along the way. For example, he advises against just taking a job in a park because you will have to start at the bottom and work your way up. An alternative approach is to work as an intern.

"Interns often have better access to management and a better chance to further their education and career," says Quintero. Internship also provides the kind of experience that will help you direct your educational efforts.

Do your homework on the agencies that interest you. Says the 15-year National Park Service veteran: "I look at other agencies and examine my career options outside the Park Service. I have no intention of leaving, but I am always thinking about options. I learn how to do my job better by looking at other agencies. I try to work within the bureaucracy without being trapped by it."

Keep the student in yourself alive, says Quintero. Keep learning—stay receptive to new ideas.

Exploring new ways of integrating the parks into society is a personal focus of Quintero's work. "There is a tendency to imply that where people and nature exist is separate—that nature exists only in isolated pockets," he says. "We are wiser to come to grips with a view of ourselves as part of the same natural systems rather than something separate. We are all products of the same biology and ecology and are impacted by the same factors, whether we live in downtown San Francisco or in a remote cabin out in the redwoods."

Angelle Cooper
Program Coordinator
Education Department
Zoo Atlanta
Atlanta, Georgia

Urban parks of all kinds serve as a vital connection between urban people and the natural world. Urban parks are far more numerous than any other type of park and are visited by many more people.

"[When I was] growing up in the inner city of Philadelphia, my mother was always trying to keep me off the street," recalls Angelle Cooper, program coordinator for the Education Department of Zoo Atlanta. "We had day camps, overnight camps, family trips to an Audubon nature center, and Saturday and summer classes."

Because of these experiences, Cooper says: "I have always had an interest in nature and the out-of-doors. I grew to appreciate these things because they are so different from where I was growing up." While earning a degree in English from Spelman College in Atlanta, Cooper worked several summers as a volunteer with the Outdoor Activity Center in southwestern Atlanta. "As a result of working with [the center] and wanting to learn more about the field, I read a book on environmental education by Bill Stapp."

The result of reading the book was Cooper's master's degree in environmental communications from the University of Michigan at Ann Arbor and the start of her environmental career. While working at one job in Atlanta, Cooper spent her weekends as a volunteer at Zoo Atlanta. Over the course of a year, the volunteer work became her full-time job.

Zoo Atlanta, Atlanta, Georgia. Educator Angelle Cooper (second from left) develops and teaches wildlife conservation programs for children who may have little or no exposure to wildlife away from the zoo.

What began as a hands-on job of planning and executing educational programs for children evolved into an administrative role in which Cooper oversees several educational programs and manages the office as well. But even so, this is not an ordinary desk job. "The environment in which I work is not formal. There are opportunities to be outdoors and see the animals and work with the children, lots of them, and to see how they react and interact with the animals. It is an opportunity to educate a large group about wildlife conservation."

"At times it can be hectic," she laughs. "There are late buses and rainy days—my best plans go awry." And clearly, there is always plenty to do. Cooper spends some 25 percent of her typical day on the telephone or answering questions and another 25 percent overseeing educational programs. Maintenance concerns take up another 15 percent of the day; marketing and administrative work each require 15 percent of her time, and the final 5 percent is spent on a teachers' workshop.

The payoff is reaching young people who may not have much access to environmental or wildlife issues other than what they receive at the zoo. Cooper recalls a rain forest presentation during an overnight program for a number of families. "The youngest child in the group stood up and very accurately summed up the key points of what I had said. It was a very special moment. You are catching and shaping young minds and instilling values in them while they are young. Hopefully, they will grow to be responsible adults."

It is these moments that make the hard work of getting to such a career worthwhile for Cooper. "It can be frustrating because not everyone realizes how important this work is," she says. "But don't give up on your visions. Take advantage of every opportunity, every job and volunteer project, to learn and do as much as you can. Summer jobs and internships can give you an idea of what a job in that field would really be like. They give you an inside look at whatever the job, organization, or facility may be."

Cooper wants to broaden her efforts as an environmental communicator to encourage minority group members to get into environmental and science careers. "It is important that minorities see other minorities in this field. Until I went to the ECO conference, I did not know there were that many minorities involved.

"I want to allow all children, but especially inner-city children, to appreciate nature and their environment. I want them to know they have a stake in this as well. The environment where they live is just as important and just as special as any other."

Richard Heaton
Park Planner
Cleveland Metroparks
Cleveland, Ohio

More than half of all parks and outdoor recreation employees in the United States work for state and local government agencies. Employment opportunities in the Cleveland area are found in the city park system, the Metroparks System (discussed here), the Cuyahoga Valley National Recreation Area, numerous suburban park systems, and several private nature centers and state parks, all within 50 miles of the city.

Those who read the first edition of this book learned about Richard Heaton in the position he held as manager of research and planning for the city of Cleveland's Department of Parks, Recreation, and Property. Since that time, Heaton has worked for a while as a planner with a private landscaping firm and returned to the public sector, where he is now park planner for Cleveland Metroparks.

"The Metroparks System has a similar master planning process to the city's, but the park system is very different," says Heaton. "Instead of many small parks, as in the city, in this system you are dealing with what we call the 'emerald necklace' of 12 park reservations ringing the city. We have a systemwide master plan that looks at how we are serving our region as well as a detailed master plan for each reservation."

Heaton is currently working on "Metroparks 2000," a master plan that is part of the 75th anniversary of the Metroparks System. In the master plan, he analyzes existing park facilities and their condition, the services being rendered, the quality of those services, and how those services and facilities may change in the future. The plan projects population demographics and predicts how demands for park services may change over time. "We conduct surveys of users in the parks to determine what they do and don't like and what activities they use. We've also approached nonusers to get their feedback on why they are not using the parks and what we might do to entice them into the parks."

In spite of the differences between city planning and regional park planning, there are strong similarities as well. All park systems are currently working to implement new regulations requiring effective park access for handicapped persons. While working as a city parks planner, Heaton worked on a park center that had a major goal of providing that access. Heaton researched new materials and designs to ensure full access to the center's facilities. "Park departments have not always served handicapped people adequately in the past," he says.

Before his work with the city parks department began, Heaton says, his route into the field was straightforward. "I was reading a career guidance book and thought the section on landscape architecture sounded interesting," he recalls. A bachelor's degree in landscape architecture from Louisiana State University resulted.

After graduation, Heaton moved to Houston, where he did commercial, retail, and residential planning for a design and construction firm. Then he returned to Cleveland and worked for the city as a landscape architect until the park planner job became available. In the late 1980s, Heaton again moved to the private sector, working as a landscape architect until his move to Metroparks.

Comparing his experience in the public and private sectors, Heaton says: "In the public sector, you are working on projects that lots of people can enjoy. You can see lots of people having fun with your work. I liked private work and the design of plantings, but I get more satisfaction out of interacting with park visitors, talking about recreational needs, and presenting the master plan."

Heaton advises those intending to pursue a career in park planning to decide where they would like to work and aim toward either landscape architecture or recreational planning. He adds, "Combining this with a master's degree in public administration would put you on an administrative track in a park system."

RESOURCES

Contact individual government agencies for information on the application process for full-time and seasonal employment, or contact the nearest Federal Job Information Center. Information on cooperative education programs can be obtained from agencies and schools. Each agency can provide materials that acquaint you with the agency's objectives, the range of full-time and seasonal jobs available, and the application process. For additional information on careers in parks and outdoor recreation, see the Resources sections in chapters 6, 11, 12, and 14.

American Association of Zoological Parks and Aquariums, Office of Membership Services, Oglebay Park, Wheeling, WV 26003–1698.

American Recreation Coalition, 1331 Pennsylvania Ave., NW, #726, Washington, DC 20004. (202) 662–7420.

National Parks and Conservation Association. A private citizens' organization dedicated to promoting and improving national parks. Provides extensive membership services, publishes *National Parks* (bimonthly), and organizes local groups near national parks (NPCA Park Activist Network). 1776 Massachusetts Ave., NW, Washington, DC 20036. (202) 223–6722.

National Park Service. P.O. Box 37127, Washington, DC 20013–7127. Public information number: (202) 208–4747. For information on employment opportunities in the National Park Service, check your local library for "Federal Career Opportunities" (updated biweekly), or call (800) 822-JOBS.

National Recreation and Park Association. Association of parks and recreation professionals and citizens' advocates. Holds annual meetings and conducts professional development activities. Provides technical and general information in publications and periodicals, including *Parks &*

Recreation (monthly); *Employ* (nine times a year), which is designed
to assist individuals in preparing for the job search; and *Parks and
Recreation Opportunities Job Bulletin* (22 times a year). A Job Mart is
held at the association's annual conference. 2775 S. Quincy St., Suite
300, Arlington, VA 22206–2204. (703) 820–4940.
Student Conservation Association. See the Resources section in chapter 3
for more information.
*The Report of the President's Commission on Americans Outdoors: The
Legacy, The Challenge* (1987). This report represents the federal
government's first attempt in 25 years to document Americans' need
for expanded recreational facilities and opportunities. Includes recommendations, case studies, market research, and testimony. The
Washington Post predicted that this report, with its surprising findings and controversial conclusions, would not "see the light of day."
Island Press.

14   Forestry

AT A GLANCE

Employment:
55,000 forestry professionals nationwide, including 40,000 professional foresters and 15,000 forestry technicians

Demand:
0 to 5 percent growth per year in the early 1990s; more as foresters expand into other environmental fields

Breakdown:
Public sector, 43 percent (26 percent federal, 17 percent state and local)
Private sector, 45 percent
Nonprofit sector, 2 percent
Education, 10 percent (includes both public and private sectors)

Key Job Titles:
Consulting forester
Environmental consultant
Forest entomologist
Forester
Forest hydrologist
Forest manager
Forest pathologist
Land manager

Natural resource manager
Procurement manager
Urban forester
Urban planner

Influential Organizations:
American Forestry Association
Association of Consulting Foresters
International Society of Arboriculture
Society of American Foresters

Salary:
Entry-level salaries range from $15,000 to $25,000; most experienced
foresters earn $30,000 to $35,000. Top salaries can reach $60,000 to
$70,000 or more, although there are very few of these.

"There are five traditional management uses of the forest: timber, water,
wildlife, recreation, and grazing," says Greg Smith, director of science and
education for the Society of American Foresters. "In the past, timber
received most of the attention. Now there is a significant shift toward
considering integrated uses of the forest. Attention is now given to other
aspects of forest resource management, such as wilderness and other
noncommodity values. This necessitates curriculum changes at the forestry schools to produce a forester who has a broader base of skills."

Once typified by the jack-of-all-trades forester, the timber cruiser, and
the fire fighter, forestry today is a diverse, specialized profession. Smith
remarks: "The range of opportunities is tremendously expanded from just
15 years ago. You might say we have finally turned the corner on the
'Smokey the Bear sitting in the fire tower' image."

Foresters are moving into the cities, helping to stem the loss of urban
forests and protect watersheds; they specialize in such areas as entomology, forest genetics, forest hydrology, soils, planning, and forest economics; foresters work in Third World countries on tropical reforestation
projects as well as harvesting operations; and they are involved in providing recreational opportunities and wildlife habitats. Today's foresters cannot get by with just a technical background: They are learning and using
management skills and skills involving computers, economics, and communication. Even in an age of specialization, there is a call for foresters to
obtain a broader ecological base in their training.

WHAT IS FORESTRY?

Forestry is the maintenance and management of forests with a variety of objectives in mind. The definition is likely to differ according to who is talking.

Some 45 percent of all foresters belong to the private sector and have as a primary objective the healthy growth of forests as a source of wood products. Private foresters work for companies that manage forests for lumber, pulpwood, and other products; paper mills; suppliers of forestry equipment and materials; and urban tree care companies.

Another 26 percent of professional foresters belong to the federal segment of the public sector. These agencies work to balance their responsibility to preserve forests with their obligation to make some forest resources available for exploitation. According to Greg Smith of the Society of American Foresters, the percentage of foresters working for the federal government is shrinking. Federal employers include the Forest Service, which manages 191 million acres in 156 national forests, the Soil Conservation Service, the Bureau of Land Management, the Bureau of Indian Affairs, the National Park Service, and the Army Corps of Engineers.

Another 17 percent of foresters work for state and local government— primarily the former, though local government is probably the fastest-growing category of forestry employers. In local government, however, foresters are often called on to do other work as well, such as managing watersheds or parks. Like federal foresters, state and local forestry professionals seek to balance preservation and exploitation interests. The results of their efforts in both of these areas are likely to be less consistent from one locale to another than is true for federal foresters. They may preserve much more or much less.

Consulting firms account for only a few percent of all foresters. Consulting foresters manage timber sales for both private landowners and public agencies. They supervise planting and spraying, survey forests, and perform other tasks for companies that find it more cost-effective to use consultants than to employ in-house specialists. Most consultants have previous experience in the public or private sector. They represent both exploitation and preservation interests.

Educators, depending on their specialty, may lean toward exploitation or preservation of forests or a mix of the two. Nonprofit organizations will also vary in intent, although a number of these lean toward preservation.

About one-third of the United States is forested. Of this land, 58 percent is owned by private individuals; 14 percent, by corporations; and 28 percent, by federal, state, and local governments. There are approximately 40,000 foresters employed in the United States, 15,000 forestry technicians, and many who perform the work of forestry technicians without having the formal designation. The male-to-female ratio among forestry undergraduates is currently 7 to 3.

HISTORY AND BACKGROUND

Professional forestry in the United States dates back to 1893, when Gifford Pinchot opened an office in New York City and called himself a consulting forester, based on his training in Europe. His ideas so impressed Presidents William McKinley, Grover Cleveland, and Theodore Roosevelt that he was able to transform the nation's forest practices and establish the Forest Service.

Forest practices in the 1800s for the most part amounted to disorganized pillaging of forests without regard for sustaining timber production or wildlife. The U.S. Land Office was responsible for federal lands, but corruption and lack of funding and skilled workers made management virtually impossible. During the 1890s, federal lands gradually came to be seen as endangered by indiscriminate use. New forestry legislation was a direct response to these excesses.

Forest Organic Act of 1897. This act began to make a science of forestry. It established forest reserves to provide "favorable conditions of water flow, and to furnish a continuous supply of timber. . . ." Pinchot, who helped write the act, became head of the Forestry Division in the Department of Agriculture.

Agricultural Appropriation Act of 1905. This act put the force of law behind forestry by giving foresters the authority to enforce violations of forest regulations. The Forestry Division then changed its name to the Forest Service. By 1909, the service controlled 148 million acres and had become a highly regarded government agency. Pinchot, whose ideas still guide much of what we consider forestry to be, wrote: "Conservation is the foresighted utilization, preservation and/or renewal of forests, waters, lands and minerals for the greatest good of the greatest number of people for the longest time."

National Forest Management Act of 1976. This is the predominant modern legislation controlling federal timber management.

Highly regarded foresters now work for timber companies as well as for the Forest Service, and forestry professionals are working for state and local governments and in foreign countries.

ISSUES AND TRENDS

Current issues have a profound effect on what environmental programs get the most attention and, often, funding. Keeping track of new trends allows you to increase your value to prospective employers and improve your chances of getting hired for the job you seek.

ENDANGERED SPECIES

Although the northern spotted owl has gotten the most media exposure (see this chapter's Case Study), many other endangered species are at risk as well. In many cases, resolution of the conflict requires further research to determine just what habitat is essential to sustain specific species. Foresters equipped to conduct research on the interdependence of wildlife and forests will be needed as long as these concerns remain.

WETLANDS

Nearly every forest tract of any size has a wetlands component, and certain very large forests are considered by some to be entirely wetlands. Growing recognition of wetlands as a mechanism to provide water quality, fish stock replenishment, wildlife habitat, and human enjoyment gives them an important place in the ecosystem management of forests.

MULTIPLE-USE FORESTS

More demands are placed on less forest today. Demand for forest products has grown by 70 percent in the past three decades, and the rate is expected to accelerate until the turn of the century. At the same time, recreational and other consumptive and nonconsumptive uses of the forest have steadily increased.

CITIZEN INVOLVEMENT

"I see a steady rise in the concern of people for forests," says Jim Stone, silviculturist with the Forest Service in Oregon. "Citizens demand more participation in the planning of forest management; the days of managing forests without public scrutiny are over." Andy Stahl, a forester with the

Sierra Club Legal Defense Fund in Seattle, observes, "A small cottage industry has been created whose mission is to appeal forest management plans proposed for the 156 national forests managed by the Forest Service." Concerns about these plans vary by region and involve below-cost timber sales, construction of roads in wilderness areas, clear-cutting of timber rather than selective harvesting, logging of old-growth timber, monoculture plantings in areas that previously had a variety of trees, and lack of wildlife protection.

PRESSURES ON PRIVATE FORESTS

Increased scrutiny by citizens is also affecting the management of privately owned forests. Timber companies that own land are more sensitive to public opinion and a mobilized constituency of people concerned with forests and wildlife. A number of states, including New York, Massachusetts, and New Jersey, provide tax abatement incentives for small landowners who adhere to forest management plans. This in turn creates a new market for consultants who help landowners develop and implement these plans.

POLLUTION

The effects of pollutants on forest health is an issue of growing concern among foresters. Acid rain, groundwater toxins, smog, and other pollutants are now thought to harm forests. Even though the source or identity of particular pollutants or the manner in which they damage trees is not clearly understood, few can argue with the results. One prime example is the decline in sugar maples on the eastern seaboard. The need for more information about the effects of pollutants on forests is one reason for the trend toward a broader ecological component to undergraduate education.

URBAN FORESTRY

Although mixed-use forests in urban areas cover more acres than all of the land managed by the Forest Service, they are currently dwindling. Nationwide, only one tree is planted for every four removed. But as part of the trend toward concern for environmental issues closer to home, municipalities are increasingly hiring foresters and arborists. In addition to the aesthetic value of urban trees, they help purify the air, provide shade, moderate temperatures, improve water quality, and reduce flooding.

INTERNATIONAL FORESTRY

Increasing concern about global deforestation and the lack of forestry management in many less developed countries creates new opportunities for those interested in international forestry. Both government agencies and timber companies need foresters to help shape forestry management practices abroad. Working for the Peace Corps, which has many reforestation projects in Third World countries, will earn you one year of noncompetitive eligibility for federal jobs.

CAREER OPPORTUNITIES

Employment prospects for foresters have been rather cyclical and are tied closely to the economy as well as to the demand for forest products. There are three factors that permit cautious optimism. First, demand for forest products continues to grow. Second, many foresters, especially in the Forest Service, are nearing retirement age. Third, the number of students entering forestry programs has dropped dramatically.

According to the Society for American Foresters' Greg Smith, there has been a 50 percent decline in students entering undergraduate programs in forestry or forestry-related programs since the late 1970s. One reason for this has been dismal reports, not accurate, about job prospects. Another reason is that newer natural resource management programs, such as water resource management and environmental conservation, today draw students who ten years ago would have gone into forestry.

Entry-level jobs in state and federal agencies often involve foresters in recreation, wildlife, and watershed management. This might mean talking to hikers, campers, and hunters and carrying out trail maintenance, wildlife surveys, or multipurpose management of a piece of the forest. Working with a supervisor, foresters maintain boundary lines, conduct surveys, determine what needs to be cut, manage timber sales and logging, and oversee regeneration activities. This work is usually done with the assistance of a number of forestry technicians.

Those considering a career in natural resource management often want hands-on fieldwork. Such work is performed by technicians and does not generally require a bachelor's or graduate degree. Forestry technicians, who usually have two-year degrees and sometimes bachelor's degrees in forestry, serve as timber cruisers, recreation area custodians, fire dispatchers, tree nursery workers, tree maintenance staff members, research aides, and log scalers. In short, they spend most of their time in the field.

Hiawatha National Forest, Michigan. Roger Jewell photographs a recently constructed swinging bridge on the North Country Trail, which runs along the shore of Lake Superior. Photograph courtesy of the Forest Service.

An entry-level position in forestry can lead to several different career paths managing larger parcels of land and supervising the foresters assigned to these parcels. You might move to a corporate office or develop a specialty. Some possible specialties include database development, forest entomology and pathology, forest economics, forest hydrology, forest recreation, silviculture, planning, fuels management and fire suppression, bioengineering, forest ecology, contract administration, public relations, and soil science. Many of these specialties require an advanced degree; given the amount of basic forestry that must be learned in college, it is difficult to do much specialization as an undergraduate.

PUBLIC SECTOR

As in other segments of the environment, the most sought-after employers are often those with the least number of new job openings. However, there are several federal agencies with need of foresters other than the Forest Service. Greater growth is taking place on the state and local levels.

Federal government. The United States government employs about one-quarter of the professional foresters in the United States. The majority of these work for the Forest Service in the Department of Agriculture. The next largest federal employer of foresters is the Department of the Interior, which employs foresters in its National Park Service, Bureau of Land Management, and U.S. Fish and Wildlife Service. Significant numbers of federal foresters also work for the Soil Conservation Service.

Substantial growth took place in federal forestry during the 1970s, creating a large group of professionals moving through their careers in a rather homogeneous age group. As these people begin to reach retirement age in the mid- to late 1990s, increased hiring will take place. However, federal forestry has become more specialized, and not all retiring foresters will be replaced by professionals with the same backgrounds. Many will be replaced by people who can provide specialized expertise in related environmental fields.

State and local government. State and local governments, though making up one of the smaller blocks of forestry professionals, are probably the fastest-growing segment of the industry. State and local forestry currently accounts for some 17 percent of foresters nationwide. A growing appreciation for the benefits of urban forestry, although tempered by economic difficulties, will probably continue to expand this area for new entrants.

PRIVATE SECTOR

Nearly half of all foresters who work in the private sector are employed by timber companies or consulting firms.

Private industry. Private sector forestry employs 45 percent of all professional foresters and continues to grow. Private timber companies experience boom and bust cycles, but overall, demand for timber products continues to grow. Increased demand for forest products in turn creates demand for professionals to help get the most available timberlands. Private sector companies manage forests for lumber and pulpwood, produce paper and other wood fiber products, supply forestry equipment and materials, and provide care for urban parks and forests.

Ermine Venuto, vice president for woodlands and solid wood products for Mead Corporation in Columbus, Georgia, says: "Entry-level foresters are putting their names on agreements involving hundreds of thousands of dollars. They also must oversee the work of three or four hardened logging contractors who were probably working before [the foresters] were born. This is responsibility; many thrive on it.

Consulting firms. Although consulting firms have never employed large numbers of foresters, they have experienced significant growth in recent years. "Municipalities are going out and hiring forestry consultants," says Greg Smith of the Society of American Foresters. "This is particularly true in the Northeast and in other urban areas throughout the country. In many cases, planning departments want forestry statements and forestry inventories that go into the plans." Forestry consultants work with private landowners to acquire standing timber, make volume estimates, and authorize purchases. Consultants also develop forest management plans for privately held lands.

NONPROFIT SECTOR

Forestry in the nonprofit sector is a very small segment of the field, perhaps accounting for 2 percent of the total number of professionals. This segment includes industry associations as well as forestry professionals within larger environmental organizations.

SALARY

A 1992 salary survey conducted by the Society of American Foresters shows average salaries of experienced foresters ranging from $30,000 to $35,000. The results of the survey were as follows:

- Entry-level salaries ranged from $15,000 to $25,000.
- Salaries for field positions ranged from $20,000 to $35,000.
- Salaries for mid-level positions ranged from $35,000 to $50,000.
- Top management salaries ranged from $50,000 to $70,000 or more.

Entry-level positions in private sector forestry generally pay in the $17,000 to $20,000 range. Larger companies tend to pay higher starting salaries than do smaller companies. Consulting firms pay entry-level foresters less, typically a base salary of $12,000 to $15,000 with a draw-plus arrangement, which is a financial incentive to bring in customers. In the private sector, an M.S. degree will command a slightly higher starting salary.

GETTING STARTED

Because of technological advances, today's forester is moving out of the forest and into the office. Much of the work of foresters has become less labor-intensive or has been farmed out to forestry technicians. Where maps and surveys were once used, computers and aerial photography or computerized geographic information systems now do a quicker and more accurate job.

Consequently, today's forester must have a high degree of skill with computers, statistics, and accounting, along with good interpersonal skills. The latter are necessary because foresters are not only communicating more with a variety of colleagues and coworkers but also are more in the public eye than ever before. Their job increasingly entails public relations and public education.

EDUCATION

A blend of education and experience is the best pathway to a successful career in forestry, but the most effective mix will vary widely according to the path you choose into the profession.

Undergraduate degree. Foresters have a tall order to fill. As one forester acknowledges, "We are trying to pack into four years of school what realistically should take seven." This is where experience and graduate school increasingly come into the picture.

Most foresters obtain a B.A. or B.S. from one of the 45 forestry schools accredited by the Society of American Foresters. Most schools require students to hold at least one field position. Do not, however, limit your fieldwork to the bare requirements—obtain as much experience as you can. This not only will help you direct your interests and studies in the field but also will make you more attractive to prospective employers.

Keep in mind that all schools, even those that are accredited, are not created equal; it is quite legitimate to ask professionals about a school's reputation. Many schools have a tendency to specialize either in a particular application of forestry (forestry management, recreation, economics, forestry engineering, ecology) or in the type of forest in the region in which the school is located. Decide whether you are interested in a particular focus or want a more general background. Finally, spend some time comparing the courses offered and required by the various schools.

Liberal arts background. All professionals stress the value of a strong liberal arts background for a forester; some go as far as to put liberal arts courses above forestry course work. Says one forestry consultant: "Ultimately, what separates the technicians from the foresters is not the forestry expertise as much as the liberal arts skills: written and oral communications, management, political science, accounting, and economics. These are the skills that will make or break your forestry career."

Specialization. There is no consensus on specialization in forestry education. Employers are looking for broadly educated graduates, but there is a pull toward specialization once a forester starts working, and some employers want to see an inclination toward a specialty before they hire. Some foresters feel that undergraduates can hurt themselves by being "a mile wide and an inch deep"; others say that specializing early in a career can limit your options before you have a chance to learn about the field and make career decisions based on experience. The latter camp advises that specialization be left to graduate school.

One approach is to get a minor or possibly a second major in addition to your forestry degree. This could be in a technical area—soil science, wildlife, or surveying—or might be oriented more toward liberal arts—business, economics, political science, or computer science. A similar route is to pursue one of the forestry tracks offered by many schools, such as forest economics, management, hydrology, or economics.

Field experience. As is the case with all natural resource management professions, seasonal or part-time work experience is necessary to obtain a full-time job. Your first experience may be as a volunteer. Use this as an opportunity to test out various types of forestry work, build up skills, make contacts in the profession, and collect letters of recommendation.

A variety of volunteer and seasonal work programs are available through agencies, institutions, and universities. You may want to consider broadening your work experience with a stint in a nontraditional setting, such as doing policy work with a nonprofit organization, research with a botanical garden, or interpretation with a park system. Formal cooperative education programs with state and federal agencies offer you the best odds of getting full-time entry-level employment on graduation.

Graduate degree. Many forestry specializations now require graduate study. A graduate degree is also an opportunity to broaden your skill base. For example, foresters may go back to school to obtain M.B.A.s, master's degrees in public administration, and even law degrees.

A master's degree will probably be useful later in your career. Whether it helps early on depends somewhat on the demand for foresters. One employer in industrial forestry points out: "There is currently an abundant supply of foresters. One way to choose is to see whether they have a master's degree. In the last few years, two of every three persons we have hired have had graduate degrees."

ADVICE

Many of the best ideas on how to prepare for your career come from those who have already had success. Here is some of the advice gathered from forestry professionals.

Consider specialized training in urban forestry. If urban forestry interests you, you can prepare by completing a traditional undergraduate forestry program. However, you may want to attend one of the growing number of schools that have special programs for urban forestry or find a school that offers a minor in urban forest management. The urban forester must be able to identify and know the characteristics and requirements of literally hundreds of types of trees. Urban foresters must also be well versed in entomology, pathology, herbicide and pesticide applications, communications, landscape architecture, and public relations.

Much of the work on urban trees is performed by arborists and horticulturists. Most prepare for these professions by combining a two-year technical degree and on-the-job training or by completing a four-year program.

Develop some hands-on skills. Be on the lookout for opportunities to develop some of the skills specific to forestry, such as inventorying and timber cruising, grading lumber, identifying species, using aerial photographs and maps, administering contracts, and controlling pests. Demonstrating your knowledge of these hands-on skills is your best assurance of obtaining an entry-level job.

Gain computer expertise. Because forestry involves determining conditions and planning uses for large areas of land, it is particularly well suited to computer-aided tools such as geographic information systems and database applications. Look for opportunities to become familiar with these systems and get over any "computer phobia." Training employees to use these systems can be costly and time-consuming, so your experience in this area will be very attractive to potential employers.

Accumulate as much diverse experience as possible. Says a forestry professor: "We are no longer just cruising timber and cutting trees but [are also] telling our story to the public and providing for their recreation.

Don't let a summer pass without a forestry job. Get a different job each summer, in the field and in an office."

SUMMARY

Much of the near-term future for forestry employment depends on court decisions on endangered species, economic conditions, retirement of current foresters, and other events that are difficult to predict. On an individual basis, entrants to the field can choose to move to related environmental fields to avoid the tight hiring market of rural forestry. Urban forestry, meanwhile, should continue to grow through the 1990s.

Not everyone agrees with the projection of healthy long-term hiring prospects for forestry graduates. But there will always be a steady supply of positions for the best and most persistent applicants.

CASE STUDY

The Spotted Owl Controversy

Is the purpose of forest management to preserve all of a forest's species, regardless of the inconvenience, or is a forest a materials storehouse and is species preservation a secondary concern? Or is there a middle ground where the two approaches can meet?

The controversy over the fate of the northern spotted owl in the old-growth forests of the Pacific Northwest encapsulates a decades-old economic and philosophical disagreement about the purpose of wild places. Should all wildlife in them be preserved and disturbed as little as possible—that is, are the wild places and the organisms they house valuable in their own right? Or are wild spaces resources to be used as befits the needs and desires of mankind, with preservation of species a secondary concern?

The expert who directed the study of the northern spotted owl for the Forest Service cautions against misunderstanding the real issues. "The issue is far bigger than the spotted owl and jobs," says Jack Ward Thomas, chief research wildlife biologist for the Forest Service. "That trivializes it. The important topic is really the larger issue of whether we are going to preserve a particular ecosystem. About 10 percent of the old-growth forest is left in the Pacific Northwest. How much of that do we want to preserve?"

By the late 1980s, dramatic losses in old-growth timber had reduced the spotted owl population in the United States by 80 percent, to an estimated 3,000 to 6,000 pairs. Environmental groups protested the timber cutting and resulting danger to the owl, and in 1989 a federal district court judge in Seattle ordered the U.S. government to produce a careful study of the owl. Jack Ward Thomas agreed to lead the effort.

Thomas is a transplanted Texan with a degree in wildlife biology from Texas A&M University and a Ph.D. in forestry from the University of Massachusetts–Amherst. He is well known for his work with range and wildlife issues in the Oregon woodlands. "My first love," Thomas says, "is big game population dynamics, diseases, interactions between game and livestock, and game reactions to forest manipulations."

Thomas is also known for his work with songbirds, which, together with his extensive knowledge of the Northwest's timber country, made him the choice to lead the spotted owl study. Predictably, not everyone was pleased with the resulting report. Preservationists are angry that the report suggests allowing some further cutting of old-growth forest. Those in the timber industry are incensed that millions of acres of old growth would be set aside, unavailable for harvest.

The Thomas report recommended a logging ban on 30 to 40 percent of public timberland in the Northwest to ensure survival of the northern spotted owl's ecosystem. Some continued cutting is allowed, however, which will cause a further decline in total owl population. Congress responded to the report in 1991 by reducing Forest Service cutting by about 25 percent, and the Bureau of Land Management reduced cuts on its lands as well.

The timber industry is the victim here of multiple trends, all pointing toward difficult changes in the industry's cutting practices. In his book *Earth in the Balance,* Vice President Al Gore writes: "Ironically, if those wishing to continue the cutting had won, their jobs would have been lost anyway as soon as the remaining 10 percent of the [old-growth] forest was cut. The only issue was whether they would shift to new employment before or after the last remnant of the forest was gone."

Time magazine notes: "The life cycle of the Pacific Northwest's primeval woodlands is measured not in decades but in centuries. The industry's reforestation practices have markedly improved over the past decade, but the investment is too little too late." The Forest Service predicts that technological changes will cost the jobs of 13 percent of the timber work force during the next 15 years while exportation of whole logs cuts mill work further and high timber costs in the Northwest put the region at an economic disadvantage compared with Southeast and Canadian timber companies.

Job losses resulting from the logging ban, on top of what was already a slow period for the timber industry, generated strong protests, along with angry predictions of lost employment for anywhere from 20,000 people (Bush administration estimate) to 100,000 (timber industry estimate).

Although the decisions of Congress and the changes in allowed cutting are not yet the final word in the spotted owl controversy, Thomas is encouraged and credits Congress with "beginning to look at the old-growth ecosystem in a more appropriate framework. You can't have just pockets, where the birds and animals cannot move from one pocket to the next. You have to look at how the old-growth forest is arranged from the Canadian border down to northern California."

Nobody in this controversy gets away without shouldering a bit of the blame. Some environmentalists have antagonized timber interests with antics to get attention for their cause, yet the attention was needed. Environmental groups still do not agree on the best course of action. Some are unwilling to consider anything other than complete old-growth preservation, accusing more moderate groups of selling out.

Government agencies took too long to take the issue seriously, with early reports on endangered species routinely sanitized to avoid making waves. Some within the Forest Service allege that more studies were requested just to stall for time.

In the end, the discussion inevitably finds its way back to the core issue of habitat preservation. Choices must be made about what we wish to preserve and how much we are willing to pay to preserve it.

Thomas reminds us that the northern spotted owl is not the issue. "The spotted owl is thought of by the Forest Service as an indicator species," he says. Because the owl is at the top of its food chain, requires a large home range, and has a long life span, its presence in a forest indicates stability. "If it is okay, then the other species in the old-growth ecosystem are okay." Efforts to protect endangered species will probably focus on such indicator species in the future because the cost of studying the large numbers of species placed in peril is simply prohibitive.

What Thomas sees in the future of forest management is a shift in the philosophical basis of forestry decision making. In the Forest Service, this new philosophy is called "New Perspectives in Forestry," while others in the field refer simply to "New Forestry." "Forestry is more than timber production," says Thomas. "It includes the treatment and manipulation of forestlands to meet a new mix of objectives. There is nothing new about multiuse forests, but we have used wood as the primary function and other uses as secondary. Now other things besides wood may be equally important, or dominant, or less important."

There will always be intensive forestry on some lands, where trees are raised as a monoculture crop, called "fiber" in the trade. At the other extreme, says Thomas, there will be habitat preserves of old-growth forest for the spotted owls of the natural world. And in between will be a mix of forests with a range of objectives.

The spotted owl controversy illustrates the importance of effective research—not to find out who is right and who is wrong but to determine enough of the facts to allow intelligent thinking, discussion, and decision making. Continued wrestling with endangered species issues requires professional work of the highest caliber by foresters and the professionals who work with them. Without question, there will be increased demand for the highly trained people who can conduct these efforts.

When will the spotted owl issue be settled? Thomas says with a laugh: "Two years ago, I would have said six months. Here we are two years later, and I would still say six months to a year." But whatever the final outcome, Thomas assures us, the northern spotted owl will forever change the way we view forests.

PROFILES

Elizabeth Buchanan
Executive Vice president
ACRT, Inc.
Kent, Ohio

Urban forestry presents almost an inverse picture of job opportunities when compared with traditional forestry. It is a growing field with need of new professionals and comes complete with a supply of urban trees in need of help, as well as urban areas in need of more trees.

An entry-level job is the route urban forester Elizabeth Buchanan took to her current position as executive vice president of ACRT, Inc., an environmental consulting firm that specializes in urban forestry.

Buchanan talks in her soft southern accent about completing her bachelor's degree in biology and botany at Maryville College, Tennessee, and finding that she "didn't have a clue" about what she wanted to do. She earned a master's degree in biology at Appalachian State University in North Carolina and then found that there were no jobs. After completing her Ph.D. in aquatic ecology at Kent State University, she taught a number of courses to make ends meet. "I had classes all over the place," she recalls.

The job that led to her current position was a temporary job as a caller in a state telesurvey to determine if there was a market for firewood vendors. That work ignited her interests in urban forestry, which led her to a private tree maintenance company that provided consulting services.

When the consulting services were shut down in 1985, Buchanan and her colleagues formed ACRT, an independent consulting firm in Kent, Ohio.

"We pooled our savings and said, 'Let's do it,' " she recalls. The firm tied into a national trend toward managing the growth of urban trees at a crucial time, and now it has business across the United States and Canada.

Urban forestry is fundamentally different from traditional forestry, says Buchanan. "While woodland trees are managed as tree populations, urban trees are managed on a tree-by-tree basis. Urban trees are managed for environmental benefits such as cooling, shade, and aesthetics. The goal is to have a population of trees that are healthy and will live as long as possible. You need diversity as well as quality."

Whereas woodland forestry is dominated by concerns of large government bodies such as the federal government or states, urban forestry is the province of local governments. Several states, such as Ohio, have departments of urban forestry, but the vast majority of the work and jobs reside at the local level, in both the public and private sectors.

Buchanan notes that the two primary types of urban foresters are degree-toting professionals, who manage programs and work with the scientific knowledge in the field, and arborists, the workers who actually get into the trees. Those desiring careers in this field must seek out the city maintenance departments; the contractors who work with those departments; and the public works, parks, or forestry department or whatever organization is home to the local program in urban forestry.

Urban forestry programs across the country range from municipalities in which practice is limited to picking up tree limbs when they fall down after storms and few, if any, new trees are planted to locations where full programs are in operation, complete with planning, planting, and maintenance. Utility companies are another source of urban forestry jobs. Foresters direct the work of contractors to keep utility lines clear. ACRT employs 50 entry-level foresters on contract to utility companies to do this work.

Urban forestry is currently the fastest-growing segment of the forestry field, and there are indications that it will grow more rapidly still in the years ahead. Buchanan cites the efforts of the American Forestry Association's Urban Forestry Group, which lobbied for federal money and has initiated a Global ReLeaf program to promote tree planting in urban areas.

"Now there is increasing attention because of the America the Beautiful program," Buchanan adds. In this program, "states that establish a state urban forestry coordinator and develop an urban forestry council can get grants. If a city decides it wants technical assistance in urban forestry, it can share costs with the state." This is very likely to generate new forestry jobs as states work to qualify for these federal funds.

The technical arguments for urban forestry are worth noting, says Buchanan. "One large tree has the same cooling effect as 15 room-sized air conditioners." This means significant savings for buildings near tree plantings. Combining windbreak, cooling, and weather moderation effects can generate 4 to 22 percent savings in energy costs for buildings near trees, she points out. Finally, in terms of larger environmental issues, "carbon sequestering," the pulling of carbon dioxide from the air, is now considered an important argument for growth in urban forestry.

Federal funding and growing attention for urban forestry make this field particularly attractive for would-be foresters. On preparing yourself for a career in urban forestry, Buchanan says: "If you know early that you want urban forestry, then get a degree in the field. If your degree is in botany, horticulture, or biology, then go for a master's degree in urban forestry." She notes that many excellent graduates in the Midwest come from Michigan State University and from the University of Wisconsin–Stevens Point.

But, as noted elsewhere in this book, additional skills beyond those traditionally learned in a forestry program are just as important as any scroll from a school. "Computer, writing, and organizational skills are all crucial for success," says Buchanan. "If job applicants have those and they know a bit about trees, we can teach them the rest."

Richard Wilson
Director of Forestry and Fire
Protection and State Forester
Resources Agency
Sacramento, California

California is home to unique stands of old-growth forest, a large forestry industry with a constant appetite for new lumber, and a contingent of preservationists. Balancing political, economic, and natural resource issues in this state is a huge task.

"I have been in a lot of battles," declares the former rancher. "I don't look for them, but the battles always seem to find me." He has gone up against dam projects, developers, and those who he believes would overcut timberlands in the state of California. The former rancher is Richard Wilson, California's director of forestry and fire protection and state forester.

Wilson became an active environmentalist in the 1960s by fighting construction of a dam and reservoir proposed by the Army Corps of Engineers for the Eel River in northern California's Mendocino County. The dam would have covered a small town, the second largest Indian reservation in the state, and Wilson's own ranch under 300 feet of water. The Eel became first a state-protected river, then a federally protected river.

Wilson went on to defeat a large housing development project and served seven years on the California Coastal Commission and another five years on the California Forestry Board, during which time he developed his expertise on forestry issues. As California's state forester, Wilson believes strongly in timber harvest reform.

Whereas the federal government and its agencies control timber cutting on federal lands, Wilson's agency must work with multiple entities on both sides of timber issues. He works to keep timber companies as happy as he can while enforcing regulations concerning the use of private lands for cutting.

California's private woodlands are a mix of woodlots maintained as private investments and others preserved for the peace and quiet of their owners. "Just because the timber is merchantable does not mean it will come on the market," says Wilson.

On the other hand, many landowners allow their trees to be cut too early, due in part to encouragement from timber companies. Mill capacity is continually upgraded and increased to the point where it exceeds the ability of the trees to meet demand. "To meet mill capacity, the timber companies migrate down through old growth to younger and younger stands, and then they want to chip them because they are too small for lumber," says Wilson. "But if you cut too often, you reduce it all to sticks and stones. In these timber stands, you need rotations of something like 60 to 70 years to get it up there in its maximum growth. It's the accountants versus the foresters, and the accountants want more than the foresters can produce."

Federally controlled timber cutting in California was recently reduced from 1.5 billion board feet per year to 600 million, partly in response to endangered species issues and partly for timber management. However, Wilson has been stymied in his efforts to reduce state-controlled cutting. "We have a good set of forestry rules from 1973, but they are not enforced," he says. "The rules call for a balance between cutting and growth and consideration of wildlife and their habitat."

In the control of timber cutting, as in the resolution of disputes over endangered species, wetlands, and other crucial environmental issues, lack of knowledge is the primary impediment to progress. Ironically, because of the overlap between wildlife and forestry issues, Wilson regards biologists as the new experts most needed in forestry now.

"Biology is a ripsnorting good field right now," he says. "State forestry has a real need for qualified people to sort out the differences between scientific evaluation and dogmatic assumption. We need good fieldwork and studies of how the environment really works so that we can make statements and back them up with solid data."

Dave Mumper
Director of Environmental Affairs
Weyerhaeuser Company
Tacoma, Washington

The private sector timber industry employs nearly half of all forestry professionals, with a full range of environmental specialties.

"I grew up in southern California, right up against the mountains, and I spent a lot of time up there. I thought, 'Boy, I would like to work up there for the Forest Service,' " recalls Dave Mumper, director of environmental affairs for timber industry giant Weyerhaeuser Company.

"I was, and am, very environmentally oriented," he says. "I was very interested in what the Sierra Club was doing on environmental issues, and I knew I was going to escape Los Angeles!"

Mumper escaped to Humboldt State University, "in the heart of the redwoods" just north of Eureka, California, where he earned a bachelor's degree in forestry. He earned a master's degree in forestry economics from West Virginia University and then faced the rare and delightful task of deciding which of many job offers to accept. "Weyerhaeuser was the example held up all the way through school as [a company that was] making an attempt to practice and invest money in good forestry," he says.

In his first assignment for Weyerhaeuser, Mumper worked out of Coos Bay, Oregon, doing timber inventory and appraisal work. "What hit me [in that job was that] I am a people person, and I was spending day after day in the woods looking at trees and bushes . . . I decided I had to be around more people."

By 1971, Mumper was chief forester for Weyerhaeuser's Snoqualmie tree farm, some 40 miles east of Seattle. There, his job was indeed much more of a people-oriented occupation. "I spent 70 percent of my time convincing people in Seattle that what we were doing was okay and that more than likely this would still be a tree farm 50 years from now and not a development." Mumper went back to the woods in the late 1970s as a logging manager at Weyerhaeuser's Twin Arbors tree farm, but again he "missed the exposure to people."

When a corporate job became available in 1984, Mumper became a "people" person once again at company headquarters in Tacoma, first as manager of timberlands resources and more recently as director of environmental affairs. He has worked extensively with wetlands, which appear on every tree farm owned by Weyerhaeuser.

His specialty is one that barely existed in timber companies a few years ago: identifying and resolving timber controversies and developing effective compromises. "There are a lot of people in forestry who say the very last thing they want is to be involved in politics. That means there are a lot of technical graduates who have only one piece of what they need to be successful in the environmental arena. The people who have an appreciation for and have worked on both the politics and the science of forestry have an advantage that I would not trade for anything."

These days, Mumper divides his time about evenly between meetings outside the company, during which he keeps up on the latest issues, and meetings within Weyerhaeuser in which he disseminates that information to the people who need it.

"I enjoy being involved in the resolution of controversy," Mumper says. "If you can't walk up to an industry person and an environmentalist without having an uncontrollable urge to take a side, then you probably shouldn't get into this line of work. It puts a burden on you to look at creative solutions.

"I think the thing that gives me the most satisfaction is to take an issue that seems to be going nowhere and move it a little bit so people's eyes light up and they say, 'Yes, this is moving in the right direction.' "

RESOURCES

American Forest Council, 1250 Connecticut Ave., NW, Suite 320, Washington, DC 20036. (202) 463–2455.

American Forestry Association. A national citizens' organization devoted to trees, forests, and forestry. Publishes educational materials on forests as well as *American Forests* magazine (monthly). Other publications include *So You Want to Be in Forestry* (single copies free) and *Proceedings of the National Urban Forestry Conferences* (every other year). P.O. Box 2000, Washington, DC 20013. (202) 667–3300.

Association of Consulting Foresters. Publishes *The Consultant* (quarterly). 5410 Grosvenor Ln., Suite 250, Bethesda, MD 20814. (301) 530–6795.

Conservation Directory (annual). See the Resources section in chapter 2 for a description.

Directory of the Forest Products Industry. $197 (1992 edition). This 748-page hardcover book, updated biennially, is a comprehensive listing of forest products industries (including sawmills, wood treatment plants, and plywood mills) by state and province. Includes addresses, products and volume, and names and telephone numbers of key personnel. Miller Freeman Publications, Circulation Department, P.O. Box 7339, San Francisco, CA 94120. (800) 848–5594.

Forest Farmers Association. Publishes the *Forest Farmer Manual* ($13, includes postage). Featured are lists of southern consulting foresters, pulp and paper mills, pulpwood dealers, federal and southern-state forestry agencies, and forestry schools. P.O. Box 95385, Atlanta, GA 30347. (404) 325–2954.

Forest Service. P.O. Box 96090, Washington, DC 20090. (202) 447–3957.

International Society of Arboriculture. A scientific and educational organization devoted to the dissemination of knowledge in the care and preservation of shade and ornamental trees. Prints a listing of colleges and universities offering forestry and other arboriculture courses. Publishes bimonthly *Journal of Arboriculture*. 303 W. University, P.O. Box 908, Urbana, IL 61801. (217) 328–2032.

Municipal Arborists and Urban Foresters Society. Publishes a bimonthly newsletter. P.O. Box 1255, 17 Lafayette Pl., Freehold, NJ 07728.

National Arborist Association. Publishes *The Reporter* (monthly). Meeting Place Mall, Route 101, P.O. Box 1094, Amherst, NH 03031. (603) 673–3311.

National Council of the Paper Industry for Air and Stream Improvement, 260 Madison Ave., New York, NY 10016. (212) 532–9000.

Opportunities in Forestry Careers, by Christopher M. Wille (1992). Details how you can become a forestry professional. Published by VGM Career Horizons, 4255 W. Touhy Ave., Lincolnwood, IL 60646–1975.

Peace Corps. Peace Corps volunteers are needed in countries in Asia, Africa, the Pacific, South America, Central America, and the Caribbean to help restore and maintain forest resources. There are former Peace Corps volunteers working in most national forests and parks. Call (800) 227–4675 to find the Peace Corps office closest to you.

Save America's Forests. Volunteers are needed to organize congressional districts and build a coalition throughout the United States. 4 Liberty Ct., SE, Washington, DC 20003. (202) 544–9219.

Society of American Foresters. National organization representing various segments of the forestry profession, including public and private practitioners, researchers, administrators, educators, and students. Publishes *Journal of Forestry* (monthly) and *Forest Science* (bimonthly) as well as other publications. Accredits undergraduate and graduate forestry programs (write for a list of institutions). 5400 Grosvenor Ln., Bethesda, MD 20814. (301) 897–8720.

The Northern Logger and Timber Processor. Subscription: $10 per year. The December issue contains a listing of nearly 400 industrial mem-

bers of the Northeastern Loggers' Association. P.O. Box 69, Old
   Forge, NY 13420. (315) 369–3078.
Timber Harvesting (monthly). Each January issue contains a listing of
   personnel employed by the wood supply and forestry departments of
   all major pulp and paper companies and industrial timber firms in the
   United States. Hatton-Brown Publishers, P.O. Box 2268, Montgomery, AL 36102. (205) 834–1170.

Index

Also Available From Island Press

Balancing on the Brink of Extinction: The Endangered Species Act and Lessons for the Future
Edited by Kathryn A. Kohm

Better Trout Habitat: A Guide to Stream Restoration and Management
By Christopher J. Hunter

Crossing the Next Meridian: Land, Water, and the Future of the West
By Charles F. Wilkinson

Death in the Marsh
By Tom Harris

The Energy-Environment Connection
Edited by Jack M. Hollander

Farming in Nature's Image
By Judith Soule and Jon Piper

Ghost Bears: Exploring the Biodiversity Crisis
By R. Edward Grumbine

The Global Citizen
By Donella Meadows

Green at Work: Making Your Business Career Work for the Environment
By Susan Cohn

Healthy Homes, Healthy Kids
By Joyce Schoemaker and Charity Vitale

Holistic Resource Management
By Allan Savory

The Island Press Bibliography of Environmental Literature
By The Yale School of Forestry and Environmental Studies

Last Animals at the Zoo: How Mass Extinction Can Be Stopped
By Colin Tudge

Learning to Listen to the Land
Edited by Bill Willers

The Living Ocean: Understanding and Protecting Marine Biodiversity
By Boyce Thorne-Miller and John G. Catena

Nature Tourism: Managing for the Environment
Edited by Tensie Whelan

Not by Timber Alone
By Theodore Panayotou and Peter S. Ashton

Our Country, The Planet: Forging a Partnership for Survival
By Shridath Ramphal

Overtapped Oasis: Reform or Revolution for Western Water
By Marc Reisner and Sarah Bates

Rain Forest in Your Kitchen: The Hidden Connection Between Extinction and Your Supermarket
By Martin Teitel

The Snake River: Window to the West
By Tim Palmer

Spirit of Place
By Frederick Turner

Taking Out the Trash: A No-Nonsense Guide to Recycling
By Jennifer Carless

Turning the Tide: Saving the Chesapeake Bay
By Tom Horton and William M. Eichbaum

Visions upon the Land: Man and Nature on the Western Range
By Karl Hess, Jr.

The Wilderness Condition
Edited by Max Oelschlaeger

For a complete catalog of Island Press publications, please write: Island Press, Box 7, Covelo, CA 95428, or call: 1-800-828-1302

Island Press Board of Directors